Smuggling Law

SMUGGLING LAW

Unsettled Sovereignties in Turkey's Kurdish Borderlands

Fırat Bozçalı

Stanford University Press
Stanford, California

Stanford University Press
Stanford, California

Library of Congress Cataloging-in-Publication Data

Names: Bozçalı, Fırat author
Title: Smuggling law : unsettled sovereignties in Turkey's Kurdish borderlands / Fırat Bozçalı.
Description: Stanford, California : Stanford University Press, 2025. | Includes bibliographical references and index.
Identifiers: LCCN 2025018708 (print) | LCCN 2025018709 (ebook) | ISBN 9781503644113 cloth | ISBN 9781503644496 paperback | ISBN 9781503644502 ebook
Subjects: LCSH: Smuggling—Law and legislation—Turkey—Van İli | Smuggling—Political aspects—Turkey—Van İli | Kurds—Turkey—Van İli—Government relations | Borderlands—Political aspects—Turkey—Van İli
Classification: LCC KKX3698 .B69 2025 (print) | LCC KKX3698 (ebook) | DDC 345.561/023360956628—dc23/eng/20250421
LC record available at https://lccn.loc.gov/2025018708
LC ebook record available at https://lccn.loc.gov/2025018709

Cover design: Michele Wetherbee
Cover art: Bahar Demirtaş
Typeset by Newgen in 10.5/15 and Adobe Garamond Pro

The authorized representative in the EU for product safety and compliance is: Mare Nostrum Group B.V. | Mauritskade 21D | 1091 GC Amsterdam | The Netherlands | Email address: gpsr@mare-nostrum.co.uk | KVK chamber of commerce number: 96249943

CONTENTS

ACKNOWLEDGMENTS

I COULD NOT HAVE WRITTEN this book without the support of and intellectual exchange with numerous interlocutors and scholars over many years. I am deeply indebted, above all, to my interlocutors in Kurdistan and Turkey, who generously and courageously shared their time and experiences. After I left the field, the counterinsurgency war resumed in Kurdistan and the oppression of Kurdish people and other dissident circles in Turkey intensified once again. Some of my interlocutors—whose names I have withheld to protect their anonymity—were forced to flee Turkey, were imprisoned, or have lost their lives while defending their communities, advocating for human rights, smuggling to earn their livelihood, or simply living their lives.

During my field research, several individuals offered me their generous support and accompanied me through border villages, town centers, court sessions, military checkpoints, and even snowstorms. I am especially grateful to Kenan Abi and the Abi family, Fatih Aras, Fırat Aslan, Mahmut Bilgin, Muazzez Çağlar, Sami Görendağ, Nazmi Gür, Turan Ece, Ulaş Erkıran, Kudbettin Fırtına, Cüzeyir Özkaplan, and Murat Timur. I owe particular thanks to Kenan for journeying with me across borderlands from southern Kurdistan (Başûr) to northern Kurdistan (Bakur)—even after we were trapped in a car that flipped over three times.

My interest in the politics of smuggling began at New York University, particularly with the guidance of Timothy Mitchell, whose work has had a lasting effect on my intellectual journey. I designed and conducted the research that forms the foundation of this book at Stanford University, where I was fortunate to have the support of key mentors and fellow scholars. The late James Ferguson not only helped me situate my scholarship within political and legal anthropology but also supported this project and my intellectual curiosity when Stanford's IRB consulted an anonymous Turkey-based expert who questioned the project. I am grateful to Thomas Blom Hansen, who rigorously challenged my grounding in social theory. I owe him particular thanks for helping me develop the concept of sly legality. Sylvia Yanagisako provided invaluable support as I navigated research, writing, and the complexities of the academic job market. Kabir Tambar helped me deepen my analyses so that they were more precise and eloquent. I continue to be inspired by every conversation with Miyako Inoue, Liisa Malkki, Sharika Thiranagama, Paulla Ebron, S. Lochlann Jain, and Joel Beinin. I am deeply thankful to Ali Yaycıoğlu for his intellectual companionship and support, especially for our spontaneous in-depth conversations at Coupa Café on Turkish politics, social theory, and Ottoman history. I also appreciate the generous support of Burçak Keskin Kozat, Shelly Coughlan, and Ellen Christensen during my time at Stanford.

My colleagues at Stanford—Jess Auerbach, Jacob Doherty, Maron Greenleaf, Yasemin İpek, Jenna Rice, and Johanna Richlin—offered valuable feedback on the early drafts of several chapters. Nikhil Anand, Hannah Appel, Elif Babül, Şamil Can, Aisha Ghani, Vladimir Hamed-Troyansky, Heather Hughes, Eda Pepi, Alissa Walter, Anna West, and Kerem Uşşaklı provided insightful perspectives that enriched my research. I am also grateful to Moyukh Chatterjee, Rebecca Galemba, Serra Hakyemez, Yunus Doğan Telliel, and Dilan Yıldırım for their thoughtful comments on earlier analyses of the material presented here.

At the University of Toronto, I discovered a welcoming and intellectually stimulating home and am surrounded by a vibrant community of scholars and friends. I am deeply thankful to the Department of Anthropology for warmly welcoming me, especially, Francis Cody, Heather Miller, Andrea Muehlebach, Todd Sanders, and Jack Sidnell, whose support made my transition to

Toronto and U of T much smoother. Andrea, who has been an inspiring mentor since my arrival, generously provided feedback on earlier iterations of this book. I am also grateful to Waqas Butt, Francis Cody, Cassandra Hartblay, Sumayya Kassamali, Alejandro Paz, Jesook Song, and Zoë Wool, who have been invaluable intellectual companions and supportive friends. I feel fortunate to be part of a community grounded in intellectual exchange and solidarity and fostered by colleagues in anthropology, including Sandra Bamford, Naisargi Davé, Tracey Galloway, Nisrin Elamin, Katie Kilroy-Marac, Chris Krupa, Tania Li, Amira Mittermaier, Valentina Napolitano, Esteban Parra, Shiho Satsuka, Janelle Taylor, and Krista Maxwell, and across the U of T campus, including Hülya Arık, Filiz Kahraman, Shahrzad Mojab, Nada Moumtaz, and Kevin O'Neill. Conversations with Abdulla Majeed, Ferda Demirci, Rachel Levin, and many other graduate and undergraduate students have been both refreshing and inspiring. I am also indebted to my Toronto friends—Metin Gün, Gülay Kılıçaslan, Ömer Özcan, Sardar Saadi, and Çağrı Yoltar—for making this city truly feel like home.

I owe special thanks to Nicole Watts, Peter Andreas, and Marc Lynch for reading and providing valuable feedback on an early version of this book during the Project on Middle East Political Science's Junior Scholar Book Development Workshop. Allison Brown helped me rethink and revise my book project. I am deeply thankful to Paola Bohorquez, Rory Donnelly, and Eric George for meticulously and insightfully reading my work and helping me refine my prose. I am especially indebted to John Ramsey, who read the entire manuscript multiple times to ensure clarity and eloquence in my writing.

I was very fortunate to work with Kate Wahl at Stanford University Press, who believed in this book project and offered exceptionally generous guidance. I am deeply thankful to the two anonymous reviewers whose insightful and carefully crafted feedback helped me refine the book's arguments. I also appreciate Thane Hale, Erin Ivy, Chris Peterson, and other staff of the SUP, whose efforts ensured a smooth submission and production process. I am thankful to Bahar Demirtaş for the cover art and to Erin Greb for designing the maps included in the book.

My deepest gratitude goes to several close friends for their unwavering support and care throughout the writing and rewriting of this book. Yasemin

İpek has been a close intellectual companion, always willing to read my work and offer insightful feedback. From the very beginning of this project, she has helped me sharpen its conceptual framework. Hayal Akarsu read most of the manuscript and provided thoughtful and engaged comments. Kerem Uşşaklı helped me refine my framing of evasive engagement. I greatly benefited from my conversations with Çağrı Yoltar on the politics of evasion and sovereignty.

The research, writing, and revision of this book were made possible through the generous support of the Wenner-Gren Foundation, the National Science Foundation, the Mellon Foundation, the Stanford Humanities Center, Stanford's Abbasi Program in Islamic Studies, and the Center for Russian, East European, and Eurasian Studies, as well as the Office of the Vice Provost for Graduate Education and the Anthropology Department at Stanford University. Portions of Chapter 3 were previously published as "Probabilistic Borderwork: Oil Smuggling, Nonillegality, and Techno-legal Politics in the Kurdish Borderlands of Turkey," *American Ethnologist* 47, no. 1(2020):72–85, https://doi.org/10.1111/amet.12866. Additionally, parts of Chapter 4 appeared in "Proving Injustice: Smuggler Killings, Impunity Work, and Vernacular Counterforensics in Turkey's Kurdish Borderlands," *American Anthropologist*, 126, no. 4 (2024): 567–80, https://doi.org/10.1111/aman.28015.

Finally, I express my deepest gratitude to my mother, Muzaffer Mete; my late father, Hikmet Bozçalı; and my sister, Evin Bozçalı, for their unwavering love, support, and understanding throughout the years. My heartfelt thanks go to Deniz Duruiz; without her boundless love, care, and constant encouragement, this book would never have been completed.

I dedicate this book to my late father, who taught me the meaning of commitment to a cause and, in his final struggle against terminal illness, embodied that dedication one last time; to my mother, who encouraged me to dream bigger; and to my interlocutors, who so generously welcomed me into their worlds.

ABBREVIATIONS

AKP	Justice and Development Party (*Adalet ve Kalkınma Partisi*)
BDP	Peace and Democracy Party (*Barış ve Demokrasi Partisi*)
CHP	Republican People's Party (*Cumhuriyet Halk Partisi*)
DDKD	Revolutionary Eastern Culture Associations (*Devrimci Doğu Kültür Dernekleri*)
DDKO	Revolutionary Eastern Culture Hearts (*Devrimci Doğu Kültür Ocakları*)
ECtHR	European Court of Human Rights
EConHR	European Convention on Human Rights
EPDK	Energy Market Regulatory Authority (*Enerji Piyasası Düzenleme Kurumu)*
HDP	Peoples' Democratic Party (*Halkların Demokratik Partisi*)
HEP	People's Labor Party (*Halkın Emek Partisi*)
İHD	Human Rights Association (*İnsan Hakları Derneği*)
ISIS	The Islamic State of Iraq and Syria
KCK	Kurdistan Communities Union (*Koma Civakên Kurdistanê*)
KRG	Kurdistan Regional Government
MHP	Nationalist Action Party (*Milliyetçi Hareket Partisi*)
MİT	National Intelligence Organization (*Milli İstihbarat Teşkilatı*)
PDK	Kurdistan Democratic Party (*Partiya Demokrat a Kurdistanê*)

PDK/Bakur   Kurdistan Democratic Party/North (*Partiya Demokrat a Kurdistan/Bakur*)
PKK   Kurdistan Workers' Party (*Partiya Karkerên Kurdistan*)
PYD   Democratic Union Party (*Partiya Yekîtiya Demokratîk*)
SHP   The Social Democratic Populist Party (*Sosyal Demokrat Halkçı Parti*)
TESEV   Turkish Economic and Social Studies Foundations (*Türkiye Ekonomik ve Sosyal Etütler Vakfı*)
TİP   Workers' Party of Turkey (*Türkiye İşçi Partisi*)
TOHAV   Foundation for Society and Legal Studies (*Toplum ve Hukuk Araştırmaları Vakfı*)
TÜBİTAK   National Metrology Institute of the Turkish Scientific and Technological Research Council (*Türkiye Bilimsel ve Teknolojik Araştırma Kurumu*)
YDG-H   Patriotic Revolutionary Youth Movement (*Yurtsever Demokratik Gençlik Hareketi*)
YPG   People's Defense Units (*Yekîneyên Parastina Gel*)
YPJ   Women's Defense Units (*Yekîneyên Parastina Jin*)

NOTE ON NAMING

THIS BOOK EXAMINES A DISTINCT form of politics at the intersection between smuggling and legal courts in Kurdistan, a geography that has been historically divided and ruled by non-Kurdish nation states. As the ruling governments have denied the Kurdish people any political and cultural status, even going so far as rejecting their existence as a distinct people—a position that Turkish authorities have upheld for decades—the identification, demarcation, and naming of Kurdistan, the historical home-land of Kurds, has become deeply contentious. In Turkey, state officials have strictly denied and criminalized the use of the term "Kurdistan" and instead introduced terms such as "southeastern" and "eastern Anatolia" to refer to provinces predominantly populated by Kurds. These terms have rendered non-Turkish populations and cultures invisible, while simultaneously perpet-uating an undeclared colonial rule in Kurdistan that racializes Kurds and erases their homeland without explicitly naming them.[1] As part of this colo-nial rule, Turkish authorities have systematically replaced non-Turkish place names with Turkish ones.

In the face of this colonial domination, Kurdish people have continued to use Kurdish place names and refer to their homeland as "Kurdistan." To dis-tinguish different parts of Kurdistan under the rule of various nation-states, some have combined the names of the ruling states with the specific parts of Kurdistan, such as "Turkish Kurdistan" or "Turkey's Kurdistan." Alternatively, others have used cardinal directions as politically neutral references, calling the Kurdish region in Turkey "Northern Kurdistan" (Bakurê Kurdistanê) or simply "the North" (Bakur). Similarly, Kurdish lands in Iran are called "Eastern Kurdistan" (Rojhilatê Kurdistanê) or "the East" (Rojhelat), those in Iraq "Southern Kurdistan" (Başûrê Kurdistanê) or "the South" (Başûr), and in Syria "Western Kurdistan" (Rojavayê Kurdistanê) or "the West" (Rojava). While using cardinal directions is a decolonial strategy that refuses the identification of Kurdistan with any of the colonizing governments, this approach still references the division these governments impose rather than mere geographical distinctions. Consequently, this way of naming may still be limited as a decolonial strategy. For example, "Northern Kurdistan" may not only refer to the area of Kurdistan under Turkey's jurisdiction but also to Kurdish lands currently under the control of Armenia and of the Azerbaijani Autonomous Republic of Nakchivan—a region some may prefer to call "Red Kurdistan" (Kurdistana Sor), the vernacular name for the autonomous Kurdish province (Kurdistan Uezd) that existed under the Soviet Union from 1923 to 1929.

As this book primarily attends to the politics around the exchanges among Kurdish communities living in different nation-states of Kurdistan's colonized geography, it notes the analytical and political significance of approaching the various areas of Kurdistan as interconnected through relations of inter-coloniality. Accordingly, I refer to the northern Kurdistan located within the borders of Turkey as "Kurdistan" rather than "northern Kurdistan" (Bakur) to acknowledge the fact that this region remains connected, influenced by, and influencing other areas of Kurdistan, especially in the context of smuggling economies. When referring to the entire Kurdish geography, I use the term "greater Kurdistan (geography)." When it is analytically necessary to differentiate parts of Kurdistan, I then refer to them as "northern Kurdistan" (Bakur), "southern Kurdistan" (Başûr), "eastern Kurdistan" (Rojhelat), and "western Kurdistan" (Rojava). In so doing, I also avoid the mistaken presumption that Kurdistan ever existed as a bounded territorial entity, akin to a Kurdish nation-state, before the division of the Kurdish homeland. Instead, I refer to Kurdistan as a geography, which is imagined as existing without and beyond fixed territorial borders and which has historically been home to various ethnic and religious groups, such as Armenians, Arabs, Turks, Jews, Assyrians, and Chaldeans, among others. This is why, in the map of greater Kurdistan geography provided here, the edges of Kurdistan are blurred to avoid representing the geography with fixed boundaries.

Throughout the book, I also refer to my field site as "the Kurdish borderlands" or simply "the borderlands," designations that should not be understood as lands located along the borders of Kurdistan, particularly because I understand Kurdistan as a geography without and beyond fixed borders. Instead, "the Kurdish borderlands" refers predominantly, though not exclusively, to Kurdish-populated areas that have been transformed into militarized zones by the nation-state governments that rule Kurdistan, in order to demarcate each other's jurisdictional limits. These governments have imposed imagined borderlines, marking them with border stones, barbed wire, cement blocks, and land mines, while heavily policing the movement of both human and more-than-human actors around and across these lines.

As part of my efforts to counteract the colonial grip on Kurdistan, this book uses Kurdish place names. That is, I provide (Kurdish or Turkish) alternatives when commonly used in vernacular contexts with the official (Turkish) version provided in parentheses upon first mention.[2] For example, the largest Kurdish city and its province, which is also my hometown, is more commonly referred to as "Diyarbekir," a Turkish name, which was also its official Turkish name until 1937, while its Kurdish name, "Amed," is also used. Accordingly, I refer to it as "Diyarbekir/Amed" (Official [hereafter abbreviated as "Off."] Diyarbakır). To refer to the city and province where my fieldwork was centered, I use "Wan" (Off. Van). While I refer to Wan's northernmost border district as "Çaldêran/Ebex" (Off. Çaldıran), "Çaldêran" is the most widely used Kurdish version. In English translation, Çaldêran means "forty churches," a name that highlights the district's Armenian-Christian heritage, which was largely erased during and in the aftermath of the 1915 Armenian genocide. I therefore prefer to retain this name, both to acknowledge that erased Armenian/Christian presence and to reflect its widespread use on the ground.

Lastly, throughout this book, I use the English term "smuggling" to refer to the Kurdish word *qaçax* [pronounced khachakh], which my interlocutors commonly used to describe their commerce of contraband. Unless I am specifically referring to a Turkish legal text, such as the Anti-Smuggling Law, or to a court file, my use of "smuggling" should be understood as a translation of *qaçax*. In the Wan borderlands, *qaçax*—a Kurdified version of the

Turkish word, *kaçak* [khachak] (smuggled or illegal) or *kaçakçılık* [khachak-chylyk] (smuggling)—colloquially referred to Kurdish smuggling economies, while *qaçaxçî* [khachakhchy], a Kurdified version of the Turkish expression *kaçakçı* [khachakchy], denoted a smuggler. However, nearly all of my smuggler (*qaçaxçî*) interlocutors avoided using the correlative Turkish terms, *kaçak* or *kaçakçılık*, to describe their contraband commerce as a way of rejecting the state's criminalization of such economies. Far from being contradictory, this subtle distinction between *qaçax* and *kaçak* reflects how Kurdish inhabitants of borderlands identified *kaçak* as a legal category imposed by state officials—which they regarded as spurious—and *qaçax*, which they understood as a legitimate means of livelihood. In alignment with these discursive-moral positions, I use "smuggling" and "smuggler" primarily as translations of my interlocutors' colloquial use of *qaçax* and *qaçaxçî*.

During my fieldwork, I also encountered occasional claims proposing the use of the Turkish term *sınır ticareti* (cross-border trade) as an alternative to "smuggling." *Sınır ticareti* originally referred to a specific trade regime that eased custom regulations to allow the export and import of certain commodities, but which restricted their consumption within a specific borderland area. Choosing this term over "smuggling," however, would render invisible the state authorities' criminalization of the Kurdish trade activities across the border and the corresponding imposition of criminal prosecutions, sentences, and violence on those engaged in such trade. In fact, those who raised such arguments often used *qaçax* colloquially, in both Kurdish and Turkish, to refer to smuggling economies.

A Kurdish alternative to "smuggling" and "smuggler" is *kolber* and *kolberî*, respectively—terms derived from the Kurdish words *kol* (back) and *ber* (load or cargo). *Kolber* has been used to describe Kurdish smugglers who carried contraband goods on their backs across the Iraqi-Iranian border. While my interlocutors mostly used the terms *qaçax* and *qaçaxçî* for Kurdish contraband economies, several human rights activists and politicians in Wan used *kolber*. Yet, because Kurdish smugglers in the Wan borderlands often transported contraband cargo with pack animals, such as mules and horses, rather than on their own backs, the terms *kolber* and *kolberî* do not accurately describe the broad array of smuggling arrangements and actors I observed across Wan borders. For this reason, I refer to Kurdish contraband commerce as "smuggling," a translation for *qaçax*.

MAP 1. Wan/Van Province and Its Border Districts

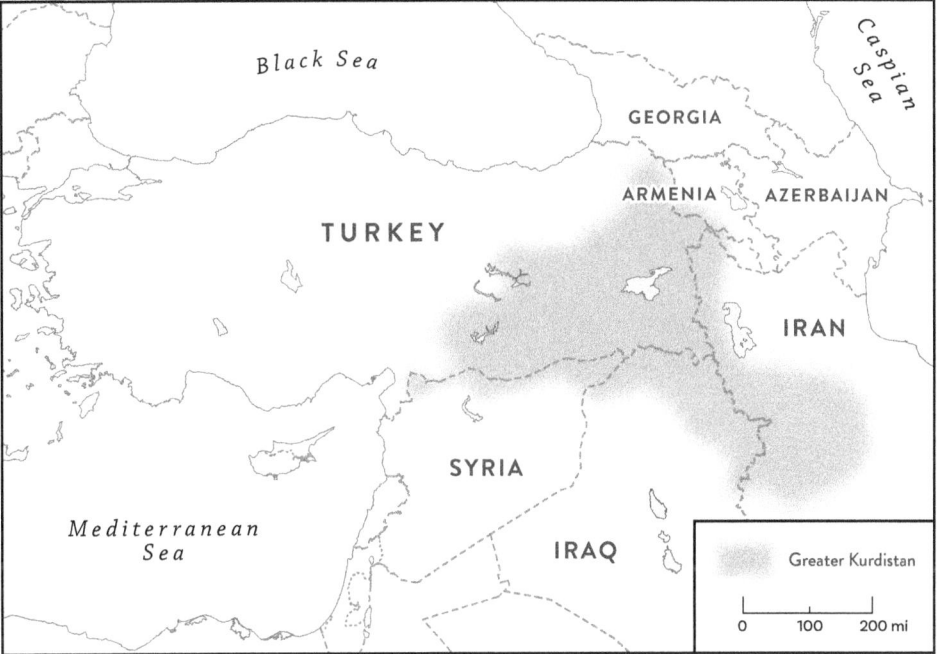

MAP 2. Greater Kurdistan Geography

Smuggling Law

INTRODUCTION

ON A SUNDAY AFTERNOON IN April 2013, Metin and I visited Baran in his village, located a few kilometers from the Turkish-Iranian border. Before moving to Wan (Off. Van) city center and becoming a subcontractor in construction a few years before, Baran had smuggled diesel fuel and cigarettes from Iran to Turkey. I met Baran through his lawyer, Metin, who was himself from another border village in the district and had defended many other Kurdish villagers in smuggling trials. As the son of a proud smuggler, Metin joined his father's smuggling journeys in his teenager years and learned about the difficulties and perils of smuggling, or *qaçax*, as it is called in Kurdish.[1] Despite being criminalized by the non-Kurdish nation-states of Turkey, Iran, Iraq, and Syria—which have divided and ruled Kurdistan, the Kurdish homeland—smuggling continued to be a socially acceptable economic activity for Metin, Baran, and many other inhabitants of the Kurdish borderlands.[2] Rather, they regarded the state borders that split Kurdistan as illegitimate.

After stopping by Baran's village house, the three of us drove on to the village's hamlet, which was even closer to the border. A few hundred meters away from the open-air yard where Baran's family held their sheep, we had a picnic. Although we could not spot the actual borderline—which was unmarked except for the border stones constructed every three to five hundred meters—we could see both an Iranian military post with a watch tower painted in the colors of the Iranian flag and the Turkish border patrol road in front of a hill. As we finished the remaining tea in our samovar, a military truck and a civilian-plated Toyota Hilux pickup pulled up next to our car. Accompanying the soldiers was the district governor (*kaymakam*), who began walking toward us. While it was not unusual for military vehicles to patrol the areas near the border, the fact that the governor had joined the soldiers, particularly on a Sunday, was significant to me; this highlighted the governor's prioritization of security and policing, as he appeared to see himself more as a military commander than a civilian bureaucrat.

The governor greeted Metin: the only one among us he knew. Metin reluctantly returned his greetings. After brief introductions, I explained to the governor that I was affiliated with an American university and was visiting the district to conduct research on smuggling cases in courts. The governor smiled sarcastically and said: "There is no smuggling case here. No sentences. Mr. Lawyer here, he makes all the cases drop. We catch the smugglers, but the lawyers save them." Metin responded immediately, "The right to defense is sacred, I am doing my legal duty." The governor dismissed Metin's response and continued: "Yes, yes, and you would also say that smuggling is a matter of livelihood, but it is not, it is a matter of security and order, the border is the foundation of the state, but the smuggling undermines that foundation of the state (*devletin temelinin altını oyuyor*) and the lawyers also facilitate that." Irritated by this comment, Baran intervened to say that many made a living by smuggling because there were no other jobs, and added, "But there is no more smuggling, the state has ended it."

"It is not like that," the governor refuted, pointing to the snowy hill that stood in front of us. He then asked whether we saw the vertical lines cutting the white, snow-covered areas of the hill. "The snow does not cover these lines because they are the paths that smugglers constantly use," he explained and then asked rhetorically, "If the smuggling was gone, why do these lines continue to appear?" Without allowing anyone to answer, the governor said, "It's getting dark, we have to go," and he left with the soldiers.

On our way back to the district center, I asked Metin about our unexpected encounter with the governor. He replied that he would do his best to defend Kurdish smugglers, making prosecutions fail and "undermin[ing] the foundation of the state," repeating the governor's exact words. This time, with the governor gone, Metin agreed with the statement that his lawyering went beyond mere legal duty, clarifying that defending smugglers was not like regular criminal lawyering, as with, for instance, "defending someone against allegations of theft." He explained that what the state officials called a crime—smuggling—and framed as a threat to state security was simply "trade with [his] tribesmen across the border." Implicit in this statement was Metin's comparison of the Turkish authorities' approach to smuggling in Kurdistan with their approach to pro-Kurdish political activism. Indeed, the authorities treated political mobilization for Kurdish self-determination, pro-Kurdish rights advocacy, or even engaging in cultural production in the Kurdish language as threats to state security and, therefore, made efforts to suppress them through the weaponization of criminal prosecutions known in the vernacular as "political trials" (*siyasi davalar*).[3] Similar to several other Kurdish borderland residents I met, Metin viewed anti-smuggling law enforcement practices in Kurdistan as an extension of the anti-Kurdish weaponization of law. Thus, they attributed political significance to both smuggling and its criminal-legal defense in courts.[4]

Metin also clarified that not all Kurdish smugglers faced the risk of smuggling trials. Spared were the few smugglers who chose to "collaborate" with the state security forces in their counterinsurgency war against the PKK (Kurdistan Workers' Party[5]), an outlawed Kurdish political organization that had led an armed struggle since 1984. The Turkish authorities knew all about the smuggling, as illustrated by the governor's words and the way he pointed to the tracks left by smugglers on snowy hills. But instead of attempting to fully eradicate these practices, the authorities made strategic use of smuggling—at least in some cases—and deployed it as a tool in their counterinsurgency efforts. "Collaborator" smugglers were invited to join the paramilitary ranks or share intelligence on the PKK guerrillas in exchange for security forces' open or tacit support of their smuggling. In doing so, the security forces made use of smuggling to undermine the PKK's support base, recruit paramilitary labor, collect intelligence on the guerrillas, finance their own military efforts, and attain personal enrichment. Many smugglers, however, refrained from such collaborations and resisted the state authorities' domination in Kurdistan. Yet, the noncollaboration stance placed these smugglers at an even greater risk of facing anti-smuggling operations, criminal investigations, or ambushes that would wound or kill them. In the context of the counterinsurgency war, therefore, whether smugglers faced smuggling trials or were subjected to ambush functioned as a sign of the smugglers' noncollaboration. For smugglers and other members of the Kurdish borderland communities, the smugglers' behavior in court and their preparations for facing the possibility of prosecution, or the families' arrangements as they filed criminal complaints in cases of slain smugglers reflected these smugglers' and their families' disavowal of the counterinsurgency war and the Turkish government's sovereignty claims over Kurdistan. Accordingly, for many smugglers, their families, and lawyers, the smuggling cases in Turkish criminal courts—both the smuggling trials and the smuggler-killing prosecutions—served as a key forum to express their pro-Kurdish political standing and to actively engage in politics.

This book examines how Kurdish smugglers and their lawyers, as members of a persecuted people, repurposed criminal trials to disrupt state authorities' ability to legally exercise sovereign powers over the enforcement of borders, sanctioning of killings, and banning certain forms of livelihood. It theorizes a distinct yet broader political strategy that allows disenfranchised actors to interact with law or other governmental (or corporate) institutions to effectively undermine these institutions' operative logics and processes, and to enable pockets of escape from their practices of surveillance, containment, and co-optation. Kurdish smugglers created a pocket of escape, for example, in proactively altering the content of contraband goods, such as smuggled oil, in order to render court provenance inspection results inconclusive in smuggling trials. This alteration curtailed the state authorities' forensic capacity to track the allegedly smuggled item's cross-border movements, which in turn undermined their efforts to enforce borders in courts. In this way, the smugglers evaded imprisonment and confiscation of contraband goods while rendering borders legally unenforceable. In cases of anti-smuggling ambushes and the security forces' killing of smugglers, the families of slain smugglers and their lawyers filed criminal complaints with the Turkish courts that repurposed criminal prosecutions to showcase legal authorities' refusal to collect evidence that could identify perpetrators and demonstrate the unlawfulness of the killings. In so doing, they revealed the judiciary's complicity in the killings and, more generally, the emptiness of the promise of universal justice upon which the legitimacy of judicial power rests.

In exploring Kurdish smugglers and lawyers' strategic use of courts to evade court-imposed dispossession, incarceration, and co-optation, I conceptualize "sly legality" as a distinct way of engaging the legal system. Sly legality occurs when disenfranchised actors adopt and rework legal procedures, rules, and reasonings to alter, interrupt, or undermine the ways in which state law and sovereignty are imposed. My articulation of sly legality builds upon Homi Bhabha's conceptualization of "sly civility," an expression Archdeacon Potts originally used to blame colonial subjects for insincerity in India.[6] Bhabha takes up the phrase to theorize a particular type of strategic engagement in which colonized subjects adopt the speech, writing, body language, and other manners of the colonizers to resist their demands for subjugation and admiration. Through sly civility, the colonized do not initially and outrightly reject engaging with the colonizer but rather mobilize the colonizers' style of speech and writing to "off-turn" them and to refuse to "satisfy the colonizer's narrative demand."[7] By generating discursive ambiguity around the colonized's expected legible submission to the colonizer, sly civility undermines the colonizer's ability to monitor and thus govern the colonized.[8]

In ways similar to how sly civility requires the colonized to adopt and repurpose the colonizers' manners, the sly legality of Kurdish smugglers and lawyers required them to closely engage with state courts to monitor, reshape, or improvise processes for collecting and validating legal evidence. Through their sly legality, smugglers and their lawyers also created discursive, material, and technoscientific ambiguity (e.g., indecisive forensic evidence on smuggled goods) to hinder the state authorities' ability to declare crossborder mobilities or killings as lawful or unlawful. State officers, particularly judges and prosecutors, were aware of the ambiguity created through legal evidence-making processes and other procedures. This ambiguity—much like Archdeacon Potts's irritation with sly civility—also frustrated Turkish officials. This frustration manifested in the district governor's annoyance with Kurdish lawyers who defended smugglers, an annoyance that he openly expressed during our encounter.

Resonating with the district governor's accusation that smugglers, and the lawyers who defend them, undermine the foundations of the state—*devletin temelinin altını oymak*—I understand sly legality as a deliberate and progressive effort to corrode legal rules, practices, and authorities. The Turkish phrase *altını oymak* is, in fact, a particularly apt expression as it literally means "digging or excavating beneath a building or another constructed structure"—an action that does not immediately make the construction collapse, but progressively erodes its foundations. In a similar vein, sly legality, as a strategic engagement with criminal courts, does not completely collapse or halt the operation of these courts. Instead, it requires the courts to operate, but it is precisely via their operation that sly legality creates cracks and openings through which actors and practices can escape the state's legal system. The pursuit of sly legality, thus, hinges on making state law work in ways to interrupt its capacity to exercise certain sovereign powers so that the state's legal machinery eventually runs idle or slips out of its (sovereignty) gear.

One way of tripping the legal machine is illustrated in how the undertakers of sly legality engaged criminal courts without adhering to the protections, remedies, and redresses recognized by the law. In performing sly legality, Kurdish smugglers and lawyers, thus, sought to disrupt how the state legal system interpellates them as state subjects who violate the law, exercise legal rights, or demand legal reparations. Even though these smugglers and lawyers did claim and benefit from particular legal rights—namely the right to a fair trial and the implementation of the Turkish Procedural Law (which establishes the principle of the burden of proof)—they did not claim these rights to pursue and ultimately establish a specific rights demand, such as rights to property, cross-border mobility, or trade. Rather than achieve legal recognition in the form of legal rights, sly legality aims to hinder such recognition.

Because of its disinterest in legal recognition and other legal remedies, sly legality exceeds the aims of human rights activism and legal advocacy that seek broader social, economic, and political changes through litigation. In so doing, sly legality compels us to rethink both the strategies and rationale of political mobilization in courts. Since the 1980s, the global trend of "judicialization of politics," in which courts are used as sites for political mobilization, has become prominent.[9] Indeed, rights advocates, grassroots organizations, and social movements have increasingly resorted to domestic and international courts to make and attain political demands that would otherwise be pursued through street protests, strikes, or civil disobedience, if not direct action and armed struggle.[10] In the same period (from the 1980s and onward) human rights lawyers and activists have developed "anti-impunity activism"—a worldwide rights defense movement that opposes crimes committed by state officials by holding individual perpetrators criminally responsible, compensating state-inflicted damages, and ensuring government compliance with human rights.[11] Yet, this recourse to law has several limitations. First, political advocacy in courts relies on the judicial authorities' capacity—and will—to recognize or authorize certain rights or protections.[12] Relatedly, judicialized politics render political struggles vulnerable to co-optation into existing ruling systems, as courts often favor incremental improvements for marginalized groups or measures that mitigate ongoing injustices without fundamentally dismantling them, thereby avoiding more radical demands for structural change.[13] Another limitation arises from the manner in which liberal law treats rights-bearing subjects as individual persons, thereby atomizing sufferings and rights demands that are inherently collective and could be more effectively addressed as such. This strategy stymies collective rights-seeking agendas while obscuring structural political and economic conditions that perpetuate injustices.[14] These limitations of judicialized politics emerge as the marginalized actors demand and embrace legal remedies. Yet, as a recourse to state law that aims at disrupting its ability to deploy its narrow remedies, sly legality offers the possibility of politically engaging with the state's legal system in ways that bypass and exceed these limitations.

Given that sly legality can only be pursued through engaging with state courts, it works as a paradoxical act of evasion from state authorities' surveillance and containment of cross-border movements in smuggling trials and from the retroactive authorization of security forces' use of violence in prosecutions for smuggler killings. Sly legality constitutes a distinct type of evasion in that it requires a strategic engagement with state authorities and their institutional rules and practices rather than their circumvention. Indeed, evasion from surveillance and control characterizes many outlawed forms of mobility and livelihood, from "irregular" migration to smuggling and piracy—whether maritime or cyberspace. Often, this evasion is achieved by bypassing the ruling authorities' monitoring. From the U.S.–Mexico border and the Caribbean and Mediterranean seas to the Kurdish borderlands across Turkey and Iran, migrants and smugglers have taken dangerous journeys through remote, mountanious, desert, or maritime territories where surveillance is limited or nonexistent.[15] When these migrants and smugglers have no choice but to pass through surveillance infrastructures—such as border crossings or road checkpoints—they often disguise their identities and actions with fraudulent documents or concealed contraband items.[16] In these cases, evasion is associated with avoiding detection, identification, and possible arrest by state authorities.

Sly legality, however, constitutes evasion by virtue of engagement. Rather than avoid the state's legal system and criminal-legal processes, Kurdish smugglers and lawyers engaged with these processes to practice sly legality. This engagement, in turn, enabled the corroding of the legal system's operative processes and capacity to co-opt, discipline, and oppress.[17] I theorize this distinct act of evasion as "evasive engagement," a political strategy in which disenfranchised actors interact with oppressive authorities and their institutional rules and practices to create pockets of evasion from these authorities' regimes of surveillance and control by altering and eventually disturbing how such regimes operate. While sly legality appears as a form of evasive engagement that Kurdish smugglers and their lawyers pursued in criminal courts, this book ultimately conceptualizes evasive engagement as a heuristic for examining how different disenfranchised groups—including but not limited to various colonized, racialized, and persecuted peoples—may engage with governmental or corporate actors in distinct contexts to curtail or disrupt these actors' operative logics and practices of containment and oppression.

POLITICS AND WAR IN KURDISTAN

Kurdish smugglers and their lawyers' sly legality, as well as the pockets of evasion they enabled, relied on and complemented the existing forms and forums of political engagement in Kurdistan. Everyday life in Kurdistan was intensely political, especially following the 1990s rise of the Kurdish Freedom Movement—a loose network of distinct political organizations across the greater Kurdistan geography and diaspora that shared the PKK-led political vision. When I began my fieldwork in 2012, armed resistance, electoral politics—both at national and municipal levels—street protests, civil society advocacy, and human rights activism were the main pillars of Kurdish liberation politics in Turkey. The Kurdish Freedom Movement was dominating the political scene in Wan. The Wan Metropolitan municipality and various district municipalities were run by mayors who had the support of the leading pro-Kurdish party and the broader Kurdish movement. This Kurdish political context shaped various aspects of everyday life in Kurdistan, including the smuggling economies.

Historically, Kurdish liberation politics in Turkey and the greater Kurdistan geography emerged in reaction to and in contestation of colonial domination. The Kurdistan geography was divided between the Ottoman and Iranian empires in the sixteenth century and, following World War I, was further partitioned among Turkey, Iran, British-colonized Iraq, French-colonized Syria, and the Soviet Union.[18] During the twentieth century and onward, Kurdistan geography remained under the rule of non-Kurdish states, which showcases a particular colonial condition that sociologist İsmail Beşikçi calls an "international colony" (*devletlerarası sömürge*).[19] A distinct feature of this colonial condition is the denial of any political or cultural status to the Kurdish people and Kurdistan, which has led colonizing authorities to establish unofficial colonial rules.[20] Another key feature is the collaboration between, rather than competition among, the colonizing governments.[21] Although these governments have competed, disputed, and engaged in wars with one another, they have often collaborated to suppress any attempts at Kurdish self-determination.[22] This collaboration makes the colonial situation in each part of Kurdistan inseparable from the others, resulting in inter-coloniality—a condition in which multiple colonial practices and legacies from different parts operate concomitantly, mostly reinforcing but occasionally undercutting one another.[23] The borders and border-enforcement regimes that divide Kurdistan have been key sites of this inter-coloniality, as illustrated by the colonizing governments' co-criminalization of political, social, and economic exchanges between Kurdish communities as smuggling.

The Turkish government's domination of Kurdistan has been based on a strict denial of the existence of the Kurdish people, effectively establishing a secret and officially undeclared colonial rule.[24] Following the foundation of the Republic in 1923, the Turkish authorities oppressed the existing political, cultural, and economic autonomy of Kurdish communities; established central state authority in Kurdish provinces; and introduced Turkification policies that denied Kurdish identity and banned the use of the Kurdish language in education and courts—the authorities even suppressed the use of words "Kurd" and "Kurdistan."[25] While centralization policies during the late Ottoman era had already began to undermine local Kurdish economies, the Republican policies brought the "de-development" of Kurdistan and destroyed the conditions for the independent development of the Kurdish economies of farming, manufacturing, and commerce.[26] Kurdish communities initially reacted to the colonial political and economic oppression with armed resistance and, from 1923 to 1938, rebelled in various provinces.[27] After quelling these uprisings, state authorities further consolidated their undeclared colonial regimes of domination and de-development in Kurdistan by forcibly displacing the Kurdish population, relocating Turkish settlers to Kurdistan, and subjecting Kurdish people and lands to routinized state violence and extraordinary laws. Through these mechanisms, state authorities imposed colonial law without declaring it so.[28] As they heightened their colonial domination, the Turkish authorities faced no or very limited resistance from the Kurdish communities in the following two decades.[29]

The political inertia in Kurdistan was broken during the 1960s by the Kurdish urban elite and university youth, who studied Kurdish history, culture, and language and formed illegal Kurdish political organizations.[30] A broader Kurdish political mobilization gained momentum from 1967 to 1969 through a series of public meetings held in Kurdish cities and towns protesting the underdevelopment of the Kurdish region and the security forces' continuous harassment of Kurdish people.[31] This rise of Kurdish political mobilization overlapped with and, to some extent, was supported by the rise of Turkish leftist politics. The military memorandum of 1971 reshaped this mobilization by banning Kurdish youth clubs and further criminalizing Turkish and Kurdish leftist politics. Since the 1970s, successive Turkish governments have increasingly weaponized the law and launched "lawfare"[32] campaigns against Kurdish activists, politicians, artists, and intellectuals, to prosecute them under charges of separatism, terrorism, and even racism for claiming a distinct Kurdish ethnic-linguistic identity.[33] By the mid-1970s, the Kurdish left began to articulate the colonized character of Kurdistan and thus to organize independently of the Turkish left, though split into different fractions.[34] While these Kurdish political groups mostly fought with each other or eventually became fragmented through internal conflicts, some of them managed, in the late 1970s, to mobilize their support base and eventually win local elections in several Kurdish cities and towns, including Diyarbekir/ Amed (Off. Diyarbakır), the largest city in Kurdistan.[35] The PKK emerged from one of these Kurdish revolutionary groups.[36]

The 1980 military coup interrupted the unfolding of Kurdish political mobilization for a few years. In 1978 and 1979, the Turkish authorities already had imposed martial rule in various Kurdish provinces, including Diyarbekir/Amed, Mêrdîn (Off. Mardin), Sêrt (Off. Siirt), and Colemêrg (Off. Hakkari), but the coup intensified state oppression in northern Kurdistan (Bakur) and Turkey,[37] leading to the destruction of most Kurdish revolutionary organizations, a fate shared by their Turkish counterparts.[38] While the military rule began to be lifted in 1984, emergency rule in Kurdish provinces replaced the junta, and an emergency rule regional governorship was established in 1987.[39] This regional governorship reasserted the colonized character of Kurdistan and re-marked its unofficial status by officially demarcating an emergency rule region governed through special laws, even as the authorities continued to deny the existence of a geography called Kurdistan and Turkey's colonial rule over it.[40]

The PKK survived the military rule of the 1980 coup, while most of the other Turkish and Kurdish revolutionary organizations lost their basis of support. The PKK leader Abdullah Öcalan and most of the leading cadres had left Turkey before the coup. Supported by the Palestinian revolutionary movements, the PKK was stationed in Lebanon's Beqaa Valley and transferred its members to Lebanon for ideological and military training via the Turkish-Syrian border and the existing Kurdish smuggling networks that operated across this border.[41] The PKK also obtained guerrilla bases in southern Kurdistan (Başûr) in the summer of 1983.[42] Following six years of preparation in and outside of Turkey, the PKK launched a full-scale armed struggle against the Turkish state on August 15, 1984, which posed the greatest military and political challenge to the Republic since its establishment. The armed resistance of the PKK also sparked broader mobilization in urban Kurdistan, which led to street protests, clashes with security forces, and days-long urban uprisings (*serhildan*) in response to the authorities' bans and attacks on Kurdish New Year (*Newroz*) celebrations or funerals of Kurdish guerrillas, politicians, activists, or other public figures.[43] Although the PKK had not fully liberated specific cities or districts from the Turkish government's control, its militia networks and support bases effectively spread across urban Kurdistan.[44]

The Turkish authorities responded to the PKK-led armed struggle by deepening the existing regimes of violence and dispossession, launching an extensive counterinsurgency campaign that forcibly displaced millions of people; destroyed thousands of villages; imposed road checkpoints, no-go zones, curfews, or food embargos; and systematically violated rights by killing, arbitrarily arresting, torturing, kidnapping, and disappearing Kurds. The counterinsurgency-led militarization of the rural Kurdistan devastated the existing agricultural and animal husbandry economies, which compelled many people to engage in smuggling, thus significantly expanding the scale of Kurdish smuggling economies in the 1990s and afterward.[45]

The PKK-led political mobilization in rural and urban Kurdistan also coincided with and expanded a new phase of pro-Kurdish electoral politics. Until the late 1980s, the electoral politics in northern Kurdistan were mainly dominated by urban and rural notables, who ran for parliament or municipalities through mainstream Turkish political parties. In 1991, however, Kurdish and Turkish socialist circles—including several deputies from the leading central-left party—founded the first pro-Kurdish legal party, HEP (People's Labor Party[46]).[47] In the 1991 general elections, HEP won seats in parliament.[48] Soon after, HEP deputies, branch members, and local supporters were accused of terrorism and faced criminal investigations, torture, kidnappings, and even killings. In July 1993, the Constitutional Court banned HEP, and over fifty pro-Kurdish party members were slain between 1991 and 1994.[49] State repression of Kurdish electoral politics increased in subsequent years. Five more pro-Kurdish parties that succeeded HEP were outlawed in the 1990s and 2000s. In June 2021, the Constitutional Court initiated a closure case against the pro-Kurdish HDP (Peoples' Democratic Party[50]), which, in October 2012, had replaced the BDP (Peace and Democracy Party[51]). The BDP was the leading pro-Kurdish party at the time I was conducting my fieldwork.

In response to the expanding scope of human rights violations in 1990s Kurdistan, a well-organized movement of human rights advocacy and a strong civil society mobilization also emerged. Kurdish human rights activism was part of the broader human rights movement that developed following the 1980 coup in Turkey.[52] While families of political prisoners established the İHD (Human Rights Association[53])—Turkey's leading human rights organization—in 1986, its third branch was established in Diyarbekir/Amed in 1988.[54] In the following years, Kurdish human rights activists established İHD branches across Kurdish provinces. During the 1990s, Kurdish lawyers—most of whom were fresh law school graduates—took leading roles in human rights activism, even though they faced arbitrary detention, torture, and death.[55] Despite ongoing state oppression, the Kurdish human rights lawyers kept İHD branches functioning, collected evidence on rights violations, and brought violation claims to the courts. By developing solidarity networks with human rights lawyers in Europe, particularly in the United Kingdom, these lawyers managed to bring the violation cases to the ECtHR (European Court of Human Rights) and, ultimately, compelled the European court to generate its own case law on armed conflicts.[56] By incorporating human rights discourse into Kurdish politics, Kurdish human rights lawyers also shaped pro-Kurdish electoral politics; some became leading figures in pro-Kurdish political parties during the 1990s and 2000s.[57]

With the recognition of Turkey's candidacy for the EU during the mid-2000s, Turkish authorities introduced democratization reforms and appropriated the human rights discourse.[58] As a result, extrajudicial killings, torture, and other rights violations decreased in the 2000s. Yet the targeting of pro-Kurdish activists, leftists, and religious minorities persisted. During the 2000s and 2010s, state authorities also maintained their practice of using anti-terrorism trials to arbitrarily imprison dissidents.[59] In this period, Kurdish human rights lawyers continued to contest the state's violations of rights, including smuggler killings, by providing legal services and organizing political mobilizations around pro-Kurdish causes.[60] As Kurdish lawyers carried on with their rights advocacy and progressively assumed prominent roles in pro-Kurdish parties and civil society organizations, they remained targets of state authorities' persecution and faced physical and legal harassment. As case in point, during the prosecutions of the Kurdistan Communities Union (KCK[61]), an umbrella organization of which the PKK was a member, hundreds of Kurdish human rights lawyers were detained and put on trials through the 2010s. In 2015, Tahir Elçi, the head of Diyarbakır Bar

Association, was shot and killed during a press conference that criticized the security forces' counterinsurgency operations in the historical city center.[62]

When I arrived in Wan for my fieldwork in 2012, I became engaged in Kurdish human rights activism. As I spent more time with Kurdish lawyers working on criminal prosecutions for smuggler killings, as well as smuggling trials, I realized that their lawyering went beyond conventional forms of human rights advocacy as they performed sly legality by resorting to state law without adhering to legal redresses. I further observed that this particular type of recourse required not only a good grasp of law and jurisprudence but also of other bodies of knowledge. These included technological and scientific expertise—which legal authorities used to collect and assess legal evidence—as well as a deep understanding of how local smuggling economies operated—particularly the specific material features of contraband goods, how the goods were stored or transported, and details of the topographical features of the smuggling paths where ambushes and killings typically happened. Smuggling trials and smuggler-killing prosecutions required the assemblage of various pieces of evidence, such as provenance tests in the former and ballistic evidence in the latter, each referring to separate sets of legislations, regulations, and technoscientific expertise. In these court cases, Kurdish lawyers and their clients also assumed different roles, joining smuggling trials as the defending party and smuggler-killing prosecutions as claimants. Yet, in both types of cases, Kurdish lawyers and their clients used tactics that combined technoscientific know-how and local knowledge of smuggling economies with legal expertise to undermine the state authorities' capacity to implement law in the courts. These technoscientific and legal tactics became the main means through which the lawyers and smugglers performed sly legality in the Wan borderlands.

TECHNOLEGAL POLITICS

Kurdish smugglers collaborated with their lawyers and other experts, such as accountants, by combining their diverse technoscientific and legal expertise to monitor and modify evidence produced in Turkish courts. This collaborative application of seemingly unrelated fields of knowledge constitutes "technolegal politics"—a separate field of politics in which technoscientific and legal knowledge bodies and practices are conjointly deployed to manipulate legal processes and accomplish political objectives that are not possible or imaginable within the confines of existing legal systems. The tactical use of legal evidentiary procedures by Kurdish lawyers and their clients undermined the state court's ability to declare specific cross-border movements legal or illegal, a political goal that would not have been otherwise feasible under the state's legal system. In this way, technolegal tactics enabled Kurdish lawyers and their clients to resort to state law without necessarily adhering to its remedies. These technolegal practices emerged as the primary mechanism through which these individuals pursued sly legality.

My framing of technolegal practices builds upon and responds to scholarship that understands the intersection of law and science as a "clash of epistemologies."[63] Because scientific epistemology holds that scientific truth can never be conclusively proven and that a hypothesis can fail when applied to a new situation, scientific knowledge is produced through ongoing cycles of objection, revision, and verification.[64] Legal decision-making, however, follows the logic of precedent and aims for a final verdict that precludes or minimizes future appeals.[65] For this reason, scholars have noted that the use of technoscientific expertise in courts often contrasts with legal decision-making by destabilizing material facts and leading to new legal controversies, rather than resolving existing ones.[66] Law and science have thus been mainly understood as disparate fields that operate through different epistemological assumptions.

My inquiry into technolegal practices, however, offers a new analytical approach. Rather than assume that legal and technoscientific knowledge production processes are necessarily disparate, my ethnography reveals how these processes can become entangled and reshape each other before, during, and after court proceedings. It further shows how these entanglements might enable unexpected and novel forms of political-legal agency.

One such form of agency is illustrated by sly legality, which Kurdish smugglers and lawyers enacted through specific, jointly developed technolegal practices that combine legal and technoscientific knowledge. For instance, in oil smuggling trials, the primary technolegal tactic that smugglers employed in cooperation with their lawyers was the mixing of oil with other chemicals in order to skew chemical tests that would identify the oil provenance. When successful, they would obtain inconclusive test results and adjust their legal defense accordingly. Through this tactic, the smugglers and lawyers conducted "disruptive borderwork"—the work of undermining and obstructing the means through which state authorities legally enforce borders. Thus, through their technolegal borderwork in smuggling trials, smugglers and lawyers performed sly legality and practiced technolegal politics.

In smuggler-killing prosecutions, Kurdish lawyers and their clients—the relatives of the slain smugglers—improvised their own forensic investigations to gather evidence that would identify the perpetrators and corroborate the unlawfulness of the killings. They also developed technolegal practices that document how judicial authorities avoided collecting such evidence by closely monitoring official crime investigations and related forensic practices. In this manner, the lawyers and the complainants conducted "vernacular counterforensics," in which they not only examined the killings but also scrutinized the state authorities' forensic investigations. Through their own evidence collection practices, the lawyers and complainants interrupted the state courts' ability to sanction such killings. Their forensic examination of the state authorities' forensics further exposed the judiciary's complicity in these state-committed crimes and defied the courts' claims of impartiality. Vernacular counterforensics, then, refers to the technolegal practices through which my interlocutors conducted their sly legality in smuggler-killing prosecutions. This constitutes another example of technolegal politics practiced in Wan courts.

My conceptualization of technolegal politics builds upon and brings together legal activism and "technopolitics"—the use of technoscientific knowledge to achieve particular political objectives. Yet, technolegal politics cannot be fully captured or performed through either legal activism or technopolitics alone.[67] Unique to technolegal politics are the ways in which technoscientific knowledge and legal expertise are brought together to work with, on, and against each other in order to effectuate unexpected political-legal outcomes or achieve potential benefits by and for disenfranchised groups. Accordingly, my interlocutors' sly legality and related technolegal practices went beyond legally defined and available remedies associated with legal activism, such as rights claims or redresses. Their practices also went beyond forms of illegal or de facto achievements, such as makeshift access to water or electricity networks, that marginalized groups gained through technopolitical practices.[68] In this way, technolegal politics offers a powerful analytical lens for explaining how disenfranchised actors seek and acquire not only illegal, covert, or precarious access to material resources but also formal, legal, or long-lasting forms of access. Such access may even extend to areas beyond legal control or sanction, as technolegal practices can open a threshold between the legal and illegal, creating a zone of undecidability. Kurdish smugglers' disruption of state border enforcement in oil smuggling trials illustrates this type of technolegal political achievement, given that they attained cross-border mobility that state courts could neither legally authorize nor punish.

Technolegal politics is not the exclusive domain of legal professionals. As my ethnography demonstrates, various other actors involved in the legal process—whether as defendants, claimants, or plaintiffs, such as Kurdish smugglers and trading company owners—or those not directly engaged in jurisprudence—like smugglers' accountants—also participate in technolegal work. This wide array of actors shows how technolegal politics is not only conducted in courtrooms and court laboratories but also in locations as varied as mountain passes, gas stations, border villages, and company offices that are not usually associated with legal practice. The diversity of these actors and sites demonstrates how technolegal politics relies on unexpected partnerships and cooperation among otherwise disparate actors and forms of expertise that go beyond the institutionalized fields of law and politics. The broad array of professions and forms of expertise that were involved in my interlocutors' development of technolegal practices further shows how smuggling economies in the Wan borderlands strategically assembled different practices, professions, locations, and communities.

SMUGGLING ECONOMIES IN WAN

Wan is a leading node of smuggling between Turkey and Iran. While its 180-mile-long land border with Iran features various mountainous border passages—which Kurdish smugglers often cross in groups and with pack animals (e.g., horses and mules)—Wan province also connects the land road network with other border provinces and districts—namely, Colemêrg, Bazîd (Off. Doğubeyazıt), and Îdir (Off. Iğdır)—to central and western Turkey. With a population that exceeded one million—the third largest center in northern Kurdistan at the time of my fieldwork—the province also provided financial, technical, and labor resources that allow various forms of smuggling economies to thrive.[69] Although it was difficult to document the exact scale of smuggling economies in the province, a 2005 parliamentary report estimated that one hundred and fifty million liters of oil were smuggled across Wan borders annually.[70] Another parliamentary report suggested that, in 2010, thirty-five thousand mules and horses worked in smuggling journeys in Wan alone.[71]

Among Wan's population, both city center and border village residents, smuggling referred to different types of work, networks, and exchanges. Cinematic works have often depicted and dramatized Kurdish smugglers—mostly men—carrying contraband on pack animals across mountainous border passages under the imminent threat of attacks from border patrols, or ingeniously avoiding minefields in the border zones.[72] This cinematic portrayal of smugglers as carriers or transporters may seem romantic, but it was not altogether inaccurate: In the Wan borderlands, many border villagers conducted their smuggling journeys this way. These smugglers, whom I call "carrier smugglers," crossed the borders to meet their Iran-based business partners, who were Kurdish and typically connected to them via kinship or tribal affiliations.[73] Turkey-based carrier smugglers often bought contraband goods from their Iran-based partners on the other side of the border and brought these goods back to their villages. Occasionally, Iran-based Kurdish smugglers would cross the border to deliver goods directly to their partners in Turkey.

Across the Turkish-Iranian border, smugglers often transported everyday consumer goods, such as gasoline, diesel fuel, tobacco, sugar, tea, and other foodstuffs. During certain periods, particular goods might have become more desirable among the smugglers because of various factors that ranged from profit margins and scarcity to the ease of physical transportation or hiding, or the prospect of more lenient punishments in case of a criminal conviction. Although contraband gasoline and diesel fuel constituted the highest numbers of smuggled items in the 2000s—because of the astronomical oil price differences across the border (up to $1.6 per liter of gasoline)—contraband cigarettes came into prominence in the 2010s. In addition to the bigger price difference (up to $2 per box of cigarettes) and hence potential profit range for smugglers, cigarettes had a broader consumer base and were easier to sell by individuals standing at street corners, working at makeshift street stalls, and ferrying around. Smugglers also transported more lucrative illegal goods, such as heroin or weapons, merchandise whose production, distribution, and trade were either banned or highly restricted. While carrier smugglers could earn up to $20 in a single smuggling journey of common consumer goods,[74] a similar amount (weight or volume) of heroin could earn carriers thousands or tens of thousands of U.S. dollars.

By capitalizing on the price differences in everyday consumer goods or banned items, Kurdish contraband commerce functioned as a form of economic arbitrage.[75] The price discrepancies emerged not only when contraband goods passed via the borders between Iran and Turkey. The distinctive aspect of arbitrage in Kurdish smuggling economies is that the price differentials were created as the contraband items moved westward after they crossed the border.[76] While common contraband consumer goods, such as oil and tobacco products, were mostly consumed in central or western Turkey, heroin—the most frequently smuggled banned item—was in high demand not only in Turkey's western provinces but even more so in Western Europe.

Carrier smugglers financed themselves the small-scale contraband commerce. This form of commerce involved a limited amount of everyday consumer goods that, at the time of my fieldwork, could be bought for a few hundred U.S. dollars. These items ranged from a few hundred liters of diesel fuel to roughly one hundred packages of cigarettes or several hundred kilograms of tea, sugar, or rice. Carrier smugglers could not afford to engage in contraband commerce in larger quantities, for instance, by transporting several thousand liters of diesel fuel or large shipments of expensive banned items, such as heroin or handguns. The smuggling of these goods was organized by district or city-based traders, whom I refer to as "trader smugglers."

The carrier smugglers could only transport a certain number or amount of contraband goods on each journey. So, they accumulated the contraband in border village stashes to be transported to city centers in Kurdistan or central and western Turkey by motor vehicles, including cars, pickup trucks, minibuses, or semitrailer trucks, depending on the kind and volume of contraband.[77] For the most part, trader smugglers organized the transportation and trading of these items westward through urban company offices, warehouses, and gas stations. The smuggled items were carried across inter-city roads and highways connecting the Kurdish provinces to the western provinces of Turkey. As trader smugglers needed to pay the entire cost of the smuggling journey from Iran to northern Kurdistan and then to western Turkey, they might also seek partners, whom I call "investor smugglers," who engaged in contraband commerce by providing financial contributions. Unlike traders, who also invested in smuggling journeys of contraband, these investors did not organize its transportation, storage, or trade. Accordingly, these actors, perhaps a construction contractor or a housewife, were not typically directly associated with smuggling activities but could invest in smuggling.

The risks and rewards of smuggling were unevenly distributed, further deepening existing inequalities among the carrier, trader, and investor smugglers. When law enforcement agents seized contraband items in anti-smuggling stings or at road checkpoints, carrier smugglers risked imprisonment and the loss of all their cargo. During the on-field, armed stings—in which security forces intercepted and often fired at the smuggler convoys on mountainous passages—carrier smugglers could be seriously injured or killed. Trader or investor smugglers did not face these stark threats, but they did risk heavy financial losses or, at most, imprisonment if their contraband was confiscated. Although the carriers took on the most dangerous risks, traders—and investors—received most of the revenue from smuggling. By smuggling consumer goods, carrier smugglers could earn up to a hundred U.S. dollars weekly, which was equivalent to the official minimum weekly pay; trader or investor smugglers could earn a few thousand dollars from a single smuggling journey. For the smuggling of banned items, particularly heroin, these amounts could increase up to a few thousand U.S. dollars for the carrier smugglers and up to a hundred thousand U.S. dollars or more for traders or investors.

The Kurdish smuggling economies also included other actors who provided technical expertise and auxiliary services. Accountants could fraudulently document smuggled items or retrospectively fix corporate books; scientists could prepare expert witness reports to show that the smuggled oil had been domestically produced; and chemists or retired state oil company workers could help smugglers mix certain chemicals with smuggled oil to make it undetectable in oil marker inspections. Contraband commerce also required other sectors and services, such as money laundering and access to automobile sales lots that sold "clean" (*temiz, kaçağa düşmemiş*)—that is, not involved in any criminal investigation—used cars. Depending on the degree and frequency of their involvement in smuggling, these actors could also come to be called smugglers (*qaçaxçî*).

Kurdish lawyers played key roles in smuggling economies through both defending smugglers in criminal courts and developing specific technolegal tactics to curtail potential trials before smugglers were caught. The criminal lawyers who specialized in smuggling cases—or, as Kurdish borderland communities called them, "smuggler lawyers" (*kaçakçı avukatı*)—often worked for investor and trader smugglers as well as for the carrier smugglers the latter employed. Because they required sophisticated knowledge of the specific techniques and logistics of particular types of smuggling and about the social and professional networks that engaged in smuggling activities, smuggler lawyers often developed long-term relations with their clients. Most of these lawyers were already intimately familiar with smuggling work. Many were from the border villages themselves, had smuggler relatives or neighbors, and some, like Metin, had themselves worked as smugglers in their youth. While the majority of these lawyers lived and ran law offices in Wan city center, a few had their main offices in district centers.

In cases of smuggler-killing prosecutions, families of the slain carrier smugglers could work with human rights lawyers. Yet, following these prosecutions and conducting their own evidence collection practices—the main technolegal tactic deployed in these cases—necessitated knowledge of the local geography and techniques of smuggling, so human rights lawyers often worked with smuggler lawyers, especially those who had their offices in border districts. A few lawyers also specialized in both smuggling and human rights cases.

While partnerships among various experts and professions, particularly between smugglers and lawyers, facilitated smuggling activities, different smugglers had varying capacities for forming such partnerships; these capacities both reflected and reinforced the uneven distribution of risks and rewards in the smuggling economies. Trader or investor smugglers could afford to hire various experts, such as accountants or chemists, to work with them and develop various strategies to evade the authorities' anti-smuggling surveillance and prosecutions. Carrier smugglers, however, could not pay for such experts, even though they ran higher risks of encountering anti-smuggling operations, criminal convictions, loss of contraband goods, and security forces' lethal attacks. For them, the main way to access such expertise was to work for trader or investor smugglers who, in return, took most of the profits from smuggling. In the smuggler-killing prosecutions, human rights lawyers often viewed these cases as part of their human rights lawyering and did not ask for a fee. Yet, for smuggling trials, only a handful of lawyers, like Metin, defended carrier smugglers who could not pay lawyers' fees. Many carrier smugglers, or those caught selling contraband goods, did not consider hiring a lawyer. As a result, these smugglers typically lost the contraband goods and faced criminal fines and imprisonment. If they had previous convictions for smuggling, the new imprisonment sentences were not deferred, which resulted in immediate incarceration.

Most of the carrier smugglers that I encountered in law offices or in court were men; however, a few women were also active in the smuggling trade in the Wan borderlands. While some women participated as investors, others supported the trade as service providers, particularly as lawyers.[78] For instance, in border district towns, I came across women investors who collected small savings, often in gold, to collectively invest in oil or cigarette smuggling.

Kurdish smuggling economies connected actors of different genders, classes, and professional networks. Because these economies bridged geographically distant locations across rural and urban Turkey, Kurdistan, and Iran, they linked families and tribes who were otherwise separated by state borders. As I continued to meet more smugglers in these borderlands and attended more smuggling trials, it became clear that smuggling played a central role in the overall economy of Kurdistan and allowed for a distinct kind of political-legal agency, sly legality, to emerge.

LEGAL PROCEDURES AND UNSETTLING SOVEREIGNTY

The Kurdish smugglers and their lawyers' sly legality hinged on closely monitoring and engaging with legal processes to turn legal proceduralism from a means of executing state sovereignty into a set of strategies geared to unsettle it.[79] The doctrine of liberal legalism posits legal procedures, due process, and judicial integrity as essential to the rule of law and to the fulfillment of its promise of justice.[80] Scholarly critique of liberal legalism, however, has convincingly shown that legal procedures, processes of evidence collection and validation, and courtroom rituals can reinforce existing power inequalities and the entrenched marginalization of certain population groups, even against the backdrop of legal reforms that promise equality and robust democratization.[81] Building on their work, my ethnography of smuggling trials and smuggler-killing prosecutions demonstrates that legal procedures and evidentiary processes are central to how state authorities claim, legitimize, and exercise sovereign power.

Modern state sovereignty has been understood as the capacity to effectuate a state of exception: a legally authorized condition in which individual or collective legal rights and protections are suspended and the right to kill with impunity is claimed and exercised.[82] Although sovereignty and exception are often associated with physical and corporeal violence,[83] a decision on exception may also refer to the authorization of different forms of state-sanctioned violence—including incarceration, restriction of mobility, and dispossession of movable or unmovable properties or commons—constituting a wider spectrum of legally permitted transgression of law. Insofar as modern state authorities claim for themselves the capacity to impose and transgress state law by exercising the power of exception, modern state sovereignty rests on the monopolization of the power of decision as the sole authority to authorize—and ban—the exception, before and after the fact. This monopolization of decision, especially the ex post facto authorization of state transgressions of law, is often performed through the monopolization of the production of legal knowledge, which is asserted and realized via legal evidentiary processes and other legal procedures. Legal proceduralism is thus essential—rather than secondary—to the claim, performance, and legitimization of state sovereignty.

The historical foundations of the law of evidence, such as the concepts of burden of proof and reasonable doubt, also demonstrate the critical role that legal procedures play in executing sovereign violence in courts. In medieval European law, for example, validating guilt or evidence "beyond a reasonable doubt" initially emerged to absolve judges of any moral responsibility for possible wrongful convictions rather than to protect the accused from unjust punishments.[84] The idea of protecting the rights of the accused only emerged in legal procedures within the framework of modern liberal law, much later than when these procedures initially began.[85] Yet, under modern liberal law, reasonable doubt and other procedures of legal evidence continue to protect judges and other members of the judiciary not from their moral responsibility, but from the very sovereign violence their decisions rely on and unleash.[86] Legal proceduralism's protection of the judiciary from the violence of sovereign power also explains why spaces of legal exception are often governed by "hyperlegality"—the proliferation of legal regulations, procedures, and institutions, such as special laws, protocols, and courts, rather than the suspension or lack of law.[87]

To elaborate on the connection between state sovereignty and legal proceduralism, particularly how my interlocutors' sly legality uses this connection to undermine the exercise of state sovereignty, I appeal to Walter Benjamin's conceptualization of lawmaking and law-preserving violence in his famous essay "Critique of Violence" (*Zur Kritik der Gewalt*).[88] Benjamin's formulation echoes the categories of constituent and constituted power, given that lawmaking violence is sovereign violence that breaks the existing law to establish a new legal order and law-preserving violence protects the law and legal order that the lawmaking violence had established.[89] Exemplary forms of lawmaking violence include war and military coups, while law enforcement by police and courts illustrate law-preserving violence. The categorical, institutional, spatial, and temporal distinctions between lawmaking and law-preserving violence are hardly maintained, however. Benjamin suggests that each form requires and begets the other: Lawmaking violence evolves into law-preserving violence to protect the constituted law, but in so doing, it strangles structural political change and paves the way for a new eruption of lawmaking violence that establishes and transforms into another round of law-preserving violence, generating a lawmaking/law-preserving cycle.[90] Furthermore, both forms become entangled in the everyday operation of law enforcement, whether by police, gendarmerie, or military. Although law-preserving violence is believed to be accountable because it is procedural, it often contains and cooperates with lawmaking violence.[91] Through evidentiary processes and legal procedures, state authorities—primarily the judiciary and the legal system—render lawmaking violence invisible and, through its legal sanctioning, retroactively reframe it as law-preserving violence.

In the context of Kurdish smuggling, Turkey's imposition of borders, criminalization of cross-border trade without state sanctions, and designation of no-go zones in the highlands constituted lawmaking acts. To impose them, law enforcement engaged in a range of strategies, including intercepting or redirecting smugglers, confiscating property or cargo they deemed contraband, and exerting armed force—injuring, maiming, or killing smugglers. These acts of enforcement were conducted in the name of upholding the law—as law-preserving violence—but they also functioned as lawmaking acts: They were operationalized with security forces' on-the-spot sovereign decisions on exceptions, which resulted in dispossessing smugglers of their holdings, limbs, and lives. By following specific legal procedures and producing legal evidence, the judiciary retrospectively transformed the unrestrained acts of killing, dispossessing, or intercepting into seemingly predictable, procedural, and accountable law-preserving acts. In this way, the courts sanctioned the lawmaking violence that is always already embedded in the law-preserving violence, rendering it invisible and untraceable.

If state sovereignty is partly exercised through a monopoly on legal procedures and evidentiary processes, my account of sly legality shows how these processes can be used to disturb the state authorities' claim, performance, and legitimization of sovereignty from within the state legal system. By challenging the authorities' monopolization of legal evidence-making through their own legal evidence-making practices and technolegal tactics, Kurdish smugglers and lawyers disrupted the judicial reframing of lawmaking violence into seemingly accountable law-preserving violence. In smuggling trials, for example, the smugglers and their lawyers managed to counteract the security forces' dispossessive acts of confiscating contraband goods, pack animals, cars, minibuses, and trucks. In smuggler-killing prosecutions, the Kurdish plaintiffs and their lawyers unsettled the sanctioning of the killings and revealed the judiciary's role in producing impunity for the perpetrators by refusing the courts' political and legal legitimacy for delivering procedural equality and universal justice. In both smuggling and killing cases, and despite assuming different roles—as defendants or claimants—Kurdish smugglers and their lawyers' pursuit of sly legality curtailed the courts' capacity to sanction lawmaking violence and to reframe it as law-preserving acts. In so doing, their sly legality interrupted the state authorities' exercise of sovereign power over Kurdish lives and livelihoods.

POLITICS OF REFUSAL AND RESISTANCE IN COURTS

By interrupting the exercise of sovereign power in courts, sly legality brings together political refusal and resistance. In the context of Indigenous, Black, and stateless peoples' struggles, scholars have conceptualized political refusal as political action that rejects sovereign subjugation by disengaging from unequal relations of power to assert, instead, "a relationship between equals."[92] Political refusal is framed as a response to the liberal politics of recognition, wherein sovereign-supremacy-claiming authorities—colonial or settler-colonial—identify colonized peoples as distinct cultural groups, grant them nonreciprocal rights, and condition their claim to these rights on adherence to specific cultural practices that the authorities unilaterally associate with essentialized cultural identities.[93] Against these unequal forms of recognition, refusal politics is based on the repudiation of any hierarchical relationship by not engaging with actors who assert sovereign superiority and impose their own conditions for engagement.[94] Thus, political refusal differs from a mere rejection of the supremacy-claiming authorities, their rules, or the compromises they offer in negotiating with disenfranchised groups. It is instead a rejection of those authorities as legitimate interlocutors, not only in negotiations but in all kinds of interactions, including contestation.

In refusal politics, the practice of disengaging from supremacy-claiming authorities—rather than protesting, opposing, or contesting them—constitutes a political act in its own right. Yet, this disengagement does not necessarily mean a strict avoidance of any contact with the authorities who claim sovereign supremacy. Disenfranchised actors may also engage in political refusal by interpellating these authorities in ways that disavow their supremacy claims while simultaneously remaining disengaged from unilateral interactions dictated by those authorities.[95]

Political refusal is also conceptualized as a form of politics that differs from resistance politics.[96] Because the latter allows oppressors to set the conditions of engagement with resistors—whether through contestation or negotiation—it reproduces the oppressors' sovereign logics and superiority, even when resistors disavow and contest such supremacy. Refusal politics, in contrast, rejects unequal relations of sovereignty and employs disengagement to compel relations between equal sovereigns. In so doing, however, the disengagement strategy tends to place the onus of determining the course and success of refusals on actors who claim supremacy and who may not be willing to give up such claims.[97]

I would argue, however, that sly legality circumvents the limitations of disengagement strategies through the practice of evasive engagement. As a political strategy, sly legality deliberately contests the supremacy-claiming authorities' ability to control the terms and course of interactions they would have with these authorities. Because sly legality aims to create patches of escape within regimes of surveillance and control imposed by the authorities, it frames refusal not as an act of disengaging from unequal relations of sovereignty, but as an act of evading such relations by engaging with the authorities who impose them. To achieve evasion from unequal relations, pursuers of sly legality do not openly deny, at least initially, the legitimacy of these authorities. Instead, they interact with these authorities to corrode their operative processes and disrupt their capacity to surveil, control, or oppress. In this way, sly legality constitutes a distinct form of political refusal, one practiced through evasive engagement rather than disengagement.

Sly legality is also based on the resistance politics of engaging with supremacy-claiming authorities—namely, criminal courts and other institutional authorities—even though these authorities strive to impose the conditions and rules of these engagements through, for instance, legal procedures and evidence-making processes.[98] Yet rather than operate under these conditions of engagement while contesting or negotiating them, pursuers of sly legality engage with courts on their own terms and seek to contest and corrupt the way the courts operate. Sly legality aims to neither sabotage nor fully stop the operation of the state legal system. Rather, sly legality makes the state courts work so as to bend and repurpose the ways evidence-making processes operate. As an act of refusal politics, the practice of sly legality rejects sovereign relations and actively seeks to undercut the enactment of these relations. In this way, it performs both political refusal and resistance politics in courts.

EVASIVE ENGAGEMENT AS METHOD

As a specific form of evasive engagement, sly legality was systematically practiced as a method of political refusal and resistance in courts by my smuggler and lawyer interlocutors. But evasive engagement was also a widespread approach to interact with state officials, outsiders, and locals suspected of collaborating with security forces—a method of living and earning a livelihood for many in the Kurdish borderlands, which had been shaped by decades-long counterinsurgency warfare. During my fieldwork, I also adopted and adapted evasive engagement as a method of ethical and nonextractive research, as well as a way of inhabiting and navigating the borderlands.

This book is based on twenty months of ethnographic fieldwork that I conducted among Kurdish smugglers, traders, lawyers, law clerks, and court personnel in Wan province from 2012 to 2014. I also visited the region in the summer of 2015 and stayed in contact, through email and other internet-based messaging services, with several lawyers, rights activists, and smugglers from Wan. During my fieldwork, I was mainly based in Wan city center and regularly drove to the four border districts of Çaldêran/Ebex (Off. Çaldıran), Qelqelî (Off. Özalp), Mehmûdî (Off. Saray), and Elbak (Off. Başkale), as the investigations and initial smuggling or smuggler-killing trials were processed by prosecutors' offices and criminal courts based in these districts.

Given that both smuggling and criminal lawyering required a high level of professional confidentiality and trust, smugglers and lawyers were reluctant to allow outsiders into their professional and social worlds. Because Kurdish smuggling economies operated in an unstable and contentious political environment against the backdrop of the counterinsurgency war, it was particularly difficult for a researcher to access the everyday unfolding of these economies. As a Kurdish researcher, my previous pro-Kurdish advocacy facilitated my initial access to the field. During my undergraduate years in Istanbul, I volunteered to translate court files before they were submitted to ECtHR for TOHAV (Foundation for Society and Legal Studies[99]), a leading human rights organization. This work connected me to Kurdish human rights activists and lawyers in Istanbul and in my hometown, Diyarbekir/Amed. During my initial visits to Wan city center and its border districts in the summers of 2010 and 2011, my Kurdish human rights activist and lawyer contacts in Istanbul and Diyarbekir/Amed introduced me to their colleagues in Wan, who then introduced me to the smugglers. Thus, my lawyer, activist, and smuggler interlocutors already knew of my record of activism and viewed me as a patriotic (*welatparez* or *yurtsever*) Kurdish researcher, a supporter of broader Kurdish liberation politics, if not necessarily affiliated with any particular organization or party. In fact, on a few occasions in border villages, I was mistaken for a Kurdish human rights lawyer, and I was once mistakenly identified as one of Öcalan's (the PKK leader's) lawyers (*parêzerê serok*; the leader's lawyer)—Kurdish lawyers who had high political credibility within the Kurdish Freedom Movement.[100] I also connected with a few senior criminal lawyers, some of whom were renowned smuggler lawyers, through my father, who was a Diyarbekir/Amed-based criminal lawyer and defended Kurdish activists in political trials during the 1980s and early 1990s.

The referrals by human rights lawyers and activists did not always successfully connect me to other people in the field, however. Tensions among lawyers and activists, based on family and tribal affiliations or political ambitions, occasionally blocked or delayed my meeting with some people or access to some court cases. Few locals, including a smuggler who accused me of spying for the U.S. because of my affiliation with an American university, also questioned my presence in the field.

During my fieldwork, I worked as a clerk in several law offices that specialized in smuggling cases and that systematically observed smuggling trials held in Wan city center and the four border districts. The trials for individuals who had smuggled common consumer goods, such as oil, cigarettes, tea, or sugar, were held at the first-degree criminal courts (*Asliye Ceza Mahkemeleri*), while the cases for smuggled heroin or arms were processed at the high-degree criminal courts (*Ağır Ceza Mahkemeleri*). The court hearings were open to the public unless the judges decided otherwise. In Wan courthouses, the majority of the hearings at the first-degree criminal courts—up to nine of eleven hearings that a court typically held in a morning—were about cases of consumer goods smuggling. Given this frequency, I had the opportunity to systematically observe many first-degree criminal cases in the Wan city center and four border districts courts. I also attended the hearings, at the high-degree criminal courts, for the specific heroin smuggling cases and the smuggler-killing prosecutions I followed.

Since the hearings were held before noon, I mainly spent my mornings in courtrooms. In the afternoons, after the hearings, the judges, prosecutors, and court staff examined the upcoming cases, conducted the necessary correspondences, and finalized the interim and final court decisions. Lawyers often spent their afternoons in their offices, working on cases and meeting their clients. Thus, I spent a few afternoons each week in these law offices and volunteered as a clerk. In this capacity, I participated in the preparation of court documents and attended lawyer-client meetings. This work allowed me to gain a deeper understanding of the law offices' daily operations and the intricacies of the court cases. Unlike lawyers, lawyer clerks did not need any particular academic credentials or professional affiliations to the Bar Association, but my experience working as a clerk in my father's law office during high school had trained me to navigate court files, courthouses, and legal casework.

On some afternoons, I had arranged interviews with other lawyers and human rights activists, as well as judges and prosecutors. In fact, before the systematic observation of the hearings, I first visited judges to introduce myself and explain my research, and to ask for their permission to attend court hearings, even though the sessions were open to the public. I often conducted follow-up meetings with judges and arranged interviews with prosecutors to talk about their approach to the anti-smuggling law and its implementation in the Wan borderlands. The initial meetings with judges and prosecutors were surprisingly welcoming.[101] Some judges and prosecutors even shared with me the smuggling techniques they found particularly creative. I also visited Kurdish defendants (in smuggling trials) and complainants (in smuggler-killing cases) in their border villages, spent nights in their village houses (often with their neighbors), followed them in their daily routines and in their errands at government offices and marketplaces, and accompanied them to the gatherings in coffeehouses and in the pro-Kurdish party branches in the town centers.

As part of my research, I also joined Van Bar Association's Human Rights Commission. I attended meetings, participated in fact-finding human rights reporting, and received human rights law and forensic trainings offered by Istanbul- and EU-based rights advocacy NGOs. My affiliation with the Bar further facilitated my movement across various locations, including military checkpoints, city centers, border villages, and courthouses. Having grown up during the harsh years of the counterinsurgency war in Diyarbekir/Amed in the late 1980s and early 1990s, I also knew a few ways of navigating the politically and militarily unstable Kurdish borderlands. These included always notifying two or more people about my whereabouts and itineraries and avoiding driving in front of or behind military vehicles, which could become targets of guerrilla attacks.

My focus on legal practice is grounded on theoretical and methodological considerations. Theoretically, I identify criminal courts as a key site of border enforcement and border contestation and discuss how smugglers use courts to challenge and rework state borders in ways that are not possible at other sites of border enforcement, such as border gates, borderlines, or checkpoints on land roads, airports, and city centers. While scholars have examined various practices through which smugglers bypass the state surveillance and security infrastructure, thereby transgressing state borders,[102] criminal courts are rarely identified as sites of evasion for smugglers. Accordingly, the illegality of smuggling and other economic activities that authorities strive to criminalize is often presumed. In contrast, this study attends to how smugglers and lawyers contested and undercut the technolegal capacities for such criminalization, and to how they turned criminal courts into pockets of evasion from surveillance and containment.

Methodologically, examining smuggling cases in Turkish courts mitigated, though did not completely eliminate, the grave and ever-present risk that my fieldwork might unwillingly facilitate the authorities' anti-smuggling efforts—a significant concern that influenced all my decisions concerning the design, implementation, and writing of my research. Entering the field through court cases and law offices meant that I was working on cases that were already identified by security forces and were being processed in courts. In fact, I learned more about smuggling from the court files and legal personnel than from the smugglers themselves. I had not expected to meet judges and prosecutors so well versed on the always shifting smuggling techniques and networks—including knowing the specific mountain passes that smugglers preferred—or the techniques of chemical manipulation of contraband oil. Observing the legal authorities' close knowledge of smuggling economies in Wan made me even more rigorous in my efforts to protect the confidentiality of my interlocutors. Accordingly, I have used pseudonyms and changed place names, event dates, and other information that might reveal my interlocutors' identities. While I maintained the factuality of incidents, I have chosen at times to exclude or ambiguate information—both in my fieldnotes and this book.[103]

As I followed my interlocutors from courtrooms to law offices and participated in their sly legality and other practices of evasive engagement, I also developed an evasive mode of engagement in my ethnography and writing. My ethnographic evasive engagement is twofold. First, I practiced "ethnographic refusal," adhering to my interlocutors' rejection of ethnographic inquiry.[104] I respected their decisions to not share certain stories or documents and to decline meetings with me. I also avoided asking my interlocutors for certain information, such as the technical details of making contraband oil chemically unintelligible to forensic tests or for the specific chemicals they mixed with it. When they wanted to share these details with me, I listened but also omitted the information from my fieldnotes. Second, I refrained from writing about the specific technolegal arrangements and other practices of sly legality that were neither directly depicted in specific court files nor mentioned by the judges or prosecutors in interviews and court hearings. In this sense, this book covers, and thus reveals, as much as my interlocutors—smugglers and lawyers—disclosed to the judiciary and other state officials.

As I lived and traveled across the Kurdish borderlands during my fieldwork, it became evident to me that evasive engagement was the primary mode of interaction with state authorities—and their surveillance and prosecution infrastructure—among the borderland residents, whose lives and means of subsistence, including smuggling, unfolded against the backdrop of the counterinsurgency war. Because of the ongoing war and the shifting political positions and alliances within Kurdish and Turkish politics, smuggling emerged as a paradoxical site of both co-optation by and resistance to state authorities. The next chapter delves into this by examining how smuggling economies turned into a site of multiple political, economic, and armed struggles among various actors and across different spatiotemporal registers.

ONE

A SITE OF MANY
STRUGGLES

WHEN I VISITED THE CITY of Wan for the first time in the summer of 2010, I found it easy to orient myself while walking or driving. The city lay between Mt. Erek in the east—which could be seen from various locations across the city—and Lake Wan in the west. The earliest settlements in Wan emerged in the 800s BC, and the first city center was built next to the Wan citadel, which perched on a hilltop and overlooked the lakeshore. The city center, however, had been completely destroyed during clashes between the Ottoman forces and the Wan Armenians' resistance—clashes that began with the onset of the Armenian genocide in April 1915 and continued until April 1918.[1] The Republican authorities, which replaced the Ottoman Empire in 1923, relocated the city center and began the rebuilding project in the 1940s. While the old city center remained leveled, Turkish, Azeri, and Kurdish settlers from the countryside gradually repopulated the city center. Almost a half century later, in the 1990s, the city witnessed another wave of migration, as the Turkish authorities' counterinsurgency campaign forcibly displaced Kurdish villagers from the Wan countryside and the neighboring provinces of Colemêrg (Off. Hakkari), Agirî (Off. Ağrı), Bedlîs (Off. Bitlis), and Mûş (Off. Muş).

The bustling crossroads of the city center were located between the lake and the mountain. Cumhuriyet (Republic) Avenue—running north-south and intersecting Maraş Avenue in the south and Beşyol (Five Roads) junction in the north—was the administrative and commercial center of the city. The governor's building, which used to host the courthouse, was located near the Beşyol intersection. The customs building along with the main branches of the central bank, the state investment and development bank as well as other state-owned and private banks, lined Cumhuriyet Avenue. Commercial buildings, including restaurants, hotels, and shops, were all located on the avenue or on neighboring and connected streets. This urban center was also a regional financial hub that had accumulated, circulated, and re-channeled the revenue and wealth that various economic activities in Wan and neighboring provinces generated. These activities ranged from agriculture and animal husbandry to those of the service sectors, including education, health, transportation, and trading. But above all, smuggling was the main driver of economic life not only in Wan province but in the entire region across Colemêrg, Agirî, and Bedlîs.

Indeed, the smuggling economy was all too visible to non-locals. For example, contraband cigarettes were sold at makeshift vendor stalls on the streets connected to Cumhuriyet Avenue—not more than a few hundred meters from the governor's office—and the shopping arcades were filled with contraband goods that ranged from tea and sugar to chinaware and electronics. After spending several weeks in Wan, I learned about stores, just a few blocks away from the customs building, where I could even buy contraband gasoline. Through my many visits to border districts and villages, I also began to recognize the specific village houses in different districts where contraband fuel was sold.

Despite these rather obvious signs of the contraband commerce in the city center streets and distant border villages, the actual volume and breadth of the smuggling economies were difficult to gauge. Yet, expensive cars or real estate prices could serve as important indices of smuggling activity in the Kurdish borderlands. On Cumhuriyet Avenue, one could often spot expensive sports cars, luxury sedans, and SUVs, which were rumored to be driven by heroin smugglers. Likewise, Cumhuriyet Avenue was notorious for over-inflated commercial rental prices, especially on its tiny jewelry stores, which many locals speculated laundered money. Real estate investments, particularly commercial buildings, shopping arcades, and hotels, were also identified as a means of storing and disguising the contraband origins of wealth that smuggling generated.

The omnipresence of smuggling was puzzling given that the state security forces closely monitored northern Kurdistan (Bakur), its city centers, inter-city roads, and countryside because of the counterinsurgency war against the PKK. The contraband items—such as smuggled cigarettes that one could buy from the makeshift stalls on streets near Cumhuriyet Avenue—must have crossed the border and made their way to the city center after traveling through several military road checkpoints. As smuggling defied state laws, regulations, and borders, one might assume that the security forces would attempt to prevent smuggling activities and investigate the smugglers. In fact, the hundreds of court cases I saw during my fieldwork illustrated that security forces had pursued and detained smugglers, at least some of them.

I myself observed one incident in which the police attempted to catch a young Kurdish boy for selling contraband cigarettes at his makeshift stall on Sanat (Art) Street. The street, lined with shops, was open only to pedestrians, and street vendors sold a numerous variety of items, including textiles, shoes, phone accessories, and smuggled cigarettes. It was also directly connected to Cumhuriyet Avenue, a few hundred meters away from the governor's office and constantly surveilled by security cameras. On that occasion, as I was walking on Cumhuriyet Avenue and just after I turned into the street, I witnessed the attempted arrest. The boy seemed about ten years old and was standing next to several boxes of cigarettes on a stall made of two wooden fruit boxes. One police officer held one of the boy's arms and several individuals—other pedestrians—held his other arm and argued with the police officers in Turkish. As more onlookers arrived, a crowd began to form around the officers. After fifteen more minutes of heated exchange, the police officers backed off and left without the boy or the contraband cigarettes. The incident exemplified the broader social and political legitimacy of smuggling in Kurdistan. Many Kurds viewed state borders and laws to be socially and politically illicit because they arbitrarily divided the Kurdish homeland, families, and tribes and severed ancestral trade networks. Smuggling also played a key role in the regional economy as many earned their living directly or indirectly from the contraband commerce.

The smuggling economies' wider social legitimacy and their broader role in the overall economy of Kurdistan may explain why Turkish authorities tolerated certain smuggling activities. These economies were too central to the regional economy of northern Kurdistan and dismantling these activities might further provoke the Kurdish population and increase the popularity of the PKK-led armed struggle. In fact, by turning rural Kurdistan into a battleground, imposing no-go zones and forced village evacuations—and thus heavily undermining the economies of agriculture and livestock—the government's counterinsurgency war compelled many to turn to smuggling to earn a living. As the incident on Sanat Street demonstrated, the state officials could always target Kurdish smugglers, however. There was no taken-for-granted tolerance by the state authorities for smuggling. For this reason, many smugglers often bribed state officials—from unranked lay soldiers to mid-ranking military officers—to secure their ability to transport and sell contraband items. Despite these bribes, many smugglers still faced anti-smuggling operations and ambushes. Although the authorities' enforcement of anti-smuggling laws seemed inconsistent, it was never fully absent in the Kurdish borderlands. This inconsistency, in fact, emerged as a feature of colonial control of Kurdish lands, lives, and livelihoods.

Soliciting bribes from smugglers was not the only way Turkish security forces benefited from smuggling—they also sought to appropriate certain smuggling networks and a share of the contraband trade. On several occasions and since the heyday of the counterinsurgency war in the 1990s, members of the security forces had been caught and accused of arms and heroin smuggling. During my fieldwork, I came across many smugglers who accused village guards—paramilitary groups recruited by the government from Kurdish villagers and tribes to fight against the PKK—of offering their paramilitary service or intelligence on the guerrillas in exchange for the security forces tolerating or even facilitating their smuggling. Instead of pursuing and dismantling Kurdish smuggling networks, the security forces appropriated some of these networks and made use of smuggling to fund their counterinsurgency efforts, both directly and indirectly. However, the authorities' control over smuggling remained partial, and many continued to engage in contraband commerce independent of networks aligned with the security forces. In the 2000s and 2010s, the coexistence in Kurdistan of smuggling

networks co-opted by state authorities and contraband commerce that operated outside of the authorities' control transformed smuggling economies
into a key node of economic activity, as well as political and armed confronta-
tions. To explicate how Kurdish smuggling economies became crucial sites of
these struggles, this chapter traces multiple actors and histories from the late
Ottoman period and early Republican years to the 1990s counterinsurgency
war and beyond, connecting the Kurdish highlands to urban centers in western Turkey, Europe, and North America.

A BRIEF HISTORY OF SMUGGLING IN
TURKEY AND KURDISTAN

For most of the nineteenth and early twentieth centuries, smuggling had
been an established means of subsistence across the Ottoman Empire's ex-
pansive borders. During this period, smuggling focused on the commodities
whose production and trade had been jointly monopolized by the Ottoman
state and European merchants whose commercial enterprise was to aid the
Empire in repaying its increasing foreign debts.[2] A prominent example of an
otherwise monopolized contraband good was tobacco. In 1873, the Ottoman
state first monopolized the tobacco trade, and, in 1883, the tobacco monopoly
rights were given to the joint company *Société de la Régie Co-Intéressée des
Tabacs de l'Empire Ottoman*, also known as the Régie Company. The company
was established by the Ottoman Public Debt Administration and received
direct investment from three European Banks.[3] Against the backdrop of this
monopolization, tobacco smuggling emerged and expanded across Ottoman
lands; consequently, the Régie installed armed surveillance forces (*kolcu*) to
combat smugglers. Similarly, the salt monopoly—which originated in 1862
and was later assigned to the Debt Administration—also incentivized smuggling, especially across the Empire's Black Sea and Aegean shores.[4] In 1925,
two years after the establishment of the Turkish Republic, the monopolies
were nationalized and maintained until the 2000s, as the smuggling of the
monopolized goods continued and grew.[5] While cigarette (roll) papers, salt,
matches, and sugar were smuggled into the country, tobacco and sheep were
smuggled out of Turkey.[6] Opium was another key commodity during the
nineteenth-century smuggling trade and has remained significant to this day.
In this period, the opium produced in Ottoman lands obtained a significant

place in the world's market and eventually came to supply 10 percent of the opium consumed in China.[7]

At the turn of the nineteenth century, European and U.S. authorities began restricting the trade and consumption of raw opium and opium products, including heroin, while the Ottoman state and its successor, the Republic of Turkey, remained hesitant about abandoning the trade. Legally produced opium and opium products in Turkey were mainly smuggled to European countries, the U.S., and Egypt. In response to the League of Nations' impositions of restrictions on the international opium trade in 1924 and 1925, heroin factories began to open in Istanbul in 1926.[8] By 1930, three heroin factories were active in Istanbul and supplied heroin to international heroin smuggling networks.[9] Despite international pressure, the Republican authorities were reluctant to close these factories until late 1932, when Turkey joined the League of Nations and was forced to shut them down. A leading reason for this reluctance was the economic difficulties wrought by the Great Depression of 1929—indeed, as foreign demand for locally cultivated cash crops, such as cotton, tobacco, and hazelnuts, declined, the Republic faced a scarcity of foreign currency, for which the opium trade emerged as partial relief.[10]

The Great Depression marked a turning point in Turkey's economic strategies: authorities began enacting policies for an increasingly protectionist and government-controlled economic order. Yet, these policy changes also set the stage for the resurgence of smuggling. As protectionist policies introduced import limitations and bans, high customs fees, and rigid foreign currency restrictions, smuggling networks increasingly thrived through the selling of goods whose production and trade were restricted by the government. In this period, smuggling across the Turkish-Syrian border burgeoned, as the French mandate in Syria continued its liberal foreign trade regime and provided low-cost Japanese textiles that were heavily smuggled into Turkey.[11] Opium trade also emerged across Turkey and Syria. Following the closure of heroin factories in Istanbul and the imposition of controls on opium production, small-scale, black-market workshops arose and, during the 1940s and 1950s, provided morphine and other opium products to the global (contraband) heroin market via Syria and Lebanon. These networks sold raw opium and morphine to Corsican mafia groups who processed these substances in their heroin laboratories in Marseille. This opium-heroin trade, known as the French Connection, was active until the 1970s.[12]

Following the Kurdish rebellion led by Shaikh Said in February of 1925, Turkish authorities began to tighten their border enforcement across the Syrian and Iraqi borders.[13] Given that the rebellion posed a significant political and military threat to the Republic, the authorities also viewed the spread of news and ideologies that heightened Kurdish political consciousness across Syria, Iraq, and Iran as a national security issue.[14] Accordingly, the Turkish government specifically targeted Kurdish smugglers—the key actors who facilitated the circulation not only of commodities, but also of news, ideas, and ideologies across Kurdish communities living in different parts of Kurdistan—as a threat to state security, a concern that still persists today. Since the merchants who supplied the smuggling networks out of Syria were mainly of Armenian and Assyrian descent (i.e., former nationals of the Ottoman Empire who escaped from persecution and genocide in Anatolia), Turkish authorities particularly suspected the potential of smuggling activities to foster alliances between Kurds and other former Ottoman nationals.[15] The Turkish officials conveyed such concerns to French colonial authorities in Syria. For example, in one incident, the Turkish government warned of an impending conspiracy led by Kurdish and Armenian groups in Syria and accused the French of providing them with aid.[16] Relatedly, the Turkish government also perceived the smuggling trade as an obstacle to the creation of a national economy. In 1931, the interior minister prepared a report on smuggling across the Turkish-Syrian border and complained about the economic influence of the Syrian province of Aleppo in Turkey's southern and eastern regions, indirectly referring to northern Kurdistan.[17] In 1936, another report by state authorities recommended tightening border enforcement, raising the prices of tobacco and cigarettes—because the state monopoly sold these items for a low price, they were mainly smuggled to Syria—and expanding domestic textile production to offer affordable alternatives to smuggled fabrics and materials.[18] Despite the Turkish government's efforts to frame smuggling as a threat, contraband commerce across the Syrian-Turkish border continued to expand until the outbreak of World War II.[19]

From the 1950s onward, the Turkish state continued tightening the enforcement of its southern and eastern borders. In the 1950s, the government installed barbed-wire fences, built watch towers, and laid mines across the Syrian border.[20] Despite these intensified security measures, the contraband commerce continued and rapidly adjusted to the changing nature of regional and international trade. Illegal border crossings to Syria increasingly came to be led by experienced smugglers who knew the routes and how to avoid surveillance and land mines. These smugglers often bribed border patrols to establish safe passage to Turkey. The need for specialized knowledge about border crossing, border passage arrangements, and the idiosyncrasies of the landscape, however, undermined small-scale smuggling journeys that individual border villagers used to organize and finance across the Turkish-Syrian border.[21] From the 1960s onward, this new border regime resulted in the emergence of a network of district- and city-based traders—trader smugglers—who became the primary organizers, investors, and beneficiaries of smuggling activities. These traders' dominance of the smuggling economies allowed them to accumulate capital and invest in city-center arcades to sell their smuggled goods.[22] Meanwhile, villagers participated in smuggling as carriers—day workers who transported the contraband for the traders.

The late 1950s and 1960s also witnessed a major transformation in the opium trade, which left its mark on the smuggling economies in the region. In response to pressure from U.S. authorities, opium production was banned in Iran in 1955. This ban resulted in increased opium cultivation in Turkey, Afghanistan, and Pakistan as well as in the rise of a new wave of smuggling into Iran itself, which historically had been home to a developed domestic opium market. As opium smuggling to France continued in the 1960s—via the French connection through Turkish-Syrian border and Beirut ports—Kurdish smugglers also began transporting to Iran opium and opium products, in addition to contraband sheep, through Turkish-Iranian borders.[23] Particularly, the smugglers based in Licê (Off. Lice) district of Diyarbekir/ Amed became a dominant force in the contraband trade. Since the district's rugged landscape connected different regions—such as the Black Sea, Syrian, Iraqi, and Iranian borderlands—the district emerged as a key smuggling hub despite its distance from the official borderlines.[24]

The 1960s also witnessed the rise of arms and ammunition smuggling from Western Germany, Spain, France, and Czechoslovakia to Iran, Iraq, and Syria, via Bulgaria and Turkey.[25] The shipment of contraband weapons and ammunition from Europe to Turkey was organized by smugglers who were based in western and northern Turkey, especially Laz smugglers from the Black Sea region. These ventures were key in supporting the Kurdish rebellion in Iraq, led by Mullah Mustafa Barzani during the 1960s and the 1970s.[26] In the 1970s, arms and opium smuggling became entangled with and controlled by the same criminal networks.

Whereas Iran reauthorized the cultivation of opium in 1969, Turkey banned it in 1971. This had the effect, for much of the 1970s, of reversing the trajectories of opium smuggling between the two countries. While Kurdish smugglers based in Wan, Colemêrg, and Diyarbekir/Amed's Licê district organized the transportation of opium from Iran to Turkey, Black Sea smugglers delivered the smuggled opium to European—primarily, Italian-Sicilian—mafia to be processed into heroin and eventually sold in Western Europe and North America markets.[27] The very lucrative smuggling of arms and opium enabled Turkish and Kurdish smugglers to accumulate enough financial capital to venture into legal businesses and create "front" companies, such as inter-city bus companies, trucking services, hotels, clubs, and construction firms. Thanks to the increased accumulation of capital and an effective money laundering operation, their smuggling activities expanded significantly.[28] Istanbul-based smugglers became leading crime bosses in the city's underground, which had already been dominated by racketeers who ran their own coffeehouses, clubs, and gambling casinos.[29]

The 1970s also marked a crucial era in the smuggling trade, as arms and ammunition were increasingly funneled toward conflicts between right-wing, ultranationalist militants, on the one hand, and leftist groups in Turkey, on the other. The smuggler bosses who had right-wing political affiliations supplied arms to the ultranationalist militants—who were mainly affiliated with the MHP's (Nationalist Action Party[30]) youth organization, Idealist Hearts (Ülkü Ocakları), popularly known as Grey Wolves (Bozkurtlar).[31] During the late 1960s and 1970s, the Turkish military's Special Warfare Department—which had been established in 1953 under the auspices of the CIA after Turkey's accession to NATO—recruited some of these ultranationalist youth into its counterguerrilla program and mobilized them as a proxy paramilitary force against leftist activists, intellectuals, and labor organizers, as well as minorities, particularly the Alevi and Kurdish communities in Turkey.[32] In the late 1970s, the ultranationalist militants themselves engaged in arms and drug smuggling.[33] Istanbul-based smuggling networks occasionally allowed some leftist Turkish and Kurdish students access to contraband handguns to protect themselves against these ultranationalist militants.[34]

The nature and scope of the smuggling economies in Turkey changed once again with the military coup of September 1980. The Turkish army heavily restricted arms smuggling, which forced smuggling networks to revert back to the trade of opium and heroin. Simultaneously, the Iranian Revolution of 1979 had already increased deterrence measures on opium smuggling in Iran, which gradually led to the relocation of heroin laboratories to Turkey, mainly in Kurdish borderlands along the Iranian border and Diyarbekir/ Amed's Licê district. The military junta and subsequent civilian governments also introduced neoliberal economic reforms in the 1980s. By replacing the import substitution economic model with an export orientation model, they lifted capital controls and eventually allowed trade in foreign currency. As a result, the domestic market became flooded with high-quality imports— such as electronics, textile products, and foreign currency—which, in turn, shrunk the smuggling market. The domestic production of textile products also increased, which led to a decline in the smuggling of such goods during the 1980s.

The 1990s saw a dramatic increase in the smuggling of everyday consumption items, especially oil, cigarettes, tea, and sugar. This expansionary trend continued through the 2000s. A 2005 Turkish parliamentary report, for instance, estimated that a billion gallons of smuggled oil entered Turkey every year.[35] The apparent reason for this increase was the price differences in oil between Turkey and its neighbors. At the time of my fieldwork, for example, the gasoline price in Turkey (around $8 per gallon) was one of the highest in the world, even though prices were significantly lower in oil-producing neighboring states, such as Iran ($2 per gallon) and Iraq ($3.5 per gallon). The same applied to cigarettes, with a package costing around $3 in Turkey, compared to $1 in Iraq and Iran. These price differences resulted from successive increases in sales taxes throughout the 1990s, which financed the government's internal and external borrowing to fund the corrupt ventures of state officials and the military expenses associated with the counterinsurgency war against the PKK.[36] Thus, the explicit economic motive behind the increasing smuggling of everyday consumption items in the 1990s—namely increased sales taxes—was thus closely related to the counterinsurgency war with the PKK. Indeed, the counterinsurgency war profoundly reshaped smuggling economies in Kurdistan and Turkey. To explain this impact, I now turn to rural Kurdistan, particularly the highlands as the key site of smuggling logistics, to trace how and why this particular region became the stage for the PKK guerrillas' armed resistance campaign, while the security forces attempted to regain control over the area.

THE RISE OF THE PKK AND THE COUNTERINSURGENCY WAR

The PKK was one of the few Kurdish political organizations to survive the military dictatorship responsible for the 1980 coup. Most other Turkish and Kurdish revolutionary organizations lost their leadership, membership, and support bases during this period. The PKK's leading cadres fled Turkey before the coup, establishing themselves in Lebanon's Beqaa Valley and securing guerrilla bases in southern Kurdistan (Başûr) through the first half of the 1980s. Following a six-year-long preparatory period in and outside of Turkey, the PKK launched a full-fledged armed struggle against the Turkish state in August 1984. To this day, the PKK has posed the most enduring military and political challenge to the Republic.

In their first attack, on August 15, 1984, PKK guerrillas targeted military bases and state buildings in the town centers of Dih (Off. Eruh), a district in Sêrt province, and Şemzînan (Off. Şemdinli), a district in Colemêrg province. The PKK commanders had planned to attack Wan's Şax (Off. Çatak) district as well in an attempt to delimit a specific region—the Dih-Şemzînan-Şax triangle—which corresponded to the main highlands that interconnected Kurdish regions in Turkey, Iran, and Iraq.[37] The PKK commanders had selected these highlands as a foundational region for the establishment of guerrilla bases that could gradually expand their presence into other highland areas. Although the Şax attack was called off, the PKK forces were stationed in the Kurdish highlands, from the Dih-Şemzînan-Şax triangle to northern Amed—Diyarbekir/Amed's Licê, Pasûr (Off. Kulp), and Hezro (Off. Hazro) districts—and the Serhad highlands—Tendürek and Ararat Mountains as well as Wan's border districts—during the second half of the 1980s.[38] By the early 1990s, the PKK had secured temporary and permanent guerrilla camps in the highlands of northern Kurdistan and had achieved the capacity to conduct ambushes and raids on Turkish security forces and military stations; they could even impose temporary road checkpoints on the land-road network. The PKK also built city-based networks of support.[39] A senior Turkish journalist, for example, reported in 1992 that a high-ranking Turkish military commander had confessed to him that "there [was] a dual authority in many parts of the Southeast [northern Kurdistan]; the state [was in charge] in the daylight and another authority [the PKK] at night."[40]

Because of the harsh, mountainous terrain that characterizes the Kurdish highlands and the limited communication and transportation technologies of the time, the Turkish authorities could only establish partial rule over the area during the 1980s. Thus, the PKK commanders decided to use the highlands as a launching point for their broader guerrilla strategy—a decision that resonated on the ground and garnered widespread support from the local residents. These highlands were mainly populated and navigated by villagers, shepherds, and nomads (*koçers*) who took their flocks into the highlands during the spring and summer seasons. By the end of the 1980s, the guerrillas became the Kurdish highlands' new residents and navigators.

The topographical features of the region, with its deep valleys and caves, allowed the guerrillas to hide from the security forces and to navigate the region swiftly and stealthily.[41] The mountains allowed the guerrillas to orchestrate multiple attacks while keeping a distance from the military's armored ground vehicles.[42] With the help of pack animals, guerrillas transported food, ammunition, heavy weapons—such as trench mortars and anti-aircraft weapons—and other types of equipment. The small mountain creeks and the subterranean reservoirs provided the guerrillas with much-needed water, thus enabling several-days-long journeys during which they carried very small amounts of food. A former guerrilla whom I met in a border district, for example, told me how they could walk for days with just a handful of salt, which they ate to regulate their blood pressure. The guerrillas used the mountain caves—some of which could extend hundreds of meters underground—as subterranean bases where they could furnish different levels with dormitories, kitchens, or computer rooms.[43] The persistent guerrilla presence in the highlands transformed the signifiers "the mountain" or "being-on-the-mountains" into powerful political symbol of Kurdish resistance and liberation.[44]

Against the PKK's rising popularity and influence in rural Kurdistan, the Turkish government initiated a multistage counterinsurgency campaign that employed a new military approach known as "the field domination concept" (*alan hakimiyeti konsepti*). This approach superseded the preexisting strategy of holding and protecting land through the presence of a steady military force. Rather than being stationed in military bases, the military forces continuously navigated the highlands, searching for and collecting intelligence on the guerrillas, and fighting them using the guerrillas' own combat tactics.[45] This novel strategy had two goals: to reorganize the security forces into an armed force that could effectively combat guerrillas, and to depopulate the Kurdish highlands to undermine the PKK's use of Kurdish villages and hamlets as logistical bases for obtaining intelligence and food.

The first goal of creating a military force that could deploy guerrilla tactics involved training regular, conscripted soldiers to become resilient to long walks while carrying heavy equipment and to spending weeks in the mountains without adequate food or sleep.[46] The military also deployed its commando brigades, which were originally based in central and western Turkey (Kayseri and Bolu provinces), to the Kurdish highlands. In time, the military established new commando brigades in Kurdish provinces, including Colemêrg, Sêrt, Bedlîs, Çewlîk (Off. Bingöl), and Dersim (Off. Tunceli). By the late 1980s, the Turkish authorities had successfully formed paramilitary forces among the Kurdish villagers under the post of village guards (*köy korucuları*).[47] The village guards system aimed to extend the Turkish military's reach into the mountains and into rural Kurdistan by creating an armed force that could contest guerrillas and collect information on them.[48] The village guards participated in the military operations alongside the conscripted soldiers. In an effort to undermine the guerrilla forces, the Turkish parliament also introduced a law in 1988 that offered PKK members legal immunity and public posts as an incentive to repent, desert the guerrilla ranks, and surrender to the security forces.[49]

The leading guerrilla-like military force that the Turkish government deployed in its counterinsurgency efforts was named the JİTEM (the

Gendarmerie Intelligence and Counter-Terrorism Organization[50]), a military unit founded around 1987 to 1988 and whose existence was officially denied until the 2010s.[51] The JİTEM operated through special teams, which included former and active-duty officers, as well as PKK repentants (*itirafçılar*).[52] Unlike the military's regular forces, JİTEM teams wore guerrilla clothing and were deployed in the mountains for weeks at a time. They visited villages and hamlets and disguised themselves as guerrillas to gather intelligence on PKK forces and their militia (*milis*) networks, which consisted of civilians who provided regular logistical and intelligence support to the guerrillas. These teams also identified ordinary villagers who supported guerrillas with food and shelter, targeting them for threats, harassment, or torture.

To target individuals who were allegedly associated with the PKK, the state authorities also formed death squads among the JİTEM units as well as among the village guards, the army's counterguerrilla teams, the associates of the MİT (National Intelligence Organization[53]), and the police special forces.[54] Several ultranationalist militants who had been recruited by the government's counterguerrilla units against the leftist youth movements of the 1970s and 1980s also joined these death squads.[55] Moreover, the government officials clandestinely supported the outlawed Hizbullah—an armed Kurdish Islamist organization that rivaled the PKK—and directed it to physically target PKK members and supporters.[56] In the 1990s and early 2000s, these death squads engaged in political killings, enforced disappearances, kidnappings, torture, and extortion, as well as heroin and arms smuggling. They were blamed for the loss of thirty thousand lives in Kurdistan and Turkey during the war with the PKK.[57] These squads turned daily encounters with security forces and paramilitaries—including one's neighbors or acquaintances who had become villager guards—into chilling experiences and, in doing so, installed "fear as a way of life" in urban and rural Kurdistan.[58]

The Turkish government also equipped the army with technologically advanced military equipment, such as armored and four-by-four personnel carriers, night-vision and thermal imagining equipment, as well as transportation and attack helicopters. This equipment allowed security forces to conduct surveillance and offensive operations at night and, therefore, to undermine the PKK's nighttime rule of Kurdistan.

The use of night vision and thermal imaging by security forces substantially changed how guerrillas and other residents of the highlands, such as smugglers, sensed and navigated the Kurdish highlands. Focusing on the daily rhythms of the highlanders, a "rhythmanalysis" could offer insights into how the counterinsurgency war reshaped human and nonhuman mobility across day and night, as well as seasonally.[59] Equipped with night vision, helicopters allowed security forces to navigate and monitor Kurdish mountains around the clock. As a former guerrilla told me, this led the guerrillas to restrict their movements at night and to seek shelter to avoid the risk of starting a fire. They also became attuned to weather conditions, such as snowstorms, which could limit the use of helicopters. The presence of helicopters further transformed the soundscapes of the Kurdish highlands. Nomads and their animals, smugglers, and guerrillas became used to the sounds of hovering helicopters and even began to differentiate the sounds of (Sikorsky) cargo helicopters from that of (Cobra or Super Cobra) attack helicopters. At night, especially in foggy weather, the distinctive hovering sounds served as warnings of the presence of military patrols, surveillance expeditions, potential aerial bombings, or nearby special teams.[60] During their nocturnal movements, smugglers or guerrillas would visually scan the landscape for any light sources that might indicate the presence of security forces and would listen intently to the soundscape for any auditory signs of unseen aerial vehicles.

The soundscapes of Kurdish highlands changed again in the 2010s when state authorities adopted the use of surveillance and assault aerial drones in their counterinsurgency war. By the mid-2010s, Turkey, relying on the technological support from its NATO allies, had developed the capacity to locally manufacture advanced surveillance and assault drone systems.[61] Compared to other aircrafts, these drones—offering lower operating costs and the ability to fly for extended periods (around twenty hours)—allowed for much longer time blocks of uninterrupted surveillance of the highlands. While the drones were not always visible from the ground, the highlanders learned to detect them through their distinctive buzzing sound—a more distant yet higher-pitched sound than that of helicopter hovering—and by their smell—reminiscent of burnt diesel fuel. After spending a few months in mountainous border villages, I even began to recognize the drones' sounds and smells myself. Identifying a drone lingering in the sky above invoked chilling experiences for Kurdish highlanders, as it was difficult to predict whether the drone was conducting surveillance or preparing for an attack. In this way, drones had a terrorizing effect in the Kurdish borderlands similar to that of death squads, as the targets, timing, and location of an attack remained unpredictable.[62]

To achieve the second goal of the field domination strategy—namely, the depopulation of rural Kurdistan—security forces initially imposed embargos on the villages to limit the amount of food, such as flour or bread, that villagers were allowed to bring into their locales. While seeking to limit the amount of food that villagers voluntarily or involuntarily shared with the guerrillas, the embargo primarily aimed to harass, intimidate, and make life unbearable for rural inhabitants in the highlands. Accordingly, the gendarmerie and village guards established checkpoints at the entrances of certain villages or regions to confiscate food cargos that exceeded the permitted amounts. Later, the Turkish government implemented a broader, more systematic plan to depopulate rural Kurdistan.[63] Under this plan, security forces evacuated villages and hamlets, displacing millions of people, and destroyed the emptied villages, including houses, furniture, foodstuffs, animals, and agricultural fields, to prevent the villagers from returning.[64]

The village evacuations were closely tied to the expansion of the village guard system, as authorities often forced Kurdish villagers to either join this paramilitary force or leave their homes.[65] With no other options, some villagers became guards to protect their communities from being evacuated. However, these guards often avoided or reluctantly participated in the army's clashes with the PKK. For this reason, joining the village guard force did not necessarily mean aligning with the Turkish government—although many used their government-provided weapons and status as leverage in land disputes and other local power rivalries. Additionally, security forces imposed no-go zones in nearby agricultural fields and grazing lands for those who were not forcibly evacuated. In some cases, access to privately owned land was granted only through temporary written permissions.

By dispossessing the rural populations of their land, agricultural fields, and livestock, the village evacuations generated new and unusual forms of wealth accumulation and gave rise to new economic actors in Kurdistan. While working as a clerk in a law office, I came across a man who made his fortune from the forced evacuations. Contraband cigarettes were found in a warehouse owned by a businessman who used to be a butcher. In fact, the businessman started as a butcher's apprentice when he was a young boy and later opened up his own butcher shop in 1995. During the 2000s, he had accumulated a significant amount of capital and began extending his business into other sectors, establishing a regional corporate group. While smuggling might explain his fast track to wealth, he initially needed a significant amount of money to invest in lucrative businesses, including smuggling. Where did that initial capital come from? How could a butcher generate that amount of money? At first, the entire scenario seemed very unlikely to me. Yet, as I later found out, the butcher shop had, indeed, generated the initial capital. Because of the village evacuations and forced displacement, tens of thousands of villagers were forced to move to the city center, bringing their livestock with them and whatever else they could carry. With no place to house their livestock, they had no choice but to sell the animals at significantly lower prices. Benefiting from their existing business networks across the country, a few butchers in Wan bought these animals and sold them to their counterparts in western Turkey. These butchers obtained significant profits, while the forcibly displaced villagers were dispossessed of their property and belongings. Like these butchers, several city dwellers benefited economically from the influx of the forcibly displaced people during the 1990s. In this way, a new affluent class emerged, one that invested their accumulated wealth into smuggling to generate more wealth. Throughout the 2000s and 2010s, they constituted a significant proportion of the Kurdish entrepreneurs who were engaged in many economy sectors, including trade, construction, tourism, and retail. The rise of this new business class illustrated how the counterinsurgency war and related regimes of violence and dispossession in Kurdistan led to considerable socioeconomic and demographic changes. These changes also resulted in the unexpected growth of smuggling economies.

EXPANSION OF SMUGGLING DURING THE COUNTERINSURGENCY

The counterinsurgency notably enhanced the Kurdish smuggling economies' social, geopolitical, and financial scopes. The forced village evacuations and the imposition of no-go zones wreaked havoc on existing farming economies in rural Kurdistan and forcibly displaced millions to the Kurdish cities first and eventually to those in central and western Turkey. The arrival of the forcibly displaced population further overwhelmed the already "de-developed" urban economies of Kurdistan.[66] Because of the devastated rural economies and deepening unemployment and poverty in the cities in 1990s Kurdistan, an increasing number of people entered the smuggling trade to earn their daily subsistence, which resulted in an unprecedented expansion of the smuggling economies. This expansion also overlapped with and was reinforced by the rising prices of everyday consumption items, such as oil, cigarettes, sugar, and tea across the whole country, given the increasing sale taxes that the government imposed to finance budgetary deficits and counterinsurgency war expenses.[67] As daily consumer goods became increasingly less affordable in the 1990s, Kurdish smugglers began to supply their contraband equivalents to northern Kurdistan as well as to central and western Turkey.

In the 2000s and 2010s, contraband commerce continued to flourish and became increasingly entangled with economic transactions that would have not otherwise involved smuggling in the Kurdish borderlands. On various occasions, not long after I moved to Wan city center in August 2012, I observed how participating in the city's economic life inevitably meant engaging in everyday debt and exchange relations with smugglers. The dispersed economies of smuggling occasionally meant that smuggling transactions and debt conflicts implicated people I would have not expected. I came across such a story through a neighbor, Zeki, a construction subcontractor, who had no interest in smuggling operations.

One day, Zeki asked me to meet to go over some court documents together. The case was about a land dispute. Although I insisted that I was not a lawyer and that he needed to consult one, he still wanted me to look over the documents. Since I spent my mornings in the central Wan courthouse following the court sessions, I asked him to meet me in the afternoon in the city center. We agreed to meet in front of my favorite tea garden. Zeki did not like the meeting point, however. It was Zeki's landlord's favorite tea garden too. "The landlord is not here," I said to lighten his anxiety. As a construction subcontractor, Zeki worked for larger construction companies on various projects. His business had recently incurred financial problems, and he had been unable to pay his rent for the last five months. Following the devastating earthquake in late 2011, new business opportunities emerged for the construction sector, as hundreds of buildings needed to be demolished because of structural damage. However, Zeki's business suffered because payments and reimbursements from a contractor were significantly delayed.

"I could not deal with the landlord today," Zeki said. I asked if he had any good news about his payments from the contractor. "There is some news, but I am not sure whether it is good or bad." The contractor had actually paid the debt. That was great news. Maybe Zeki could pay all of his debts after all, including his unpaid rent. Yet, the contractor had offered to pay his debts in the form of smuggled cigarettes, and Zeki had accepted the offer. "I became a part-time smuggler," he said, combining the English word "part-time" with the Kurdish *qaçaxçi*.

As far as I knew, Zeki was not involved with any smuggling network. Without any connections, it would have been very difficult for him to trade the cigarettes for cash. But there was more to the story: The cigarettes were intercepted and confiscated by the police. According to Zeki, a month before the confiscation, the contractor had transported the cigarettes to Westan (Off. Gevaş), a town twenty miles west of the Wan city center. He had hoped to find a buyer from the western parts of the country who could easily transfer them to central and western Anatolian cities through the mountain pass near Westan, as transporting the smuggled cigarettes in and out of Wan city center would have been challenging. Yet, the contractor failed to find a buyer and, under increasing pressure from Zeki, offered the cigarettes to him as payment for the debt. After Zeki accepted the cigarettes as payment, the contraband was reloaded on a truck and put back on the road from Westan to Wan. Yet, just before the truck entered Wan, it was stopped at a police checkpoint, and the smuggled cigarettes were seized. The trucker was sent to court under an allegation of smuggling. But who was legally—criminally—responsible for the smuggling operation? And who was financially responsible for the confiscated cigarettes? Was it Zeki's responsibility or the contractor's? These were all important questions that were eventually resolved through negotiations between the contractor, Zeki, the trucker, his family, and some mediators. Both Zeki and the contractor agreed on equally sharing the financial loss and made a payment to the trucker's family in exchange for his silence regarding their involvement.

In addition to demonstrating the omnipresence of contraband commerce in the economic life of the Kurdish borderlands, the case demonstrated how smuggling economies operated on and generated new debt relations, especially given the added risks of being caught in a militarized region and potentially losing the contraband cargo. For Zeki and the other contractor, the material loss was around a few thousand dollars (a few thousand packages of cigarettes at $1 per package). Depending on the smuggled item, however, the financial scope of the venture could reach a few million dollars. While a package of smuggled cigarettes cost around $1, a smuggled smartphone (e.g., an iPhone) was worth more than $500 at the time. If Zeki had engaged in smuggling a few hundred smartphones—which would have taken a volume of space similar to that of a few thousand cigarette packages—he would have faced a material loss of a few hundred thousand dollars. If it had been a case of heroin smuggling, not only would the material loss had been significantly more substantive, but the criminal punishment would have been considerably more severe—more than twenty years of imprisonment.

THE APPROPRIATION OF KURDISH SMUGGLING

While the counterinsurgency war expanded Kurdish smuggling economies, security forces also attempted to contain these economies and redirect the smuggling-generated wealth toward their counterinsurgency efforts. During the early 1990s, as the counterinsurgency forces traversed the Kurdish highlands and achieved a regular presence in urban life, they began to exert control over Kurdish smugglers. The forces targeted the smugglers known to support the PKK, while also employing the accusation of "aiding terrorism" as an unofficial pretext to co-opt or eliminate certain smuggling networks. The first group of Kurdish smugglers whom the security forces set their sights on was the heroin traffickers. During the 1980s, after heroin laboratories were relocated from Iran to Turkey, mainly in rural Kurdistan, Kurdish heroin smugglers significantly increased their share of the global heroin market. They began to organize long-range, high-volume heroin smuggling operations, procuring opium and heroin from Afghanistan, transporting it via cargo ships through Pakistani ports, and then transferring it to European business partners in the Mediterranean Sea.[68] To secure large-scale heroin trafficking operations, these smugglers also developed close relations with high-ranking state officials in the police and the military, regularly bribing them. These contacts, however, did not spare Kurdish heroin smugglers, including well-established smuggler bosses, from being kidnapped and killed by counterinsurgency death squads in the 1990s.

In the fall of 1993, high-ranking military officials and members of the government put together a list of Kurdish businesspeople, artists, intellectuals, and activists who were purported to support the PKK.[69] It was reported that Tansu Çiller, the head of True Path Party and then the prime minister, first mentioned the list during a press conference on November 4, 1993.[70] She declared, "The state will fight against those who provide financial support to the PKK in every possible way, just as it does with the PKK itself."[71] A week after the prime minister's statement—in a meeting held at the headquarter of the Union of Chambers and Commodity Exchanges in the capital city, Ankara—the interior minister and the head of the Turkish police "warned" a group of businesspeople who represented the trade chambers in Kurdish provinces not to provide financial support to the PKK.[72]

About two and half months after this meeting, on January 14, 1994, Behçet Cantürk—the first Kurdish businessperson and well-established smuggler boss who had been accused of supporting pro-Armenian and pro-Kurdish organizations—was killed by unknown perpetrators.[73] Cantürk was originally from Diyarbekir/Amed's Licê district and believed to be at the top of this list. He was kidnapped along with his driver; their lifeless bodies were found the following morning. In the year following this incident, at least eight other Kurdish businesspeople whom the authorities associated with smuggling, three Kurdish lawyers (one of whom was representing Behçet Cantürk), and two mid-level Kurdish state bureaucrats were kidnapped and killed in Istanbul and Ankara.[74] Hüseyin Baybaşin, another Kurdish smuggler boss, who was also from Licê, claimed to have learned about the death list from a high-ranking military officer he had bribed.[75] Shortly after finding out that his name was on the death list, Baybaşin left the country.

The killing of Kurdish businesspeople allegedly involved in smuggling, or their forced fleeing the country, particularly shocked other Kurdish smugglers, as some of these businesspeople, such as Cantürk, had been protected by armed bodyguards and armored vehicles and enjoyed close relations with high-ranking state officers. The elimination of these rich, well-connected strongmen pointed to the possible existence of a broader, albeit publicly unacknowledged, state strategy to redesign the Kurdish smuggling scene, especially given that only the counterinsurgency forces would have the organizational capacity and the state authorities' unofficial protection to carry out an operation on this scale. These killings also overlapped with the political killings and forced disappearances of politicians, activists, journalists, and lawyers in Kurdistan for which the counterinsurgency death squads have been publicly blamed.[76] These killings, vernacularly known as "the political killings by unknown perpetrators" (*faili meçhul siyasal cinayetler*), began as early as 1989, dramatically increased in 1992, and continued throughout the rest of the 1990s.[77]

The elimination of Kurdish businesspeople accused of smuggling significantly restructured the heroin and arms smuggling trade. The counterinsurgency squads expropriated and rechanneled smuggling revenues to pay for their expenses and corrupt self-enrichment. However, the Turkish government consistently denied the existence of these death squads. A 1995 parliamentary report blamed the PKK repentants, village guards, as well as Hizbullah and the PKK guerrillas for these political killings and highlighted several arms and ammunition smuggling cases in which village guards were involved.[78] In November 1996, a car accident exposed the depth of the alliances that the death squads had forged with high-ranking bureaucrats and elected politicians. A Mercedes sedan carrying the deputy chief of the Istanbul Police, a member of parliament who led a village guard Kurdish tribe, a former leader of the ultranationalist youth who later became a crime boss accused of murder and smuggling, and his girlfriend hit a truck near Susurluk district in Balıkesir province.[79] The parliamentarian was a member of Tansu Çiller's party, the former prime minister who, back in 1993, first mentioned the death list of Kurdish businesspeople and other purported PKK supporters. While the presence of these passengers in the same car was scandalous, public outrage increased when the ultranationalist crime boss was found carrying a government-issued diplomatic passport that featured his photo and a different name. In addition to the law enforcement authorities, a parliamentary commission and the Prime Ministry investigated the incident and published reports on it.[80] These reports eventually acknowledged that counterinsurgency death squads were engaged in heroin and arms smuggling.

Yet, the reports still claimed that these activities were isolated incidents committed by a few rogue factions.

The state authorities' control and appropriation of Kurdish smuggling networks at the time must be understood as part of a centrally planned and executed strategy, rather than an ad hoc development. And indeed, the mutually beneficial relations between security forces and smugglers, as well as state officials' involvement in smuggling, have been amply documented in Turkey and elsewhere.[81] These symbiotic relations range from corruption and self-enrichment schemes among individual state officers to the procurement of much-needed resources, such as money or arms, to establish a new government or allow an existing one to survive. During the counterinsurgency war in Kurdistan, the government-smuggling symbiosis followed a two-pronged strategy: eliminating Kurdish smuggler bosses identified as PKK supporters, and replacing—or subsuming—Kurdish networks of arms and heroin smuggling with counterinsurgency gangs to pay for paramilitary efforts.

The first part of the strategy materialized in the death list of Kurdish businesspeople who allegedly supported the PKK. Although death squads affiliated with different security bodies or factions, such as JİTEM, MİT, or police special forces, competed with each other over control of smuggling networks, they still maintained a broader strategy of eliminating Kurdish smuggler bosses, as well as Kurdish lawyers, politicians, and intellectuals, whom they extrajudicially listed as state enemies.

The second part of the strategy—which involved the counterinsurgency forces' involvement in heroin and arms smuggling to fund paramilitary expenses and personal enrichment—was exposed during the 1990s, perhaps accidentally or as a spillover of rivalries within the security forces and counterinsurgency gangs. One such exposure unfolded in July 1996, five months before the Susurluk accident, when a PKK repentant working for the Special Operation Unit in Colemêrg was accused of smuggling a heroin shipment in Colemêrg's Gever (Off. Yüksekova) district.[82] According to the repentant's testimony, the heroin cargo was connected to high-ranking commanders stationed in the region, including the head commander of the Hakkari Mountain and Commando Brigade. Thus, the existence of one of the counterinsurgency gangs, which would later be called "the Yüksekova Gang" (*Yüksekova Çetesi*), was identified. As a result of the public outrage that followed the Susurluk incident, the investigation of the Yüksekova Gang eventually evolved into a criminal prosecution in Diyarbekir/Amed. The prosecutor accused several on-duty security officers, including a colonel and a major, of heroin smuggling. The court documents record in detail how these officers vouched for repentants and village guards who carried heroin cargo through road checkpoints and how they organized the transportation of heroin cargos inside military trucks and helicopters.[83] Nonetheless, for both this specific case and more broadly, many questions remain unanswered about who benefited financially, politically, and personally from the counterinsurgency gangs' smuggling and in what forms and to what extent the smuggling supported the Turkish government's military and paramilitary efforts in Kurdistan from the 1990s onward.

The state authorities' appropriation of smuggling in Kurdistan remained limited, however. The security forces failed to contain all smuggling activities and smugglers in Kurdistan, especially given the expanding social, financial, and spatiotemporal scales of the smuggling economies. In fact, many carrier, trader, and investor smugglers continued to support Kurdish freedom politics—by voting for pro-Kurdish parties and joining and donating to civil society organizations that advocated Kurdish rights, as well as by providing financial and logistic support to the insurgencies and avoiding deeper collaborations with the security forces. A key factor that allowed many Kurdish smugglers to resist the security forces' efforts at appropriation was the persisting guerrilla presence that contested the security forces and interrupted their territorial control in the Kurdish border- and highlands.

CONTRABAND MOBILITY IN THE BORDERLANDS

By the 2000s, the government's counterinsurgency campaign had successfully undermined guerrilla control of Kurdish cities and some parts of rural Kurdistan by establishing an extensive surveillance infrastructure.[84] This surveillance apparatus was primarily composed of military and gendarmerie stations, watch towers equipped with night vision and thermal cameras, aerial surveillance vehicles, and road checkpoints. This apparatus also expanded the scope of anti-smuggling law enforcement in Kurdistan, as most defendants in smuggling trials in Wan had been apprehended by security forces during on-field ambushes or at road checkpoints. Upon detecting an individual or group navigating the mountainous passes, the security forces could set an ambush to intercept them. These individuals might also be detected and intercepted during on-field patrols that security forces conducted on armored four-by-four vehicles or by foot in rocky and icy terrains.[85] For the carrier smugglers, who either worked for themselves or for trader smugglers, however, the most challenging anti-smuggling law enforcement tools were permanent and temporary road checkpoints, which significantly reshaped the mobility of contraband in the Kurdish highlands.

Permanent checkpoints were established along the inter-city road network, often attached to military stations or bases. Having steady structures, such as roadblocks, stop signs, lights, parking lots, or guard houses, these checkpoints could be attended twenty-four hours a day, seven days a week, or just for a few hours. Additionally, temporary checkpoints might be set up discretionarily on the inter-city road network or village roads for a few hours, days, or weeks. Various units of the security forces and law enforcement agencies (including the army, gendarmerie, JİTEM, other paramilitary groups, police special forces, anti-smuggling police units, and even traffic police) established road checkpoints to serve shifting security purposes. At road checkpoints, specifically arranged for counterinsurgency surveillance, the security forces checked whether passengers had arrest warrants and tracked local and non-local passengers, especially if they were traveling to areas near security zones or borders. For example, a non-local passenger who crossed a checkpoint close to a PKK base and did not cross it again for some time might be listed as a potential PKK recruit. For anti-smuggling surveillance, security forces could search passing vehicles for contraband goods. When a vehicle was carrying commercial cargo, they would also inspect the transported goods and any accompanying documents, such as commercial invoices, bills of lading, insurance documents, or customs papers when the cargo was imported. Some checkpoints—such as the Yeniköprü checkpoint, which connected Gever district to Colemêrg city center and Wan province—were used for both counterinsurgency and anti-smuggling surveillance.

Beginning in 2008, the Turkish government reinforced its surveillance infrastructure in Kurdistan, including road checkpoints. The reinforcement commenced with the construction of fortified, high-security military and gendarmerie stations. The fortified stations were introduced after PKK raids on military stations in 2007 and 2008, and public criticisms of the structural weaknesses and geographical vulnerabilities of the existing stations.[86] The fortified stations, which were called *kalekol,* a portmanteau of the Turkish words for castle (*kale*) and station (*karakol*), featured bulletproof windows, steel doors, and higher concrete walls that were resistant to improvised explosive device attacks and heavy artillery, as well as attached and detached watch towers connected to the main station building through underground tunnels. The stations were also equipped with thermal cameras, night vision imagers, ground motion sensors, and remote-controlled weapon stations mounted on the station walls or towers. Wan province was one of the regions where the government had completed the construction of almost all of the planned fortified stations and watch towers in the first five years after announcing the station constructions.[87]

In upgrading the military stations, and with the aim of slowing down and redirecting incoming traffic, the government also fortified the permanent road checkpoints and furnished them with steel-and-concrete blocks. The guard houses were fortified with blast blocks as well. In 2016, the authorities began installing metal overhead canopies to cover checkpoint lanes or attached parking areas.[88] In addition to the fortifications, government officials even experimented with incorporating remote-controlled surveillance apparatuses into the permanent road checkpoints. Accordingly, in November 2016, the Bitlis Governorship announced the first "High-security Uncrewed Checkpoint" (*Yüksek Güvenlikli İnsansız Kontrol Noktası*) set at the entrance of Bedlîs city center.[89] With the aid of cameras, speakers, and remote-controlled road barriers fortified with blast walls, the security forces could now stay inside the fortified guardhouse and remain protected against possible suicide vehicle attacks while conducting counterinsurgency and anti-smuggling surveillance. The gendarmerie also announced the use of body and vehicle cameras with face detection capabilities at checkpoints to facilitate remote-controlled ID checks, which relieved them from having to collect each passenger's ID cards and manually check them against the criminal records database.[90]

The permanent road checkpoints were further supported by a network of CCTV cameras installed at the entrances of city centers and main public areas, such as squares, parks, public transportation nodes, and central intersections.

First piloted in 2001, this surveillance system was called the Mobile Electronic System Integration and was publicly known by its Turkish acronym MOBESE. By the mid-2010s, the MOBESE system was operating in almost all provinces, including district and town centers. The system was equipped with automatic license plate recognition and allowed the tracking of specific vehicles' mobility across district and city centers. The MOBESE system was integrated into both counterinsurgency and anti-smuggling surveillance.

To circumvent the state's comprehensive surveillance infrastructure, particularly the road checkpoints, the smugglers implemented several tactics.[91] The first tactic relied on having a second car—a "joker car"—that would pass through the checkpoint five or ten minutes ahead of the vehicle carrying contraband cargo. As the joker car hit the checkpoint first, the driver would signal to the contraband-carrying car whether the checkpoint was active. If they signaled that a checkpoint was on duty, the cargo car would either wait until the security forces left the checkpoint or take back roads (i.e., village or country roads) to circumvent the checkpoint. While the use of back roads would be an effective way to bypass permanent road checkpoints, these roads were not well maintained, and in rainy and snowy weather the village roads were often covered with mud or ice. In the fall, winter, and spring, smugglers often needed to use pack animals—such as mules, donkeys, or horses—or certain types of motor vehicles to operate on these tough roads—often in off-road conditions—to carry a significant amount of cargo.[92] The authorities, however, could still monitor and set anti-smuggling ambushes on the back roads.

At other times, smugglers risked driving through the checkpoints while implementing measures to thwart the security forces' surveillance. To smuggle banned items, such as arms or heroin, they installed special hidden compartments (known as *zula* in Turkish and Kurdish slang) in their vehicles. However, inspection dogs or thorough searches could easily uncover these caches. Because the special cache provided limited space, they were more suitable for lighter—and more valuable—contraband cargo, such as heroin, arms, gold, or jewelry. For larger contraband cargos—like several tons of smuggled sugar or tea, or ten thousand liters of oil—smugglers used trucks or semitrailers and obtained forged or previously used trading documents, such as company invoices, lading bills, and customs papers, to facilitate passage through road checkpoints. Given the exigency of this paperwork, city-based traders typically organized the transportation and marketing of large quantities of contraband through urban company offices, warehouses, and retail stores. In addition to these tactics, often used in combination, smugglers frequently bribed low- and mid-ranking security officers for safe passage. Yet, arranging safe passage did not necessarily protect the smugglers from being caught at the checkpoints or from facing anti-smuggling ambushes. At road checkpoints, the security forces could still seize contraband cargos from the smugglers who had bribed them.[93]

While the Turkish military's presence across the inter-city road network was heavy, guerrilla activity, particularly in the highlands, was constant. Since the late 1980s, and despite being monitored by Turkish authorities (primarily through aerial surveillance), Kurdish guerrillas dominated certain parts of the highlands, restricting the Turkish army's access to these areas by land and establishing temporary and permanent guerrilla zones. Yet, the control exerted by the guerrillas in these regions—or by the government forces, for that matter—was neither absolute nor stable. At certain times, the Turkish military managed to narrow the scope of the guerrilla zones. At other times, a surge in guerrilla activity pushed the army back, expanding their zones of control. This ongoing push and pull resulted in a dynamic stalemate between the Turkish military and the PKK guerrillas.

During these stalemates, Kurdish guerrillas occasionally opened free-passage corridors on the highlands through which smugglers could circumvent the inter-city road network and avoid the security forces' checkpoints.[94] While the exact location and boundaries of such corridors would change over time, the incessant guerrilla activity could distract security forces from attending to and operating land-road checkpoints. In the summer of 2012, at the beginning of my fieldwork in Wan, for example, the clashes between the Turkish military and Kurdish guerrilla forces escalated into what was nearly a full-scale war. The guerrilla activity mainly centered around Colemêrg province's Şemzînan district—located between Iran and Iraq and connected to mainland Turkey by two narrow mountainous passes, the Haruna and Şapatan passes. In June 2012, the Kurdish guerrillas began a military campaign to block the Turkish military's land access to the Şemzînan district by taking control of these two passes. At the peak of the clashes, the PKK guerrillas had taken control of the Şapatan pass but failed to control the Haruna. A few weeks later, the Turkish military managed to take back the Şapatan pass. Eventually, the guerrilla forces withdrew from the district center to their mountain bases and held their position along southern Şemzînan. During the guerrilla operation, which extended until the end of September 2012, I noticed, while driving around, that most of the main permanent checkpoints in Wan and Colemêrg provinces were either unattended or only partially operational during daylight hours. In fact, during my fieldwork, I encountered multiple smugglers who discussed their successful transportation of illegal goods to the western provinces through inter-city roads during that guerrilla operation in the summer of 2012. They managed to do so without the need for joker vehicles, for instance, and generally encountered fewer obstacles because the guerrillas had prevented the security forces from staffing the road checkpoints. Following the guerrillas' withdrawal, however, road checkpoints imposed by the Turkish military on the main inter-city roads of Wan and Colemêrg gradually reappeared.

The resilient guerrilla activity, however, did not always benefit the smugglers. The dynamic stalemate and the constant push and pull of territorial control significantly undermined the predictability of smuggling logistics. While security forces could lose control of a region as a result of guerrilla activity, a guerrilla attack might also draw the army's attention, leading to an expansion of the Turkish government's territorial control. I observed such a contingent expansion of state control in a case where a surprise guerrilla attack on a gendarmerie station by the inter-city road network activated— rather than undermined—the station's checkpoint, resulting in a smuggler's apprehension.[95]

A SITE OF CO-OPTATION AND CONTESTATION

In the 2010s, smuggling had already emerged as the leading economic sector in the Wan borderlands. The counterinsurgency war fueled smuggling growth. By devastating the traditional agriculture and livestock economies in rural Kurdistan, dispossessing and forcibly displacing millions to the cities, the war transformed smuggling into the main source of subsistence for the urban and rural poor and into a leading site of investment for the wealthy in Kurdistan. The security forces also co-opted smuggling operations, actors, and networks into their counterinsurgency efforts, deploying them for intelligence gathering and using them as leverage for the recruitment of locals into its paramilitary forces. The appropriation of smuggling in Kurdistan, however, remained limited. Given the increasing scope and extent of the smuggling enterprise, which was ironically driven by the ongoing counterinsurgency, smuggling economies eventually became impossible for state officials to destroy, control, or fully co-opt into their counterinsurgency. Moreover, because the PKK guerrillas maintained their presence in the Kurdish highlands and occasionally opened free passages for smugglers, they also prevented the army's complete territorial takeover of rural Kurdistan and restricted its ability to fully control smuggling operations. In the backdrop of smuggling's expanding scope and reach and partial appropriation by the security forces, many in Kurdistan continued to view smuggling as a socially and politically licit economic activity. Thus, to residents of the Kurdish borderlands, smuggling became a unique site of both co-optation by and contestation of state authorities.

The seemingly contradictory coexistence of the smuggling networks appropriated by security forces alongside contraband commerce that operated outside of these forces' control further shaped the Turkish government's anti-smuggling efforts, particularly regarding the implementation of anti-smuggling laws in Kurdistan. In this manner, state officials, including the security forces and judiciary, came to view the anti-smuggling efforts as an extension of the counterinsurgency war, and accordingly treated Kurdish smugglers who were outside of government-appropriated networks as supporters or associates of the PKK-led insurgency. Because the authorities' deployment of anti-smuggling operations as a counterinsurgency device was not explicitly expressed in the texts of laws, regulations, or court decisions, it only became visible in parliamentary debates, policy papers, and off-the-record conversations in court hearings or off-the-court interactions with prosecutors and judges. The next chapter explicates how the counterinsurgency war co-opted anti-smuggling efforts and shaped the implementation of anti-smuggling law in Kurdistan.

TWO

THE CUNNING OF LAW

IT WAS A FEBRUARY EVENING in 2014. Mustafa and I had been stopped for questioning by a Turkish soldier at a temporary road checkpoint. The soldier asked what I did for a living. When I replied that I was a researcher working on smuggling economies, he retorted, "It is not smuggling, they are all terrorists." I asked him how he knew. "Smugglers are all using terrorists' paths, and they smuggle when terrorists attack us." He added, "Yet, they cannot smuggle now because we have this checkpoint here." When I asked why they did not have the checkpoint before, he answered that "without the process [the Resolution Process], I could not even stand here, especially in the winter and at night," implying that the PKK's ceasefire had permitted the Turkish military to expand its control in the region and establish new road checkpoints like the one we were at.

We continued our drive to Elbak, the most southern border district in Wan province. The road network that connected Wan city center to Elbak went along the Turkish-Iranian border. In addition to the permanent road checkpoints, this was the second additional checkpoint that the Turkish military had recently stationed. It was also the second year of the Resolution Process (*Çözüm Süreci*), which was also called the "Peace Process" (*Barış Süreci*).[1] Amidst an undeclared yet intense bout of fighting between the Turkish military and the PKK forces in December 2012, the Turkish government declared that it had been in conversations with the imprisoned leader of the PKK,

Abdullah Öcalan, and announced the Resolution Process—a set of policy schemes that aimed at ending the armed conflict.[2] Öcalan called upon the PKK to declare a ceasefire in March of 2013. Following the declaration of the ceasefire, the PKK began withdrawing some of its guerrilla forces to the inner highlands and even retrieving some from northern Kurdistan (Bakur) to its bases in southern Kurdistan (Başûr). The parliamentarians of the leading pro-Kurdish legal parties, the BDP and the HDP, made several visits to Öcalan on İmralı Island, as well as to the PKK's headquarters in the Qandil Mountains of southern Kurdistan, to facilitate peace talks between the Turkish state and the PKK. When the PKK saw that the Turkish government was reluctant to take concrete—particularly legal—steps to further the process and begin direct peace talks, it halted its withdrawal. By the summer of 2015, the Turkish authorities resumed counterinsurgency operations, engaging in skirmishes with the PKK.

Once we left the checkpoint, Mustafa—who was originally from Elbak but had lived in Wan city center for the last fifteen years—noted: "As you saw, they are taking advantage of the Peace Process, they did not have this checkpoint before. Since the process began, the state entered everywhere in Kurdistan, they are building new military bases and preparing for a longer war." Mustafa continued to explain how his relatives residing back in the village increasingly complained about the Turkish state presence, particularly how it targeted Kurdish smugglers. Mustafa was not the only person who expressed this complaint. On various visits to the border villages, I heard people objecting to the increasing frequency of anti-smuggling ambushes. The PKK's unilateral ceasefire and guerrillas' withdrawal, my interlocutors claimed, emboldened security forces to intensify their anti-smuggling operations.

The government, in fact, announced the prioritization of anti-smuggling campaigns once they had disarmed the PKK and resolved the "terror problem." This was reflected in a speech from the Turkish prime minister during the Resolution Process:

> The Resolution Process, which has gained momentum over the past months, has brought the terrorism problem to a halt. The end of terrorism and the start of a new process dominated by peace, calm, democratic rights, mutual respect, and tolerance have led to great hope in society. When weapons fall

silent, and politics speak, Turkey, Europe, and other countries will all benefit from this. When terrorism ends, smuggling, counterfeiting, and piracy will have been dealt a heavier blow.[3]

For most of my interlocutors, however, the government's anti-smuggling campaign in Kurdistan marked anything but the end of the counterinsurgency war. Instead, it was seen as an extension of the war, which brought about new forms of surveillance and assault strategies that the counterinsurgency forces intended to test on the field. Although the increased presence of security forces in Kurdistan during the Resolution Process was initially directed at the smugglers, many interlocutors expected that the enhanced reach of the security forces would soon turn toward counterinsurgency efforts. The increased focus on anti-smuggling, thus, made the inhabitants of the Kurdish borderlands suspicious and wary of the government's intention to pursue peace and reconciliation. Furthermore, prior experience with the way in which anti-smuggling law enforcement had been deployed as a counterinsurgency tactic in the 1990s only deepened these suspicions. For a short period of time—from the PKK's unilateral withdrawal in 1999 to the early 2000s—the counterinsurgency efforts abated, and in some cases were fully paused, and moved away from public sight. During that period, anti-smuggling operations took prominence, seemingly operating independently of the counterinsurgency, in accordance with their own specific logic. In the mid-2000s and 2010s, however, the counterinsurgency war had intensified, and once again the counterinsurgency forces began collaborating more closely with, sometimes even commanding, the anti-smuggling law enforcement.

The convergence of counterinsurgency and anti-smuggling efforts significantly shaped the ways in which smuggling cases in Kurdistan were processed. Judges and prosecutors often prioritized counterinsurgency concerns in their interpretation and implementation of anti-smuggling laws in courts. However, this prioritization remained implicit and was seldom directly expressed in the court records of smuggling trials, in contrast with the explicit expression of these concerns in anti-terrorism and other political trials that criminalized Kurdish rights advocates. This chapter explicates the subtle and off-the-record intersection of counterinsurgency and anti-smuggling law enforcement in courts, demonstrating how procedural legal reasoning and mechanisms became key areas where counterinsurgency concerns shaped the interpretation and enforcement of anti-smuggling law in Kurdistan.

TIMES OF CHANGE AND REFORM

Between 1998 and 2002, Turkey and Kurdistan experienced significant transformations. These four years saw two major economic crises that led to a comprehensive neoliberal restructuring, the imprisonment of the PKK's leader, a shift in the Kurdish Freedom Movement's political vision and a unilateral ceasefire by the PKK, the acceleration of Turkey's EU membership process—bringing legal reforms to enhance civil liberties, while deepening neoliberal restructuring—and the rise of the AKP (Justice and Development Party),[4] which came to dominate Turkish parliamentary politics.

In 1998, the Turkish authorities, in collaboration with the IMF (International Monetary Fund), planned a large-scale economic restructuring program that aimed at reducing Turkey's inflation rate and government debt through fiscal discipline, structural reforms, and a comprehensive privatization plan. The entrenched problems of high inflation and unmanageable government debts emerged as a result of the 1980s neoliberal economic transformation and the—counterinsurgency—war economy of the 1990s.[5] To aggravate matters, in August and November 1999, two massive earthquakes hit western Turkey and caused more than three and a half billion dollars in damages.[6] As the Turkish economy contracted by 6 percent and the inflation rate reached 70 percent, a series of devastating financial shocks struck, first in November 2000 and then again in February 2001.[7] During this crisis, the Turkish lira devaluated by 40 percent, and between 2001 and 2004, thirteen private banks ceased operations. In response, the Turkish authorities implemented an even harsher restructuring program, which led to widespread unemployment, economic precarity, wage cuts, further currency devaluation, and an increase in privatization.

The economic crisis and the neoliberal reform phase that followed coincided with Abdullah Öcalan's exit from Syria, his capture after a prolonged pursuit, and a shift in the ongoing counterinsurgency war in Kurdistan. In October 1998, the Syrian government compelled Öcalan to leave Damascus, where he had lived for the last nineteen years, in response to Turkey's threat of military action to deploy assault forces alongside the border. After failing to find asylum in Greece, Russia, and Italy, Öcalan landed in Kenya and was received at the Greek Embassy. However, the U.S. pressured the Greek authorities, who then asked him to leave. Shortly after leaving the embassy, Öcalan was captured by CIA agents at the Nairobi airport and handed over to Turkish authorities. Öcalan was brought to Turkey, secured in an island prison, prosecuted, and sentenced to death. During his oral defense in the Turkish court, as well as in defense texts that he submitted to domestic and international courts over the subsequent years, Öcalan made an unexpected move and suggested a significant change in the PKK's strategy.[8] Departing from the goal of Kurdish nation-statehood, Öcalan envisioned a radical program for establishing a gender-equal, ecologically-minded, and culturally, ethnically, and religiously pluralistic society governed through democratically elected autonomous councils.[9] On August 2, 1999, Öcalan advanced such a strategy by asking the PKK to unilaterally withdraw its guerrilla forces from northern Kurdistan as a symbolic gesture toward peace talks. The government, however, ignored this step and instead attacked the withdrawing guerrillas. Despite heavy losses, the PKK completed its withdrawal and maintained a unilateral ceasefire until June 2004, which brought about a period of non-conflict in Kurdistan. Although this period did not yield a long-lasting settlement, it did facilitate the implementation of political and economic reforms toward Turkey's accession to the EU. As they continued to implement these reforms, Turkish authorities waited until the late 2000s to engage in secret peace talks with the PKK, resulting in a two-year-long Resolution Process at the start of January 2013.[10]

In December 1999, nine months after Öcalan's capture, Turkey's candidacy to the EU was accepted, and the Turkish authorities declared a national reform program that aimed to adopt the Union's Acquis Communautaire in March 2001. Under the accession process, the Turkish government introduced a series of legal reforms that expanded political, religious, and cultural freedoms and curbed military tutelage. As part of these reforms, the death penalty was abolished, and Öcalan's sentence was reversed to life imprisonment. These changes paved the way for the EU to launch accession negotiations in October 2005.

The main dynamic that drove the EU accession reforms forward was the tenure of the AKP government during the 2000s. In the elections of

November 2002, the AKP received around 34 percent of the general vote, securing the majority in the new parliament. Besides the AKP, only one other party won seats in the elections.[11] The remaining parties failed to gain seats because of the 10 percent national threshold, which had been imposed by the military junta of 1980 to keep left-wing and pro-Kurdish political parties out of parliament.[12] The AKP was established by former members of the Islamist-conservative *Refah* (Welfare) party, which had led a coalition government from July 1996 to June 1997 until the Turkish military pressured the government to resign.[13] Distancing themselves from the *Refah* party and its successors, the AKP founders embraced a market economy, neoliberal policies, Turkey's accession to the EU, and a close alliance with the U.S., especially in the first decade of their rule. For AKP leaders, EU and U.S. support was key to counterbalancing the military tutelage, and AKP-led government's commitment to EU reforms helped the AKP to maintain Western backing.[14]

Enjoying parliamentary majority, the AKP began a comprehensive reform program under the EU accession process and revised or replaced various laws and regulations. In July 2003, under this program, the sixty-year-old Anti-Smuggling Law (Law 1918) was replaced with a new law (Law 4926) that eased punishments for smuggling crimes and marked a significant shift in the penal doctrine toward the liberal principle of "economic punishment for economic crimes."[15] In December 2003, the AKP government passed Turkey's first Oil Market Law (Law 5015), which also facilitated neoliberal restructuring by establishing the EPDK (Energy Market Regulatory Authority[16])—an autonomous regulatory agency designed to manage quality standards and licensing services. This newly configured authority forced independent gas stations to enter into a franchising agreement with existing oil distributing companies linked to transnational oil companies, such as BP and Royal Dutch Shell.[17]

During the late 2000s and early 2010s, the AKP government continued to pass new anti-smuggling legal reforms. These reforms, however, adopted more punitive regulations, given the increased state attention to the smuggling of mass-consumption items, particularly oil products and cigarettes.[18] While prison sentences were imposed for oil smuggling in February 2007, the anti-smuggling law was once again replaced with a new law (Law 5607) in March 2007. The new law reintroduced prison sentences for other forms of smuggling.[19] During this period, the government also introduced more advanced anti-smuggling surveillance technologies—such as chemical markers added to oil products and security holograms on tobacco merchandise—in order to enhance its ability to detect contraband and more effectively combat smuggling.[20] In 2013, the minimum prison sentence for tobacco smuggling was increased from two years to three years, and in 2014, the same increase was applied to oil smuggling.[21] Raising the minimum sentence to three years made it more difficult to conditionally postpone prison sentences for a probationary period.[22] In debating the 2013 amendments in parliament, deputies from the Turkish nationalist MHP asserted a connection between the smuggling economies and the PKK and blamed the AKP government for not taking sufficient action to undermine the connection. This debate was particularly striking because these legal reforms overlapped with the ongoing Resolution Process, which Turkish nationalist circles also heavily criticized. The amending law was legislated exactly a week after Öcalan's letter—which called for Kurdish guerrillas to withdraw from Turkey—was announced during the Diyarbekir/Amed Newroz celebrations. The MHP deputies reasserted allegations that the PKK engaged not only in drug trafficking but also in oil, cigarette, and sugar smuggling. As a response, the governing AKP deputies accepted the allegations of the PKK's involvement in smuggling but claimed that the government's anti-smuggling efforts were effective in undermining the PKK's supposed command of smuggling economies.

Throughout the 2000s and 2010s, the smuggling-as-terrorism allegations became increasingly prevalent in parliamentary debates. Yet, the legal texts of the anti-smuggling reforms passed during this period did not mention such a connection, nor did they impose additional legal measures against smuggling crimes that were alleged to support terrorism. Rather, the new reforms directly prioritized neoliberal restructuring by promoting the privatization of public enterprises and the establishment of autonomous market regulation authorities. In Kurdistan, however, the anti-smuggling efforts driven by neoliberal market reforms converged with the counterinsurgency warfare.[23] This alignment had a profound impact on how judges and prosecutors handled smuggling cases and how they enforced anti-smuggling laws in courts across the region. The state officials' racialized allegations, which linked Kurdish smugglers to the insurgency, played a key role in this alignment.

SMUGGLING AS "TERRORISM" AND
RACIALIZATION WITHOUT NAMING

Since the 1990s, the Turkish authorities had accused the PKK of funding its activities through heroin trafficking,[24] and through these assertions, successive Turkish governments sought to gain support across Western Europe for their efforts to criminalize the PKK.[25] Yet, these arguments gained new political and diplomatic currency in the context of the "global war on terror." Following the 9/11 attacks, the U.S. imposed a new global security doctrine on insurgencies. As outlined in the UN Security Council's Resolution No. 1373 (September 28, 2001), this doctrine introduced counterinsurgency strategies aimed at targeting insurgency groups' military and financial capacities.[26] This renewed focus on financial capacities successfully shifted the authorities' attention to the alleged connections between insurgency and organized crime, or what some would call the "crime-terror nexus" or "crime-terror continuum."[27] Against the background of this security doctrine, Turkish authorities successfully lobbied U.S. authorities to designate the PKK as a "foreign drug trafficker" in 2008.[28]

From the early 2000s onward, governmental discourse that identified smuggling with the PKK compounded their accusations of heroin smuggling with allegations of smuggling of unbanned, mass-consumption items, primarily oil and cigarettes. The 2005 parliamentary report on oil smuggling was one of the first indications of this broader shift in governmental discourse.[29] Although the report's primary aim was to document the deleterious effects of contraband oil on the economy, human health, and environmental well-being, it included a section explicitly connecting oil smuggling to "the separatist terrorist organizations and their influence on regional politics." According to the report, the PKK benefited financially from oil smuggling by taxing Kurdish smugglers. It also asserted that the smuggling trade bolstered the PKK guerrillas' mobility, as the smugglers provided cover for the PKK guerrillas to move across borders under the pretext of selling oil. The Turkish police's annual reports in the 2000s also alleged the PKK's involvement in oil and cigarette smuggling as well as in drug trafficking.[30] In October 2011, the Turkish finance minister announced an anti-tobacco-smuggling plan that associated tobacco smuggling with the PKK, stating that the action plan "must be seen as an aspect of suppression of the financial sources of the terrorist organization and the anti-terrorism struggle."[31] The smuggling-as-terrorism discourse was further supported through frequent media reports, policy papers from the national security think tanks, and academic publications. In 2010, the Turkish media celebrated the publication of a compilation edited by two American professors.[32] Its chapters, which were mostly written by members of the Turkish Police Academy, claimed a connection between the PKK and smuggling networks by citing empirical data collected by Turkish law enforcement. As the book garnered major attention in Turkish media, a PKK leader, Murat Karayılan, publicly refuted the validity of its findings.[33]

The smuggling-as-terrorism allegations were racialized because they specifically associated the smuggling activities of Kurdish people with terrorism. The 2005 parliamentary report on oil smuggling, for example, exclusively identified terrorism with the oil smuggling conducted across the Iraqi, Iranian, and Syrian borders, borderlands that Kurds predominantly populated. In 2013, the head of the Interior Ministry's Smuggling, Intelligence, Operations, and Information Gathering Department—a high-ranking security bureaucrat who had also previously worked as a district governor in the Elbak district of Wan province—published an article that connected the smuggling in "eastern and southeastern provinces"—provinces located on Turkey's borders with Syria, Iraq, and Iran—to terrorism:

> The political instability or low sale taxes in the countries neighboring our eastern and southeastern provinces made the smuggling of various items very attractive. [. . .] The people of this region do not see smuggling as a crime, but rather treat it as a means of subsistence. For them, [illegal] border crossings became a form of profession, and "smuggling (*kaçağa gitmek*)" became an ordinary event. [. . .] The fact that most of the people who engaged in smuggling are from the terror region provinces does not necessarily mean that all of these smugglers support the terrorist organization. However, it is also a known fact that the PKK terrorists who control certain movements across borders obtain a significant share of revenue from smuggling activities. This is why it is necessary to see smuggling not just as a criminal case, but also as an activity that provides financial support to terrorism. Within this perspective, the anti-smuggling policies must be developed.[34]

The identification of the "eastern and southeastern provinces" as "terror region provinces (*terör bölgesi illeri*)," and the subsequent association of the region's inhabitants with smuggling as an "ordinary" economic activity, creates a symbolic equation between smuggling and terrorism. Although, according to the bureaucrat, not all smugglers in these provinces necessarily support the PKK, the connection between smuggling and terrorism is posed as a structural phenomenon made possible because of the PKK's territorial control and regulation of border crossings, independently of individual smugglers' political views or their support, or lack thereof, of the PKK. In this way, smuggling conducted in Kurdish-populated borderlands as a whole becomes associated with the PKK or what state authorities deemed as "terrorism."

At the same time, the security bureaucrat racializes the alleged smuggling-terrorism connections by associating both smuggling and terrorism with the Kurds, although the statement carefully avoids any explicit mention of Kurdishness. The bureaucrat, instead, deploys the terms "eastern and southeastern provinces"—provinces that were majority-Kurdish—as a racial dog whistle, standing for Kurds and Kurdistan. The effectiveness of this veiled reference rests on the fact that the eastern and southeastern provinces—or simply the geographic terms "eastern" and "southeastern"—have long served as proxies for state officials' references to Kurds, Kurdishness, or Kurdistan. The authorities strictly avoided using the terms "Kurds" or "Kurdish" and often criminalized the word "Kurdistan" under an undeclared colonial rule that denied any status or even the existence of Kurds and Kurdistan. Instead, they coined the terms "Eastern Anatolia" and "Southeastern Anatolia" to refer to these regions as two of the seven geographic regions that constitute Turkey.[35]

The racialized discourse of smuggling-as-terrorism resonated with other racialized discourses that identified Kurds and Kurdistan with specific crimes, such as honor killings, as if these killings were only committed by Kurdish men.[36] The reports prepared by Turkish police and other state institutions, for example, identified perpetrators of honor killings "as people of 'eastern' or 'southeastern' background."[37] As with the identification of Kurdish smuggling with "terrorism," these anti-Kurdish discourses also used proxy terms, such as "eastern," "southeastern," "feudal," or "tribal," rather than directly refer to the Kurds or Kurdistan.[38]

The indirect marking of Kurds/Kurdistan through proxy terms led to what sociologist Dicle Koğacıoğlu calls "nonrecognizing recognition," a peculiar "mode of racialization [that does] not involve much of articulation of race in the explicit terms of science, public policy, or the market. [. . .] Instead, it worked by silencing even the name of what it bans."[39] This racialization of Kurds without naming them was particularly prevalent in state authorities' discourse and was central to Turkey's citizenship regime, which claimed to have no ethnic, linguistic, religious, or gendered basis.[40] According to the 1982 Turkish Constitution (Article 66), "everyone bound to the Turkish state through the bond of citizenship is a Turk." In the Constitutional Court decisions or official documents given to international legal bodies, the state officials presented this formulation as evidence of the Turkish state's civic character and of its neutral stance vis-à-vis ethnic, racial, or religious identities.[41] Accordingly, the Turkish authorities and judiciary denied legal recognition to any ethnic or religious group and even occasionally criminalized the expression of non-Turkish identities.[42] Despite this neutrality claim, however, Turkish law has proposed racialized articulations of what it means to be Turkish and has explicitly made reference to such articulations—such as Turkish history, Turkish culture, Turkish language, or Turkish *soy* (ethnic or racial kin)[43]—to grant (or deny) specific rights to citizens and noncitizens.[44]

The use of proxy terms and political dog whistles goes beyond a simple denial or erasure of Kurds and Kurdistan from official discourse.[45] The proxy terms replaced and erased Kurdishness and Kurdistan but also continued to signify them, making them legible without naming them. When the high-ranking security bureaucrats or other state officials, academics, or journalists referred to smuggling in eastern and southeastern provinces, for example, they also indirectly marked Kurdish smuggling economies. Because terrorism was associated with the eastern and southeastern (i.e., the Kurdish) provinces, the smugglers who were Kurdish were reframed as de facto associates of terrorism.

In the background of this racialized discourse, state officials, including judicial authorities, associated anti-smuggling efforts in Kurdistan with their counterinsurgency efforts. In this way, the officials identified Kurdish smuggling not just as an anti-market activity that undermined the national treasury, weakened the legally operating market actors, or damaged human and environmental health, but as an action that directly threatened state security and integrity. In his 2013 article, the security bureaucrat also articulates the anti-smuggling struggle as counterinsurgency:

> Recently, cigarette smuggling provided most of the revenue that the separatist terrorist organization obtained from smuggling. The contraband cigarettes bought for their cheaper prices were similar to the bullets in the weapons used against our security forces heroically fighting. [. . .] From that perspective, with the people's support, the contradiction in smoking contraband cigarettes and drinking contraband tea while engaging in conversations in support of the anti-terrorism struggle will be noticed. It will be revealed that the anti-terrorism struggle is not just a fight against the terrorists.[46]

If not terrorists, against whom should the anti-terrorism struggle be waged? The article implies that smugglers who supplied contraband cigarettes or contraband tea, and even the consumers of such items, are those whom the counterinsurgency should target. As illustrated in the article, the smuggling-as-terrorism discourse further identifies a wide array of people, from smugglers to consumers, as potential associates of terrorism. Within this framing, Kurdish smugglers become supporters of terrorism and potential terrorists, thus legitimizing state security forces' increasingly hostile responses as exemplified in the growing violence characterizing anti-smuggling operations in the region. Identifying Kurdish smugglers with guerrillas, the security forces increasingly targeted, wounded, maimed, or even killed smugglers in the borderlands.[47] The smuggling-as-terrorism discourse also circulated among the judiciary, compelling judges and prosecutors to interpret and enforce the anti-smuggling laws more severely against Kurds. Similarly, when handling criminal smuggling cases in the Kurdish borderlands, prosecutors became more likely to request longer sentences for defendants, imposing higher penal fees—which defendants could hardly afford—and impounding vehicles that allegedly were used for smuggling. In response, judges tended to impose longer prison sentences and higher fees. In this way, anti-smuggling law emerged as a particular domain in the Turkish judiciary's deployment of a separate (colonial) legal regime against Kurdish subjects and its broader weaponization of law in Kurdistan.

THE PRISON-COURTHOUSE AND LAWFARE
IN KURDISTAN

When I started my fieldwork in Wan in September 2012, the central court-house had been temporarily moved to the old prison building. The relocation was the result of a devastating earthquake that hit Wan city center on September 23, 2011, and which had heavily damaged the courthouse. Since a new, high-security (F-type) prison had recently been completed, the old prison building was repurposed until a new courthouse could be built.[48] As the former prison had two-floor wards designed to host six, eight, or ten inmates, the first floor had been arranged to serve as court clerks' offices and the top level as judges' offices. Court sessions were held in prison wards with barred windows. On my first day at the prison-courthouse, I tried to locate specific courtrooms and offices, walking through long and dark corridors with small and barred windows, when I accidentally came across the Bar's office. Each courthouse had offices for Bar member lawyers to work in and to rest, drink tea, and hang out. On my first visit to the Bar's office, I met a Kurdish lawyer who had recently started his lawyering career. He was surprised that I managed to find the Bar's room in the maze of identical corridors and rooms locked with steel doors. The lawyer further joked that the prison-as-courthouse accurately represented the Kurdish people's widespread perception of the Turkish legal system: "For Kurds, even the courthouse is designed as a prison. . . . Even before the court decides on you, you are already jailed. . . . How would a Kurd expect justice from this [legal] system?" The lawyer was, of course, referring to how the Turkish legal system treated Kurds with suspicion and considered them a priori guilty, even when they were claimants. Kurdish citizens might eventually prove their innocence, according to the lawyer, but doing so would require a significant amount of work to contest the judiciary's historically racist and discriminatory bias. For this lawyer, as well as many other Kurdish lawyers that I came across during my fieldwork, the default approach of the judiciary was to protect the Turkish state and its security forces from Kurdish citizens rather than to protect the citizens from the more powerful state authorities.

The prison-courthouse also reminded the defendants, claimants, and lawyers of the central role that the carceral system played in Turkish authorities' colonial domination of Kurdish lands.[49] In its counterinsurgency war, particularly during the "field domination strategy" developed in the 1990s, state security forces had deployed mass incarceration practices that ranged from detention, torture, and imprisonment to forced village evacuations and the imposition of no-go zones, curfews, and food embargos. The majority of Wan city residents were subject to such incarceration practices firsthand or indirectly, through their parents or other family members. For most residents, therefore, a visit to the prison-courthouse evoked memories of prison and torture that they or their kin almost certainly experienced. Being at the courthouse, even for a short period or for a mundane bureaucratic transaction—such as obtaining a police clearance that had nothing to do with the possibility of being imprisoned—still induced anxiety in most courthouse visitors, who often reported experiencing headaches and shortness of breath. The lawyers, as well as court clerks and criers, spoke of their discomfort with spending long periods of time in the courthouse. I myself experienced visceral uneasiness after spending a few hours in the building. The long, windowless, stuffy corridors, lit with eye-hurting fluorescent white lights, and connected to various wards closed with metal doors painted in metallic gray, often gave me headaches too.

The judges and prosecutors were also frustrated at being stationed at the makeshift courthouse and at spending their workdays behind barred windows and in prison wards. A judge whom I visited in his office—located on the top level of a ten-person prison ward—expressed his displeasure about having to work inside a prison. He joked: "Perhaps some defendants had cursed us so that now, that we are in prison, [we] have to think twice the next time we decide on a prison sentence." The judge complained about how he had to use bunk beds as file cabinets and how he was forced to conduct court hearings in his improvised office. The joke illustrated that the judge, like his colleagues, was very distressed that they too were somehow imprisoned, forced to spend their workday in a setting meant for criminal discipline.

At the beginning of my fieldwork, I happened to visit the courthouse on a day when it felt even more like a prison. This was a KCK trial day. The KCK (Kurdistan Communities Union), a broader organizational framework that encompassed the PKK among other affiliated groups, was frequently invoked by Turkish authorities as a pretext to launch criminal investigations across various provinces in Kurdistan, as well as in central and western Turkey.

Starting in April 2009, these investigations led to the arrests of thousands of Kurdish politicians, activists, journalists, and lawyers, with even more facing criminal charges.

One of the hearings in the KCK prosecution in Wan happened to be scheduled on the same day I had an appointment with a judge who was serving in a first-degree criminal court and primarily handled smuggling cases. I had previously met the judge to introduce myself and ask for his permission to attend the smuggling trials. Even though most of these trials were open to the public, I often visited the judges first to introduce my research and to ask whether I could observe court hearings and trials. On this occasion, I was meeting with the judge to learn more about his approach to smuggling cases and his interpretation of the existing legislation, regulations, and binding legal precedents. I knew that the KCK trials were being held at the courthouse and, considering the extra security precautions, I arrived at the courthouse an hour before my appointment to guarantee my punctuality. Unlike other workdays, security barricades and checkpoints were set up a few hundred meters outside the courthouse, with police tanks, military vehicles, cameras, and sniper shooters stationed on nearby rooftops. Facing the security forces' overwhelming presence, thousands of demonstrators had gathered to support the defendants. A number of tents served tea and were decorated with pictures of the defendants; protestors were performing traditional hand-holding dances (*govend*) in circles and singing pro-Kurdish patriotic songs.

Amid the noise of the police sirens and military helicopters flying overhead, I managed to pass through the initial checkpoint. Those who wanted to enter for routine bureaucratic transactions were denied admission. Even the people who had scheduled court hearings struggled to convince the police officers to allow them into the courthouse. When I entered, I told the police that I had an appointment with a judge from the first-degree criminal court and clarified that my meeting had nothing to do with the KCK trials. Once I explained that I was a researcher based in an American university, he looked at my university ID with confusion and eventually decided to let me in, though I had to leave my cell phone, voice recorder, mobile scanner—which I used to make electronic copies of the court files—and camera at the gate. I was prepared for arbitrary searches, so I had wiped out the memory on my devices. Without any hesitation, I left these devices and began walking toward the judge's office. I was stopped twice and redirected because the police had closed corridors and sections of the courthouse for the KCK trials. My overwhelming sense was that I was visiting a prison. The "courthouse" not only prevented the inmates from getting out but also blocked the visitors from getting in and strictly surveilled and directed their movements inside. The prison-like atmosphere on that day showed me how the authorities could easily and swiftly deploy extraordinary security measures and restrict citizens' access to the courthouse.

In May 2013, the prison-courthouse was evacuated, and the courts were relocated to the newly built courthouse. The new facility displayed state-of-the-art architecture and larger, well-ventilated, and well-lit corridors and halls. The new building did not change my feeling of the "prison-courthouse," however. For the Kurdish citizens who entered it, the building continued to operate as a place of incarceration, punishment, and dispossession. The prison-courthouse, thus, marked Kurdish citizens' widespread view of the Turkish legal system as an extension of the state's colonial domination of Kurdistan—a legal system that considered Kurdish citizens as threats and served primarily to protect the government against Kurdish citizens.

Kurdish citizens' perception of the legal system was partially shaped by the "tutelary" relationship that the high-ranking civilian and military bureaucracy was assumed to have with the overall population in Turkey, in which the people (*halk*) were understood to be backward and in need of guidance from state officials.[50] Thus, Turkish bureaucrats could act through a particular "social imaginary" that viewed them as detached from, and superior to, the people, and as having a mission to educate (and civilize) them.[51] This society-educator imaginary was particularly prevalent among the judiciary—the judges and prosecutors, who were centrally recruited among law school graduates and centrally trained in the Turkish Justice Academy based in the capital city, Ankara.[52] Over the course of their careers, judges and prosecutors carefully cultivated a detached distance from society, a strategy that allowed them to claim judicial authority and to deploy the law, including the adjudication of prolonged prison sentences, as a means to educate and discipline people whom they viewed as backward.[53] In this pedagogical role, the judiciary embodied a fetishized image of state authority, understood as the primary driver of civilization and progress through top-down reforms across both the Ottoman and Republican eras.

In Kurdistan, the Turkish judiciary's self-proclaimed role as social educator merged with another role—protector of state security. In this role, the judges and prosecutors imagined themselves as defenders of the counterinsurgency forces, which included regular troops, gendarmerie, police, and informal agents of state violence such as paramilitaries and death squads. Accordingly, the judiciary routinely used its power to protect the counterinsurgency forces from allegations of rights violations. Through the 1990s and 2000s, and acting as auxiliaries to these forces, the prosecutors and judges launched campaigns of legal warfare, or "lawfare," against Kurdish politicians, activists, lawyers, journalists, and artists, in support of the counterinsurgency war in Kurdistan.[54] By using the coercive powers of the law, these lawfare campaigns significantly intensified and expanded the existing regimes of violence and dispossession against Kurds, specifically criminalizing, incarcerating, or forcibly displacing Kurdish subjects whom the security forces associated with Kurdish freedom politics. The social imaginary of state security also led the judiciary to implement laws even more harshly insofar as they interpret laws and regulations in their assessment of criminal allegations, which state authorities discursively, rather than legislatively, connected to terrorism, smuggling included.

The State Security Courts (*Devlet Güvenlik Mahkemeleri*)—special courts established in 1983 to address issues pertaining to national unity and security, and to the preservation of the constitutional order—came to embody the judiciary's state security imaginary.[55] Explicitly titled as "state security," these courts operated as the principal arena for counterinsurgency lawfare campaigns that targeted Kurdish freedom politics. In 1991, following the ratification of Turkey's first Anti-Terror Law, the courts' jurisdiction was extended to include terrorism-related crimes.[56] The State Security Courts were led by a panel of three judges, one of whom belonged to the military judiciary. The involvement of military judges in these ostensibly civilian courts effectively expanded martial law across the entire country, even in provinces where martial law had officially been lifted.[57] These special courts were dissolved in June 2004 as part of the democratization reforms for EU accession. However, the high-degree criminal courts—which replaced the State Security Courts and handled terrorism allegations—continued to uphold the state security imaginary and the related counterinsurgency lawfare campaigns throughout the late 2000s and the 2010s.[58] The Turkish judiciary also endorsed the state security imaginary by weaponizing smuggling court cases against the Kurdish subjects in the context of smuggling-as-terrorism allegations. What further complicates the role of these allegations in the anti-Kurdish weaponization of law is that they often remained absent from official court files, even as they were widely shared by the judges and prosecutors.

SMUGGLING-AS-TERRORISM ALLEGATIONS IN THE COURTS

Allegations that smugglers were "terrorists" routinely emerged during my interviews with judges and prosecutors in Wan, often without me having raised the issue of insurgency at all. The allegations also emerged unexpectedly in my casual discussions with members of the judiciary. My experiences resonated with the lawyers I spoke to, all of whom confirmed that they encountered the smuggling-terrorism association frequently in their casework. A Kurdish lawyer with ten years of experience shared the following story with me.

The lawyer had visited a prosecutor in a border district to discuss a court case. After their conversation ended, the prosecutor offered to walk her out. When the prosecutor stood up, he reached for a cigarette package on the table, complaining about the rising price of cigarettes. The lawyer then made a joke: "You should buy contraband cigarettes, then." Without a smile and raising his voice, the prosecutor coldly stated, much to the lawyer's surprise, that he would never buy contraband cigarettes because he would never support "the terrorist organization," implying the PKK. The lawyer was taken aback by the judge's utterly humorless response to her suggestion. She knew very well that, as a person of law, the prosecutor needed to demonstrate his adherence to the law and would never buy—or admit to buying—contraband goods. Still, the prosecutor's reaction surprised the lawyer, as she had developed a friendly relationship with him and believed there was sufficient latitude for the joke.

Not all lawyers maintained friendly relations with the prosecutors or judges in Kurdistan. Preserving a social distance from the local population which, in their view, was necessary to embody the aura of their judicial authority, judges and prosecutors socialized mainly with other non-local, mid- or high-ranking state officers, such as gendarmerie commanders, district police chiefs, medical doctors, and district governors. In Kurdish districts, this social distance was further reinforced by the fact that most of the judges and prosecutors cannot speak Kurdish. In Wan courthouses, I came across few prosecutors and no judge who spoke Kurdish, even though the majority of the courthouse staff, including court criers and clerks, were locally recruited and Kurdish speakers.[59] On certain occasions, however, the lawyers who were originally from these districts might have built friendly relationships with the judiciary. In the view of judges and prosecutors, the lawyers occupied an intermediate position between them and society at large, as they shared professional knowledge and a common law school education. In some cases, the lawyers might have attended either the same schools or schools in the same cities as the judges and prosecutors. Yet, unlike the centrally appointed members of the judiciary, the lawyers were part of the local community and might engage in local politics. Some Kurdish lawyers in Wan, for example, were active in human rights advocacy and pro-Kurdish electoral politics—pursuits that the state authorities mostly associated with the insurgency in Kurdistan. Given this context, and returning to the anecdote discussed above, the lawyer's friendly relationship with the prosecutor could be said to be exceptional. However, this unusual friendship did not prevent the prosecutor's seemingly unexpected and exaggerated negative reaction to even the imaginary consumption of smuggled cigarettes. This reaction thus demonstrated how closely state officials, including the judiciary members, identified contraband goods in Kurdistan with support for the PKK.

    Although judges and prosecutors openly and routinely made smuggling-as-terrorism claims, identifying how these arguments shaped and infused formal legal settings, particularly court files and decisions, was more difficult to pinpoint. Even as the anti-smuggling legislation became more punitive, and parliamentary debates on legislation more explicit in the smuggling-terrorism connection arguments, the actual legislation carefully avoided any mention of "terrorism" and of any direct connection between terrorism and smuggling. Although the presumed link between "terrorism," smuggling, and Kurdishness was pervasive across judicial attitudes and reasoning, it often remained off the record, and therefore it functioned in more insidious ways. In smuggling trials, for example, documents such as court records, summary minutes of court sessions, official written exchanges between state institutions, testimony statements, and court decisions made no mention of "terrorism," Kurdishness, or the Kurdish region. The specific mode of legal recording, in which judges dictated statements from all parties during a hearing, was a significant formalization strategy of legal discourse in Wan and other courthouses in Turkey. The judges did not merely summarize parties' statements but often revised and edited them so that they would be compatible with the formal legal language. In some cases, lawyers may insist on having their statements recorded verbatim, but the final decision would still rest with the judge. As a result of the judge's dictation, the court session minutes reflected the judge's account of what had transpired and not the actual proceedings per se.

While smuggling-as-terrorism allegations were excluded from the court files in all the smuggling trial records I examined, there were important exceptions. Indeed, in several smuggler killing cases, court records might associate smugglers with "terrorism" when the families of the slain smugglers and their lawyers managed to exhaust all other legal avenues in challenging the impunity of state officers responsible for these killings. The smuggling-terrorism association, thus, became a last resort for courts to justify the killings—often suggesting that security forces mistook smugglers for insurgents, as smugglers frequently crossed through regions with high insurgency activity. In a few cases, the courts even affirmed the allegations that smugglers had provided logistical support to the guerrillas and asked surviving smugglers and the families of those killed in ambushes to prove that the smugglers in question had not assisted guerrillas. Even in these instances, there was still no explicit reference to Kurdishness in the court records. Instead, the terms "terror," "terrorism," or "terrorist" were used as proxy terms for Kurds and Kurdishness.[60]

The strict avoidance of any mention of Kurdishness and of smuggling-as-terrorism allegations in court files—except, as discussed above, in some smuggler killing cases—while still allowing these allegations to permeate the processing of criminal cases enabled judges and prosecutors to mirror the state authorities' insidious racialization of Kurds without directly naming them. This indirect yet highly operative racialized marking of Kurdishness through smuggling and terrorism underscores the modus operandi of the undeclared colonial rule in Kurdistan and of the colonial legal framework it employs. This framework is based on the strict denial, though not the complete erasure, of Kurdish people and Kurdistan. Instead, it operates through indirect labeling, effectively performing a procedural equality through which impartiality and universal justice are claimed and celebrated, while implicitly deploying this racialized marking to systematically discriminate against Kurdish subjects. By identifying Kurdish smuggling with "terrorism" while keeping such identification off the record in the processing of smuggling cases, for example, judges and prosecutors could claim to uphold procedural equality.[61] Yet, such procedural equality not only failed to generate "substantive equality"—the equality enjoyed by citizens and noncitizens in their capacity to make and realize rights claims based on their legal status—but rather facilitated its denial.[62] I call this—colonial and racialized—legal strategy of imposing substantive inequality through the very means of procedural equality "the cunning of law."[63]

THE JUDGE'S DISCRETION AND LEGAL CUNNING

The lack of reference to the smuggling-terrorism connection in smuggling trials prevented Kurdish smugglers and their lawyers from legally challenging these accusations. By avoiding and dismissing any reference to the geographical context of smuggling—the Kurdish-populated borderlands—even when using the Turkish authorities' proxy terms such as "eastern" and "southeastern," judges further restricted Kurdish defendants' ability to legally articulate the structural inequalities they faced. These inequalities included the counterinsurgency-driven forced displacement and dispossession that had compelled many to engage in smuggling in the first place. In fact, judges were supposed to take into consideration the socioeconomic conditions of individual defendants when arriving at decisions. These considerations were legally defined as within the judge's discretion, or what Turkish procedural laws refer to as *hakim takdiri*, which involves assessing possible mitigating factors in determining the size of the fines, the length of prison sentences, or the postponement of convictions.[64] By allowing judges to consider the defendants' socioeconomic status—or their age—in the processing of cases, this judicial discretion may seem to have promised substantive equality. Yet, according to procedural law, these considerations must be specific to the individual defendant—or plaintiff—rather than general to a particular group or region, to be deemed procedurally impartial. This requirement, therefore, individualized otherwise systematic and structural socioeconomic inequalities that Kurdish smugglers, alongside other residents of the borderlands, collectively faced.

As a procedural legal mechanism, the judge's discretion not only restricted the legal articulation of structured and structural inequalities but also enabled judges to racialize and discriminate against Kurdish subjects without openly naming them. Judges, thus, denied Kurdish defendants legal protections and rights with no need to substantiate or even declare this denial. Although judges were supposed to treat defendants as isolated individuals when practicing their discretion, this mechanism instead allowed them to implicitly interpellate Kurdish defendants as members of a racialized community, associating them, their mobilities, and their lands with insurgency. In this way, the exercise of judicial discretion played a key role in imposing substantive inequality while claiming procedural impartiality and while ensuring racialized anti-Kurdish discrimination remained off the court records.

Because of its off-the-record nature, I first noticed the critical role of judicial discretion not in the court files or even during the court hearings, but in my interviews with the judges. After observing references to smuggling-as-terrorism allegations in several interviews that I conducted, I re-examined my notes on the specific contexts in which these assertions were made. I realized that the judges often brought up "terrorism" when I asked them about their exercise of judicial discretion—specifically, about how they assessed particular smuggling cases and determined the fines and prison sentences. The following interaction with a judge working at Wan central courthouse exemplifies how judges identified the practice of judicial discretion as a critical legal-procedural mechanism to factor smuggling-as-terrorism allegations into their criminal-legal decision-making without their explicit mention.

I entered Judge Murat's office, one of the offices that had formerly been a prison ward. I had planned the visit to be a short one—merely to introduce myself and to ask for permission to observe his court. After I explained that my research was about smuggling and anti-smuggling law, the judge mentioned that he had been previously visited by another researcher when he worked in Hatay, a province located between the Mediterranean coast and the Turkish-Syrian border. As he had already worked in a border area, the judge was very knowledgeable and experienced in smuggling cases. Thus, we began talking about recent anti-smuggling legislation and regulations, particularly regarding oil and cigarette smuggling. The judge answered all of my questions regarding contraband oil inspections, cigarette smuggling files, and related court decisions. He mentioned that there was still confusion on how to apply security hologram inspections in cigarette smuggling cases, and that he and other judges had discussed this issue the previous weekend in a seminar organized and sponsored by the Customs and Trade Ministry in Ankara. Before ending our conversation, I asked about the social and economic conditions of the region, such as economic precariousness, and to what extent he took poverty into consideration when deciding on cases, specifically when determining the final amounts of penal and administrative fines. He responded:

> I have also observed the poverty in the region and also understood how smuggling has emerged as the main and, for some areas, the only means of subsistence for the people. Therefore, I try to keep the penal fines at the minimum levels . . . but you also know that it is different here, unlike the smuggling cases in Hatay. . . . Here in Van [Wan], the terrorist organization obtains significant revenue from smuggling. We cannot let that happen and must not encourage smuggling under any condition.

The judge's reference to "terrorism" was unexpected. Although I had not asked him about the matter, he still felt the need to address it. It was also striking that he mentioned the smuggling-terrorism connection as a phenomenon unique to the Wan (i.e., Kurdish) borderlands. In his view, this connection was the main difference between the Wan and Hatay borderlands and the reason why he considered anti-terrorism concerns when reviewing smuggling cases in Wan.

Judge Murat's statement, however, did not mean he would necessarily impose the maximum fines or prison sentences on defendants in every smuggling case, even in Wan. In cases involving minors, especially those who had no prior charges, the judge indeed decreased the penal sentence or postponed it. In several other cases, though, the judge avoided considering mitigating factors and chose not to decrease the punishments. In these cases, he simply stated that the defendants did not give him the impression they would not return to smuggling. In practice, judges were not required to provide much justification for their discretionary assessments—all they had to state was whether the defendants behaved respectfully during the prosecution, convincingly appeared to be regretful of committing the crime, or had left the impression they would not commit the crime again. The judges were not required to explain what specific behaviors or statements from the defendants justified their assessments or why defendants failed to give the impression that they would not commit a crime in the future. In court decision transcripts, there was no way to detect or determine how prominently the smuggling-as-terrorism discourse had figured in Judge Murat's reasoning, even though it was clearly significant in his exchanges with me. The discretionary character of the judge's decisions served as an ideal legal means to perform legal cunning when factoring in the smuggling-as-terrorism discourse—a practice that delivered substantive inequality while asserting procedural equality.

The cunning of law was not performed without contradictions, however. These contradictions often stemmed from procedural mistakes made by inexperienced members of the judiciary. The judges and prosecutors who had recently completed their central professional training were initially assigned to district courthouses in the provinces, including northern Kurdistan. As they rotated through posts at different district courthouses, these junior judges and prosecutors deepened their knowledge of legislation and jurisprudence. When stationed in Kurdish districts, they were also socialized into the state security imaginary and learned about the cunning of law—namely the off-the-record practices of considering counterinsurgency concerns in handling the criminal-legal cases that did not explicitly involve terrorism allegations, such as smuggling trials. Underpinning the cunning of the Turkish—colonial—law as deployed in Kurdistan, these off-the-record considerations of counterinsurgency concerns needed to be subtly practiced and, therefore, required skills that needed to be learned, honed, and collectively policed. Through the learning process, junior judges and prosecutors were prone to make mistakes that could unintentionally undermine state security or counterinsurgency goals, despite their commitment to defending them. When such mistakes occurred, senior judiciary members or other bureaucrats, including ranked military officers or governors, corrected them. I witnessed such professional policing in an oil smuggling case in which a district judge substantiated his decision to ignore potentially mitigating factors given the high frequency of smuggling cases in the Wan borderlands.

I came across the case in a district courthouse. In the final court decision, the junior judge—who had been appointed shortly after he finished his judicial training and internship—denied assessing the defendant's age (the defendant was under fifteen) as a mitigating factor and neither decreased the penal fines nor postponed the prison sentence, as was often permitted in cases involving minors. The judge substantiated his decision thus: "The justice will be manifested in the real sense only in this way given that cigarette and fuel smuggling is widespread enough to become a source of livelihood in the region and that it is also necessary to show the deterrent and preventive effect of the punishment on the defendant."[65] The Appeals Court judges, however, stated that "the notion that the geography in which the defendant allegedly committed the crime" would bar the defendant from the legal rights they would otherwise have benefited from if the crime were committed in another region was incompatible with "the principles of equality before the law." The "geographic" reference thus became a technical-judicial mistake that the Appeals Court corrected to guarantee the implementation of procedural equality and uphold the claim of impartial and universal justice. The Appeals Court judges, however, maintained, rather than ruled out, the discretionary character of the judge's decision by stating that the judge's discretion needed to rely on the defendant's "personality features," "behaviors and manners during the court hearings," and the overall "impression that the defendant left on the judge as to whether they would commit a crime again." In compelling the judge to treat the defendant as an isolated individual, the Appeals Court reinstated the judge's discretion as a legal means through which judges could continue to racially mark and discriminate against Kurdish smugglers while maintaining procedural impartiality.

In addition to the mistakes made by junior judges and prosecutors, disagreements could occur among experienced members of the judiciary over how to pursue off-the-record considerations of state security and counterinsurgency concerns in smuggling cases. These disagreements typically resulted from differing or contradictory ideas among senior judges and prosecutors regarding the most effective ways to fight the insurgency. One such disagreement was expressed in the central courthouse of Wan. In considering whether the anti-tobacco-smuggling regulations were unfair and ineffective against actual cigarette smugglers, two senior judges introduced a new legal interpretation and procedure to allow defendants to benefit from "effective remorse" (*etkin pişmanlık*) as defined in the anti-smuggling law (Law 5607).[66] As I noted earlier, the 2013 amendments increased the minimum prison sentence for tobacco smuggling and made it effectively impossible to postpone these sentences—even with mitigating factors. The only way to make prison sentences for cigarette smuggling eligible for postponement was to reduce them to under twenty-four months. This reduction was possible only if the accused demonstrated effective remorse by accepting responsibility during the investigation period, which ended once the prosecutor referred the case to the court and prosecution commenced. Thus, the accused was required to confess to the crime and pay twice the customs clearance value of the contraband cigarettes before the criminal prosecution began. The law also required prosecutors to inform the accused about effective remorse conditions and to ask whether the defendant wanted to benefit from them, but prosecutors tended to send the accused to the courts without informing them of this option.

Considering the prosecutors' omission of asking for effective remorse, the senior judges in the central courthouse started inquiring whether defendants had been informed about the effective remorse conditions during the prosecutions. If defendants claimed not to have been informed, which was the case in almost all the cases that I observed, the judges then asked whether the defendants wanted to make use of this provision, confess their crime, and pay the fine. In so doing, the judges used the prosecutor's omission to effectively extend the possibility of showing effective remorse beyond the investigation (*soruşturma*) period and into the prosecution (*kovuşturma*) proceedings. In this way, the judges began applying effective remorse conditions during trials and postponing prison sentences. If the defendants did not engage in any other crime for five years after the postponement decision, the prison sentence would be canceled and erased from their records.[67] In this rather creative interpretation of the law, the senior judges thus enabled some defendants to avoid prison sentences. Yet, many continued to face sentences because they still could not afford to pay the hefty fines, particularly in cases where the confiscated cigarette shipment exceeded a few hundred boxes, which made the fine unaffordable for many.

When I separately interviewed the two judges at Wan central court-house, they each said that the law in its current state punished the poorest and most vulnerable people involved in smuggling and remained ineffective against those in charge of large smuggling operations. This fact motivated them to develop their alternative legal interpretation. The new interpre-tation, however, did not mean that these judges supported a less punitive stance toward smuggling or disagreed with the smuggling-as-terrorism al-legations. In fact, as one of the judges disclosed to me, he believed that the primary organizers of the smuggling campaigns were the real associates of "the terrorist organization" and that the current system was ineffective in the fight against "the smuggling-terrorism connection" on the ground. The judge thus used the smuggling-as-terrorism accusations to justify their seemingly more liberal interpretation of the anti-smuggling law, geared toward expanding the legal rights of Kurdish defendants who engaged in small-scale smuggling.

THE CUNNING OF LAW VERSUS SLY LEGALITY

In Wan courthouses, prosecutors and judges mostly approached smuggling activity as an extension of terrorism, yet they deliberately avoided any explicit mention of Kurds, Kurdistan, or smuggling-terrorism connections in court records. This omission allowed the judiciary to maintain claims of impartial-ity, while the implementation of legal procedures—the manners in which court minutes were prepared, evidence was collected, and judicial discretion was applied—became key mechanisms for implicitly adhering to counterin-surgency concerns and for denying legal protections and rights to Kurdish people. The dual use of legal proceduralism to both impose substantive in-equality and assert procedural fairness constituted the cunning of law de-ployed in smuggling cases at Wan courthouses.

To contest this legal cunning, Kurdish smugglers and their lawyers de-veloped technolegal practices that I have theorized as sly legality. By practic-ing sly legality—a form of evasive engagement with the legal system—they repurposed legal procedures, evidence collection, and validation processes to ultimately curtail the legal authorities' capacity to impose substantive injustice or claim procedural neutrality. The following two chapters delve into how the practice of sly legality allowed smugglers and their lawyers to challenge the cunning of law in both smuggling trials and smuggler-killing prosecutions.

THREE

BORDERWORK

IN AUGUST 2012, TURKISH POLICE officers raided a gas station in the city center of Wan. It seemed to be a random anti-oil-smuggling crack-down, a common occurrence in the region. The police seized samples from the oil storage tanks and used a mobile device to test whether the oil contained the designated level of national oil marker (*ulusal marker*), a chemical substance that was mixed with legal oil products so that police could identify contraband oil. The samples failed the inspection. The police officers then sealed the station and sent its employees to the prosecutor's office on charges of smuggling. A few weeks later, the gas station's owner, Tahir, a high-profile Kurdish oil trader who owned two other gas stations, visited Emin's law office to hire him as his defense lawyer. At the time, I was working as a clerk and conducting fieldwork in Emin's office, which he shared with another lawyer. During Tahir's visit, Emin introduced me as a clerk and a researcher. Tahir agreed to my joining them during their meeting. Following that meeting, I attended court hearings held for Tahir's case and helped Emin and his two other clerks with their casework.

Tahir was originally from a border village in Elbak district. When he was fifteen, he started smuggling a few hundred liters of diesel fuel every week. After acquiring sufficient funds, in 1996, he moved to the Wan city center and opened a tire store, a front for selling contraband oil. By the early 2000s,

Tahir opened his first gas station and launched a trading company to smuggle oil and other contraband, such as sugar, tobacco, and tea.

This was not the first time that Tahir had been sent to court on smuggling charges. Emin, a criminal lawyer with over twenty years of experience, had represented him in at least two other cases. Most of Emin's time had been spent in smuggling trials, so smugglers saw Emin as a reliable lawyer because of his expertise in law and jurisprudence, as well as his extensive insider knowledge of contraband commerce through his family networks. He was a member of a border district–based merchant family, who had lent money to local farmers. When the counterinsurgency against the PKK effectively destroyed farming in the region, Emin's family shifted the focus of their moneylending business and began investing in smuggling campaigns. In fact, the connection between Tahir and Emin was based on their family business networks back in the border district where they had been born and raised. Emin's family financed various smuggling campaigns that Tahir's family organized. Their history meant that Tahir could trust Emin with serious business matters.

In the office, Emin asked Tahir whether the oil was documented. The confiscated oil (diesel fuel) was actually smuggled from Iran, but it had been documented as having been obtained through a Turkey-based oil refinery and traded through two different companies before arriving at Tahir's gas station. The trade documents were all authentic and issued by genuine and registered companies. Although the documents were meant to be used to sell fuel oil, Tahir procured them for the contraband diesel fuel. He had collected the contraband diesel from various carrier smugglers based in border villages and stored it in his gas station before sending it to a business partner in Kayseri, a province in central Anatolia. Emin then asked Tahir if the diesel fuel was "fixed" (*ayarlanmış*). At first, I did not understand what he meant by this. I later realized that it was a special code name for mixing the smuggled oil with legally processed oil and other chemicals.

Tahir's prosecution began at a first-degree criminal court at the central courthouse in Wan a few months later. During the trials, Emin's defense relied on the claim that the police had confiscated fuel oil and not diesel fuel from Tahir's gas station, and Emin presented commercial bills with company trade books to support this. He claimed that the fuel samples had failed inspection because fuel oil and diesel fuel used different chemical markers. He added that the fuel oil might have also lost a portion of its marker because of evaporation, which could only be detected in much more exact multi-variable laboratory tests rather than the mobile marker inspections that the police and gendarmerie commonly used. He also presented decisions from the Appeals Court that required using multi-variable laboratory test reports to determine the origin of confiscated oil. Despite his initial reluctance, the judge permitted the request for further testing and sent oil samples to the central expert laboratory. Two months later, the expert laboratory sent its expert witness report. In the laboratory test, the oil samples presented chemical values very close to the limit values for the national marker, but the test results fell just beyond the confidence intervals. Given the irreducible error rates of the chemical tests, the laboratory experts concluded that it was impossible to establish if the oil samples had or lacked the oil marker. The judge thus decided that the court could not determine whether the oil was contraband or not and acquitted Tahir for a lack of "sufficient, certain, and convincing evidence (*yeterli, kesin ve inandırıcı kanıt*)."[1]

After the session, Tahir seemed very happy. Although he had evaded a criminal sentence and the confiscation of the oil at his station, and so avoided a significant financial loss, neither were the source of his happiness. As we stepped from the courtroom into the courthouse corridor, I asked him for his thoughts about the court decision. He declared that the decision, his winning of the case, was a unique achievement:

> I knew that we would win the case. By winning this case, we made the state unable to impose its own borders by using its own law. Who else could do this? Nobody! [PKK] Guerrillas are fighting against the state, but even they could not do this. We achieved this by fixing the smuggled oil and playing it right at the court.

Given his boastful tone, I took Tahir to be articulating a special role for oil traders, or trader smugglers, and their lawyers: disrupting the state authorities' border enforcement by using the legal system of those authorities. He viewed this contestation of state borders as achieving something unique, a feat even the guerrillas could not perform. The PKK guerrillas militarily challenged the security forces' territorial control of the Kurdish highlands and occasionally opened free-passage corridors to Kurdish smugglers. Yet, Kurdish oil traders and their lawyers used criminal courts to challenge and disrupt these courts' capacity to exercise sovereignty in legally sanctioning (or banning) particular cross-border mobilities and livelihoods. How could an acquittal decision by a court undermine the court's own capacity to enforce borders and law? Did the court's verdict of acquittal not reinstate its legitimacy and sovereign power, after all? In what ways could defendants' efforts of obtaining an acquittal, which every defendant hoped for, become a unique political act that counteracted the state authorities' exercise of sovereignty? I had these questions in mind after hearing Tahir's comment. As I encountered similar court decisions and contemplated them, I came to understand what the decisions meant legally and politically and how they differed from other acquittal decisions.

The acquittal decision in Tahir's case confirmed that he was neither guilty nor innocent. To be more precise, the court did not prove him to be guilty. In Turkish criminal-legal jurisprudence, there were at least two types of "not proven to be guilty" verdicts.[2] In the first type, the court is able to corroborate a criminal act but not prove that the accused either committed or did not commit the act. In the second, the court cannot validate or invalidate the crime, either the specific criminal act (e.g., the act of smuggling oil) or the object of crime (e.g., the contraband oil), even though it establishes that the accused did commit that act or hold the object.[3] While the first type of not-proven guilty verdicts focuses on the link between the accused and the crime and aims to determine whether the accused conducted the criminal act, the second type examines the legality (or illegality) of the criminally charged act or object. In Tahir's case, the court offered the second type of not-proven guilty decision. The judge did not declare the oil samples to be illegal because he could not compile sufficient evidence to corroborate a smuggling crime. But he did not determine that the allegedly smuggled oil was legally imported and processed because here too there was not enough legal evidence. Instead, the judge ruled that it was not possible to determine whether the oil samples had been legally imported or traded. At the end of the court process, the smuggled oil thus became neither legal nor illegal but nonillegal, a category that exists beyond the legal-illegal binary.[4]

At first sight, there appeared to be no distinction between the two types of not-proven guilty verdicts in smuggling trials. In both cases, the accused were acquitted and so avoided criminal penalties. Yet, in the nonillegality decisions, the court would not confiscate the allegedly smuggled goods because it failed to establish their illegality. Accordingly, not only did Tahir avoid a criminal sentence, but he was also spared a sizeable financial loss since the oil was returned. More importantly, though, the nonillegality decisions had a politically salient consequence that differentiated them from other acquittal or nonguilty decisions in smuggling trials. The decisions incapacitated judicial authorities from tracing allegedly illegal cross-border mobilities (of persons or items) and thus impeded the courts' ability to enforce borders. In contrast to nonillegality decisions, the first type of not-proven guilty verdicts still detected the illegal border crossings of trade items, which corroborated smuggling crimes and hence legally enforced state borders, even though the perpetrators of smuggling crimes remained legally unidentified since the accused were not convicted at the end. By frustrating the courts' ability to establish the foreign origin of oil cargos, however, nonillegality decisions rendered borders legally unenforceable and, in doing so, allowed Kurdish traders and lawyers to attain pockets of escape within the schemes that state authorities imposed to surveil and prosecute cross-border mobilities.

The oil's nonillegality came to be established neither naturally nor coincidentally, however. These decisions became possible thanks to a specific set of technolegal tactics that Kurdish oil traders and their lawyers developed in cooperation with other actors. Through such tactics, these traders and lawyers appropriated legal procedures and evidentiary processes to curtail the state authorities' capacity to enforce borders and dispossess traders of their freedom and livelihoods. This chapter examines how oil (trader) smugglers and their lawyers devised these technolegal tactics and eventually turned oil smuggling trials into sites to contest and interrupt the authorities' sovereign control over smugglers' means of cross-border movement and subsistence.

SMUGGLING TRIALS

Turkish public prosecutors conducted anti-smuggling investigations (soruşturma) that targeted contraband consumer goods, including oil, cigarettes, tea, and sugar, and items that were prohibited altogether, namely firearms and narcotics. Most of the anti-smuggling investigations in the Wan courts commenced after law enforcement, the police in urban areas or gendarmerie in the countryside, detained individuals whom they suspected of smuggling.

The gendarmerie surveilled against smuggling by enforcing permanent and temporary checkpoints on inter-city roads and traversing the mountain passes near the border, while the police, especially anti-smuggling units, conducted smuggling inspections in cities and occasionally patrolled the city streets.[5] During the patrols and at checkpoints, law enforcement would search for contraband consumer goods, drugs, and guns. Among these items, cigarettes without security holograms, as well as drugs and guns, were the easiest items to verify.[6] For contraband tea, sugar, or foodstuffs, the forces had to check trade documents, whose authenticity was difficult to verify on-site. The law enforcement agents tended to be especially suspicious of oil carried by mule and horse convoys in valleys near the border. However, before the introduction of the oil marker, it was difficult to detect contraband oil carried in fuel tanks of any land vehicles that passed through road checkpoints unless an additional inflated fuel tank was spotted. In fact, expediting the search process was one of the driving reasons that had led the Turkish government to develop the national oil marker system.

The law enforcement and market regulatory agency staff also conducted routine or random anti-smuggling inspections in gas stations, other retail stores, and warehouses. During these inspections, they reviewed trade documents or customs papers if the trade goods were imported, examined the trade cargos, and took samples for content analyses. Inspectors occasionally brought K-9 police dogs to detect contraband tea or tobacco in addition to heroin and other narcotics, which were also often stashed within consumer goods cargos.

The anti-smuggling police and gendarmerie units carried out undercover anti-smuggling investigations as well, collecting information on suspects through wiretaps, video surveillance, and photo evidence. The undercover investigations often took weeks or even months and mainly targeted trader smugglers who organized different stages of smuggling logistics, such as cross-border and in-land transportation or the storage and marketing of contraband cargo, and who were often involved in multiple smuggling campaigns and networks.

These investigations eventually turned into anti-smuggling raids that might include domestic, workplace, or vehicle searches and potential detentions. Law enforcement mostly launched undercover investigations after they received a tip (*ihbar*) provided anonymously or, in some cases, by a police informer inside a smuggling network. In fact, an anonymous tip was responsible for the raid on Tahir's gas station, even though Emin initially thought it was a random inspection. According to the prosecutor's indictment, Tahir was identified as a suspect after a weeks-long undercover police investigation in which the tanker trucks frequenting his station were surveyed and his cell phone calls were monitored.

If law enforcement agents discovered any possessions they suspected to be contraband in the patrols, checkpoints, anti-smuggling inspections, and raids, they prepared a file on the suspected individuals and cargo and sent it to the prosecutor's office. A prosecutor would then decide whether further criminal investigations were required. The prosecutor collected testimonies from the suspects, reviewed trading documents if any had been presented, and sent the allegedly smuggled items to expert witnesses for inspection to determine their origins. For tea, sugar, unpackaged tobacco, and oil products, inspections often involved laboratory-conducted content analyses.

Once the investigations were complete, the prosecutor decided whether to pursue a criminal prosecution (*kovuşturma*) against the suspect(s) and submit an indictment to a judge or a panel of judges.[7] The first-degree criminal courts were tasked with processing the smuggling allegations about commodities for general trading, such as oil, cigarettes, and foodstuffs, while the high-degree criminal courts handled narcotics or arms smuggling. Once a judge—or a panel of judges, if a high-degree criminal court was involved—accepted an indictment, the criminal prosecution commenced. A usual courtroom included a single judge or a panel of judges, a prosecutor, a court clerk, a court crier, the defendant, and the defense lawyers. In reaching a verdict, the judges might call upon expert witnesses to evaluate the evidence. Only experts who were centrally determined and authorized by court commissions could provide binding expert witness testimony.[8] The defending party could also present expert witness statements, but judges had discretion as to whether they considered them in their decisions.

During smuggling trials, the judges would inquire whether the allegedly smuggled item had been produced abroad and, if so, whether it had been illegally transported across the border. In determining the origin of contraband goods, the courts specifically looked at two main sources of legal evidence: the allegedly smuggled item's trajectory and its material content. While the trajectory was traced through different types of trading and cargo documents, including commercial bills, corporate books, customs papers, and even package labels, the item content was examined through material content inspections that relied on particular market quality standards expressed in scientific-technical terms.

EVIDENCE OF SMUGGLING: DOCUMENTS AND MATERIAL CONTENT

Turkish law required traders who transported commercial cargo within the country to carry certain documents, such as a commercial invoice or insurance documents as well as customs papers if the cargo was imported. These documents were controlled at road checkpoints and customs offices. If the commercial cargo was stored in a warehouse, the warehouse keeper was required to present the papers to inspectors on request. An import or export transaction might require more than ten different documents, including commercial statements (e.g., commercial invoice, packing list), government papers (e.g., certificate of origin, movement certificate), transport documents (e.g., bill of lading, forwarder's receipt), insurance records (e.g., insurance certificate), or financial papers (e.g., bill of exchange, trust receipt). Trade transactions were also required to be recorded in company books. Depending on the initial document check, security officers might refer the cargo and its carrier, keeper, or owner to the court under allegations of smuggling.

Using paper to represent movements across borders is not unique in the case of trade items. For instance, consider the history of the passport: Modern state authorities invented documents and paperwork to uphold their claim of control and monopoly on people's legitimate means of movement across state borders.[9] Through paperwork, the authorities sought to make legible, and hence standardize, the cross-border movements of goods. The multiplicity of trade documents, however, brought further diversification and ever more exceptions rather than standardization and orderly classification.

With the help of their lawyers, Kurdish smugglers and traders also used the multiplicity of trade (and border-crossing) documents to contest smuggling allegations in courts by pointing out contradictions in criminal investigations.[10] In rejecting the allegations, the traders and their lawyers, for example, would use company books, trade invoices, and bills of lading interchangeably if one of the documents was missing the required information. As a documentary tactic, the traders often kept their company books partially filled and prepared trade invoices or lading bills with previous dates so that the books could be retrospectively filled if the authorities caught contraband cargo.

In some cases, the smugglers used counterfeit trade and customs documents with fake stamps and fraudulent wet signatures. Yet, these outright counterfeit documents could easily be detected in criminal-forensic inspections. It was more challenging for judicial authorities to detect the retroactively filled company books or dated trade documents that registered companies and institutions issued. In other cases, Kurdish smugglers and traders obtained authentic trade documents and used them to circumvent anti-smuggling surveillance at road checkpoints or in courts. Although these documents were genuinely issued by individuals, registered companies, or governmental institutions, such as state-owned companies or municipalities, the trade transaction that these documents described and the actual trade transaction that traders used them to facilitate did not correspond. The first time I heard of the use of these "authentic yet false" trade documents was in a court case in which contraband diesel fuel was transported as asphalt.[11]

The case commenced when the owners of a trading company were arrested after the police tracked the company's tanker trucks' delivery of diesel fuel to two different gas stations in Gaziantep, a province in southeastern Turkey. The traders had originally obtained commercial invoices from a municipality in the province of Adana, which is west of Gaziantep. The invoices detailed that the municipality promised to buy asphalt to pave a new road. Although the invoices mentioned the sale of asphalt, the company trucks left Wan with diesel fuel and, rather than deliver the cargo to Adana, the tanker trucks stopped at two different gas stations in Gaziantep. Since Gaziantep is located on the land road route from Wan to Adana, the trucks managed to pass all the road checkpoints from Wan to Gaziantep using the commercial invoices as cover. The truckers did not know, however, that they were being monitored by police. Once the trucks left the inter-city road in Gaziantep province and arrived at a gas station, instead of the destination recorded in the lading documents, the police raided the gas station and caught the truckers dumping their cargo into the station's tanks.

Similar to the compilation of various documents required for a trade transaction, court files also encompassed a variety of documents, including crime scene investigation reports, witness testimonies, expert witness statements, and prosecutors' indictments to documents prepared by other state agencies, such as poverty papers (*fakirlik belgesi*) issued by the local governorship or statements issued by nongovernmental institutions such as chambers of commerce. Procedural mistakes or inconsistencies across these documents, including misspelled names or missing signatures from state officers, witnesses, or the accused, could enable defendants and their lawyers to refute or delay smuggling allegations if not completely annul a prosecution. The documents issued by different agencies might also contradict each other or be used beyond their initial purpose. In one case, a Kurdish lawyer used his client's membership card for a truckers' association to rework the legal status of the trucker's carrying a few hundred liters of contraband diesel. The membership card allowed the lawyer to frame the extra diesel fuel as a consumption item rather than as a trade item. As the card established that the defendant was a professional truck driver, his carrying extra diesel fuel in his vehicle seemed reasonable. In this way, the defendant came to be accused of consuming, rather than procuring and selling, contraband diesel fuel. Based on the use of the membership card, the court not only postponed the defendant's imprisonment sentence and reduced the judicial fine but also decided not to confiscate his truck. The evasion of confiscation was a relief for the trucker as he needed to pay debts on the truck for the next ten years.

Using forged, contradictory, or retroactively produced documents enabled Kurdish smugglers and traders to circumvent the road checkpoints. During the anti-smuggling trials, these documentary practices could help defense lawyers challenge and alleviate criminal sentences. Yet, these practices often failed to cause judges to drop the smuggling charges and acquit the defendants completely. In almost all the cases that I reviewed, after failing to corroborate smuggling allegations through trade or customs documents, neither the judges nor the prosecutors dropped the allegations and ended the prosecutions. Instead, judges and prosecutors turned to the material content of the allegedly contraband items to determine their origins before finalizing the prosecution.

To use the material content of trade items to determine the items' origin, the judges, however, needed certain variables as references in provenance inspections. The only available sets of material variables were commodity-specific market quality standards. Accordingly, if allegedly contraband goods failed to meet these quality standards, judges confirmed their non-domestic provenance and corroborated a smuggling crime. In the case of sugar, these standards were expressed in the Turkish Sugar codex communiqué published by the Ministry of Agriculture. To detect contraband tea, court experts used the Turkish Black Tea codex communiqué, again published by the ministry, as the main reference. And for oil, until the introduction of the national marker in 2007, court experts used the Turkish oil standards that the Turkish Standards Institution published in its communiqués. The quality standards were mostly expressed in technoscientific (i.e., chemical) terms and were often expressed within validity intervals, such as maximum and minimum invert sugar figures or polarization levels for sugar, or as minimum levels of caffeine and maximum levels of cellulose or exudation for tea.

The problem with these tests, from the point of view of the court, was that they were cumbersome and often required testing at sophisticated laboratories, many of which were located in Ankara, the capital city, and some in the city center of Diyarbekir/Amed or Wan. Therefore, the judges were obliged to send samples of the allegedly contraband sugar or tea to the city centers or even Ankara. Prior to the introduction of the oil marker system, for example, the allegedly smuggled oil samples were tested mostly in the laboratories of Van Yüzüncü Yıl University, the only university in Wan. These inspections often took several weeks or months and could significantly delay the criminal prosecutions. Despite these delays, the judges I interviewed expressed that they found these inspections reliable and sufficient for their final decisions and thus had no choice but to wait for the results unless they corroborated the smuggling allegations based on the lack of documentation.[12]

The lengthy and cumbersome material content inspections were one of the main reasons that the Turkish government developed the oil marker system. The authorities assumed that these inspections undermined effective anti-smuggling campaigns amid the increasingly frequent accusations that smuggling revenues were financing the PKK-led insurgency. In contrast, the marker system promised to accelerate the prosecutions by condensing the provenance inquiry into a single test that could be conducted remotely without a lab. Acting as a chemical security hologram or a chemical passport, the system aimed to combine the practicality of document-based anti-smuggling inspections conducted at road checkpoints, gas stations, and other retail stores with the presumed reliability of material content tests.

THE OIL MARKER AS A CHEMICAL PASSPORT

The Turkish government debuted the national oil marker system in March 2006, and the EPDK published the first national oil marker communiqué in April 2006. The national oil marker (İŞARETR[13]) was eight milliliters of a specific chemical substance added to every one thousand liters of "legal" oil. It provided basic information for provenance and determining whether oil had been imported legally or not. In a sense, the oil marker was meant to work as a chemical passport for oil products.

The EPDK authorized the TÜBİTAK (National Metrology Institute of the Turkish Scientific and Technological Research Council[14]) to produce the national marker. TÜBİTAK was also given the authority to change the exact compound of the marker at least once per year to prevent counterfeiting. Unlike the Turkish oil standards, which were available to the public and thus allowed oil smugglers to modify the contraband oil to pass the market-quality tests, the chemical content of the oil marker was kept secret.

On January 1, 2007, the first oil product cargos mixed with the national marker were distributed to retailers, and the national marker controls were instituted by the EPDK inspectors. According to TÜBİTAK, between January 2007 and April 2013, over a million liters of national oil marker were produced and distributed.[15] The EPDK enforced the system using an online data collection center that kept records on the storage tanks of the oil distribution companies. It also conducted random marker inspections in oil company facilities and gas stations. Initially, the national marker inspections were centralized and conducted by the national marker reference testing devices located at TÜBİTAK's headquarters in the capital city of Turkey. However, centralized testing drew criticism for slowing down legal processes, particularly in courts in distant border zones. In response to such critiques, a few months after the national marker system had been launched, the EPDK introduced a mobile oil marker inspection device, the Marker XP, which was also developed by TÜBİTAK.[16]

The mobile device had a key role in marker inspections. At about the size of a cash register, the device could run a basic marker inspection via its liquid reservoir and produce a test report with its attached printer. With this mobile testing technology, the marker inspections became convenient at any location, from gas stations to road checkpoints.

The mobile device was also designed to provide simplified expert witness reports for the courts. The tests were directed to restrict the provenance inspection results to two mutually exclusive findings, "valid" or "invalid," on sleek, supermarket-receipt-like pieces of paper that provided no further information (see Figure 1). By contrast, the Turkish oil standards–based laboratory tests, which had been used before 2007, generated two or more full pages of test results on ten or more different variables that were expressed and detected with probabilistic estimates. The mobile inspection device, in that sense, emerged as a "black box," which packed the technoscientific processes of chemical tests that operated on scientific uncertainty and statistical probabilities into a technolegal evaluation that rendered oil as either valid/legal or invalid/illegal.[17] By the end of 2007, the mobile inspection devices were distributed to the police, gendarmerie, and EPDK inspectors across Turkey.

The mobile marker inspections turned the oil marker system into a time- and cost-efficient anti-oil-smuggling technology that extended the geographic scope of anti-oil-smuggling surveillance and facilitated the smuggling trials. In courts, prosecutors presented the mobile inspection reports as "proof" of smuggling. Considering these reports as final and binding expert witness reports, judges began imposing sentences without calling expert witnesses to question the validity of the material evidence. For example, in September 2012, when I first met and interviewed Hakan, a judge who handled most of the oil smuggling cases at the central courthouse in Wan, we discussed the reliability of the mobile marker inspections. Judge Hakan was very confident of the mobile inspections and explained how he

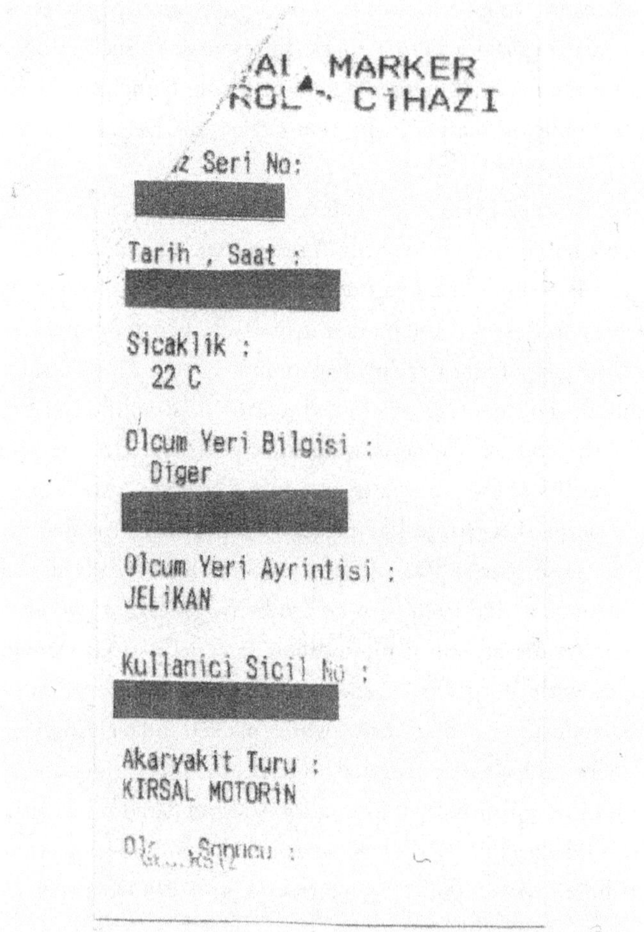

FIGURE 1. A receipt-like inspection report provided by a mobile marker inspection device at a road checkpoint near Çaldêran/Ebex, Wan, in 2010. The last line provides the test result, which says invalid (*geçersiz* in Turkish).

routinely used them to finalize smuggling cases: "It is over, the system has been consolidated, there is no doubt at all . . . if there is a mobile test device report, that is enough for me to pass a verdict." As Judge Hakan's words exemplify, the mobile marker inspection reports were initially taken as reliable and binding expert witness reports, the certainty of which was accepted without question in court.

CHALLENGING THE MARKER SYSTEM

The oil marker simplified and accelerated the prosecution of oil smuggling charges. Yet not long after it had been implemented, Kurdish oil smugglers and lawyers began challenging the marker system through technolegal tactics that exposed and exploited its vulnerabilities. Emin explained to me that "the oil marker, especially the mobile marker tests, messed things up. The state authorities strove to put an end to smuggling with these mobile tests, but it eventually backfired." In my time working at the law office, I saw firsthand how Kurdish traders and lawyers challenged and voided the oil marker system.

One way the traders circumvented the marker system was through the use of counterfeit markers. Although its chemical content was kept secret, the oil marker could still be forged, just as were passports and customs documents. While the government and the EPDK initially denied the possibility of forging the oil marker, a member of the scientific team that developed the marker confirmed that it could be counterfeited and recommended tightening its security by encrypting it with a specific DNA code.[18] Discussion of the marker's vulnerability to forgery continued even more after October 2009, when Turkish newspapers reported that a counterfeit marker had allegedly been used in a province on the Mediterranean coast. According to the reports, a bottle of counterfeit marker was discovered in the storage facilities of a private oil distribution company.[19] While the company rejected these allegations, the EPDK began investigating the incident. Upon the EPDK's request, TÜBİTAK provided a detailed expert witness report in September 2009.[20] The report stated that "the unknown chemical liquid" (i.e., the counterfeit oil marker) consisted of the 2007 oil marker (Marker 1) combined with other unidentified chemical substances. The report also confirmed that when this mixture was added to oil products in excess, the unknown liquid successfully mimicked the 2008 oil marker (Marker 2) during an inspection performed by a mobile testing device. However, according to the report, the unknown substance failed the inspection when tested with the national marker reference device. The company challenged this expert witness report by highlighting the fact that a portion of the 2007 marker (Marker 1) was also found inside the chemical liquid and claimed that the chemical compound of the marker could change over time. The EPDK was not satisfied with this explanation and announced that it would fine the company.

One could argue that this case is illustrative of the overall success of the national marker system to clamp down on the trafficking of contraband oil. Smugglers attempted to circumvent the system using a counterfeit marker, but the national marker proved effective as a chemical passport, eventually differentiating legally processed oil from smuggled oil. However, the case also illustrates the potential flaws of overreliance on the marker inspection system. As the expert witness report revealed, the sample liquid consisted of the national marker of 2007 (Marker 1) and some other substances. This finding could also lend credence to the oil company's claim that the unknown chemical liquid was merely a residual portion of the previous year's marker. And somehow, this mixture mimicked the 2008 marker (Marker 2) in the inspection test conducted with the mobile inspection device. Consequently, the case cast questions on the oil marker and its stability: Could the marker metamorphose into something else while sitting in a bottle? If so, how reliable could the overall chemical marker system be?

To answer these questions, we must turn to the material qualities of oil and the oil marker.[21] As chemical substances, oil and the oil marker were vulnerable to chemical instabilities that led to inconsistent or inconclusive results. For example, the oil marker was a volatile matter that would gradually evaporate. A barrel of legally processed diesel fuel, accordingly, would lose its level of national oil marker over time and might fail a marker inspection.

Aside from evaporation, each barrel of oil might also lose some of its contents, including the oil marker, through precipitation. Precipitation undermined the reliability of oil marker in at least two ways. First, the compounds of the marker could not be dissolved perfectly, and the non-dissolved elements of the marker could precipitate. When a sample of legally processed fuel was tested for the marker concentration level, it might fail the test. In fact, in June 2007, the EPDK acknowledged a precipitation problem in the markers that had been produced and distributed between January and March 2007. It announced that some coloring agents might not have dissolved completely, and it replaced these agents in oil marker cargos produced after April 2007.[22] Second, when a cargo of diesel fuel was kept in the storage tank of a gas station, a portion of the fuel gradually precipitated, and the precipitated substance eventually turned into oil sludge on the bottom of the tank. The oil sludge could mix with newly added oil, which would include a newer oil marker. Thus, oil tagged with a previous marker could easily be mixed with oil tagged under a new marker. This situation increased the possibility that legally processed oil products could fail oil marker inspections, especially inspections conducted through mobile test devices.

By identifying the oil marker's chemical vulnerability to evaporation and precipitation, Kurdish lawyers began challenging the use of mobile marker test results as decisive material evidence in criminal prosecutions as of 2011. They eventually succeeded in undermining the reliability of the marker system in court. Appealing to the burden of proof principle, which requires the claiming party to prove the act of crime by establishing conclusive material evidence beyond reasonable doubt, lawyers success-fully contested the mobile marker inspections first in local courts and then in the Appeals Court. Emin explained to me how he initially challenged the tests:

> The mobile tests provided a small piece of paper that only said if the oil sample had passed or failed. Yet, we knew that these tests were not highly sensitive and did not provide detailed chemical test results. For example, an oil sample that had failed in the mobile inspection device might still pass the marker inspection in a detailed laboratory test. The local courts had not accepted our request for laboratory tests, but the Appeals Court asked for these tests for the sake of revealing the material evidence and material fact.

In late 2012, the Appeals Court began overturning court decisions that relied exclusively on mobile device reports and instructed the courts to conduct detailed marker inspections using expert laboratories. By 2013, a few months after my initial interview with Judge Hakan at the central courthouse in Wan, I observed the impact of the defense lawyers' arguments on judge's decisions. Despite his reluctance, Judge Hakan began sending oil samples for extended laboratory tests. When I interviewed the judge again in January 2014, he no longer considered mobile marker inspections as the principal expert evidence and was complying with the Appeals Court decisions that required chemical analysis reports from expert laboratories. As a result of the increasingly successful defenses, the Appeals Court decisions eventually led to multi-variable laboratory tests becoming the primary expert witness evidence, replacing mobile marker inspection findings in oil smuggling cases in local courts.

PROBABILISTIC BORDERS

The use of multi-variable laboratory tests as principal expert witness evidence changed how the courts examined the legality of oil cargo. Given that a level of irreducible scientific uncertainty had always been embedded in multi-variable laboratory tests, those tests operated only within a particular threshold of probability, namely error rates and confidence intervals. While mobile marker inspections merely determined whether a sample had a marker, the expert laboratories provided a much more detailed picture. Lab experts compared chemical values for each variable with specific reference limit values that the EPDK used to identify the oil marker. By taking these tests as decisive expert witness reports in their prosecutions, judges and prosecutors shifted the defining features of the national custom zone, or the boundaries of the national oil market, from two-dimensional borderlines to a certain set of chemical values. This shift rematerialized the national borders into "probabilistic borders"—a distinct logic of bordering that frames border crossings as phenomena of degree or likelihood.[23]

Probabilistic borders contrast starkly with the common conception of national borders, which are usually understood as two-dimensional lines that demarcate one sovereign state from another or "a line in the sand."[24] Since the rise of the Westphalian state system, these two-dimensional borders have articulated national territories as being mutually exclusive and cohesive entities.[25] Accordingly, the state authorities imagined and treated national borders as definitive lines, which could be crossed or not. Even in the case of disputed or poorly enforced borders, state authorities still have treated border crossings by people, animals, or goods as definitive incidents. From their point of view, a person or a contraband good either crossed the border or not; there were no two ways about it.

At first glance, probabilistic borders might seem to rely on the same two-dimensional conception of national borders. The oil content inspection results were still evaluated in reference to (maximum or minimum) limit values for each variable. Although there was more than one limit (value), those limits were still enforced as two-dimensional lines. After all, the question was still whether one crossed those limits (lines) or not.

Yet, probabilistic borders rely on a distinct type of knowledge production, one that offers probabilistic (instead of either/or) truth claims. Because the test results provided values within a particular continuum of probability, the multi-variable chemical tests detected oil provenance with an irreducible degree of uncertainty and articulated their findings as a matter of likelihood. Consequently, the alleged border crossings by oil cargos became phenomena "that come to exist only with uncertainty."[26] Depending on the testing equipment, as well as the amount of oil used in a test, the sensitivity of test results could vary. Yet, even at higher levels of sensitivity, oil content inspections still relied on statistical estimates and thus established truth claims without absolute certainty.

Probabilistic borders should thus be understood as a distinct register of bordering that differs from two-dimensional bordering. Yet these distinct bordering registers do not necessarily replace each other, even though they may claim to enclose the same entities, such as the national (oil) market. In fact, two-dimensional and probabilistic bordering often coexist. Other bordering logics, such as racialized bordering in which national borders are designated alongside racialized categories, may also operate in conjunction with these logics such that particular border crossings or conditions of work and stay are legally banned (or facilitated) according to these categories.[27] State authorities may use different bordering logics, separately or concomitantly, to further their surveillance and containment regimes. Yet, disenfranchised groups might also deploy one bordering logic to counteract another and its associated regime(s) of control. Kurdish oil traders and their lawyers illustrate how their use of different bordering logics challenged the national marker and repurposed probabilistic borders to establish the nonillegality of contraband oil.

DISRUPTIVE BORDERWORK

In establishing oil's nonillegality through court decisions, Kurdish traders and lawyers devised their own borderwork, the work of altering and interrupting the ways in which state authorities designate and enforce borders.[28] The traders and lawyers' borderwork began with changing how criminal courts policed the oil trade: pushing the courts to replace the use of mobile marker inspections with the multi-variable laboratory tests. Referring to probabilistic estimates embedded in these tests, traders and lawyers reframed the allegedly illegal border crossings of oil cargo as incidents that could only be detected with uncertainty. Yet, the traders did not take this uncertainty as given. They, rather, developed counter-technologies, such as the technolegal tactic of chemically "fixing" smuggled oil, to enhance and govern the uncertainty.[29] This chemical work made oil samples present chemical values slightly beyond the confidence intervals within which the laboratory tests operated. Once the test results fell beyond those intervals, the results became questionable and the provenance of oil cargos could not be determined definitively. Kurdish lawyers completed the borderwork by using this inconclusive evidence as a legal counterargument that made contraband oil nonillegal and state borders unenforceable.

Borders and border enforcement has emerged as one of the most integral features of modern statecraft, as state authorities claim territorial control and monopoly on the "legitimate means of movement" and the "legitimate means of violence."[30] To uphold their claim, the authorities need to maintain borders and their enforcement on a regular basis and would often allow different actors—ordinary citizens, private companies, and NGOs—to participate in border enforcement. From Western Europe and North America to the Arabian Gulf, governments have increasingly subcontracted with private companies at home and abroad to process visa applications, conduct preemptive profile checking, and operate immigration detention centers and perform deportations.[31] Local communities also have developed their own bordering practices outside of, and in some cases in competition with, government-imposed borders.[32] Rebel groups, organized bandits, or border communities, for example, may authorize border crossings that governments deem illegal, impose their own checkpoints and tolls on cross-border trade, or exclude non-local groups from engaging in such trade activities.[33] In doing so, however, these groups mimic and reproduce, rather than reject or resist, the logic of exclusion and extraction through which the state authorities and international trade regimes control access to cross-border trade.[34]

Rather than strengthen or mimic the state authorities' border enforcement, Kurdish traders and lawyers aimed to curtail it. In doing so, the traders and lawyers performed "disruptive borderwork." They did not aim to achieve a legal authority over border crossing that was an alternative to, or in competition with, that of Turkish authorities. By rendering oil's origin unintelligible to the authorities, traders and lawyers voided the material and legal capacity the Turkish government had in claiming and executing sovereignty over specific mobilities and livelihoods within and across the borders.

The disruptive borderwork was the result of collective technolegal work, even though it was deployed in individual court cases. Kurdish traders and their lawyers developed these tactics in close cooperation with each other and with other experts, such as accountants and chemists. For example, Tahir, as an established, high-profile oil trader, knew that smuggled diesel fuel would cause the oil marker inspection to provide inconclusive results if legal oil was mixed with other chemicals at a particular ratio. After the court dropped the charges in the diesel fuel case, I asked Tahir how he learned to chemically "fix" the oil to nullify the oil marker inspections. Apparently, Tahir got the trick from a fellow trader, who had originally obtained it from a retired chemist who had worked at an oil refinery. Tahir did not tell me exactly what other chemicals he mixed in, and I did not ask him for details. But these tricks, the technolegal practices, were known to and exchanged among Kurdish traders and lawyers, even though these smugglers and lawyers might compete with each other in their respective careers. When I asked Emin if he felt comfortable sharing his legal tactics with other lawyers, Emin also expressed a sense of collective work and an ethos of political cooperation among traders and lawyers that facilitated each other's borderwork: "Winning a case does not only benefit my defendants, that case would become a binding precedent and be used by other lawyers and their clients." Once a case became a binding precedent, other traders and lawyers also benefited. For this reason, lawyers often exchanged court files from nonillegality decisions with one another to facilitate their use as precedents.[35]

The collective character of the disruptive borderwork in smuggling trials, however, did not mean that it would allow every citizen to counteract the state authorities' border enforcement. It still required very specific, substance-based know-how that most smugglers in the region did not have; it also required specific legal skills, such as up-to-date knowledge of binding precedents published by the Turkish Appeals Court, that not all lawyers necessarily possessed. Therefore, almost all of the cases that successfully destabilized the oil marker system and finally established the nonillegality of contraband oil involved high-profile smugglers and "smuggler lawyers", experienced criminal lawyers who specialized in smuggling trials. In fact, in many cases in which an inexperienced lawyer was involved or in which the lawyers failed to request detailed laboratory tests, judges ignored the Appeals Court decisions and simply relied on the results of oil marker inspections performed by the mobile devices. Thus, even the Appeals Court's binding decisions became effective mostly because of the involvement of lawyers who actively reminded the judges of these decisions.

The nonillegality decisions, expectedly, deeply frustrated judges and prosecutors. The judicial authorities were aware of the traders' and lawyers' technolegal tactics and resultant borderwork. In our last interview, for instance, after explaining that he had reluctantly changed his jurisprudence in light of the Appeals Court decisions, Judge Hakan complained about the court decisions that were based on the inconclusive material evidence that expert laboratories had provided. He expressed that if these laboratories were incapable of detecting smuggled oil, it was neither his nor the prosecutors' responsibility to fix it and added that the government and the parliament must continuously revise and reform the anti-smuggling laws, regulations, and measures. Based on this frustration with the inconclusive marker inspections, state authorities might introduce other anti-oil-smuggling technologies to rematerialize the borders of the national oil market as definite limits in the future. In response, Kurdish traders and lawyers may (or may not) develop counter-technologies or other ways to perform disruptive borderwork to maintain the nonillegality of smuggled oil. Yet, by contesting oil markers materially and legally, Kurdish traders and lawyers have already identified the technolegal political field and demonstrated the possibility of rendering state borders legally unenforceable. The frustration of the judges and other state officers further underscores the political significance of this field.

A POLITICAL ACHIEVEMENT IN COURT

Kurdish oil traders and their lawyers viewed their borderwork and nonillegality decisions as a unique political achievement. Tahir's comments following his final court hearing illustrated this view. The nonillegality decisions became politically meaningful as a way to disrupt the enforcement of state borders in courts. Because the borders divided broader Kurdistan geography

among non-Kurdish nation-states and subjugated Kurdish people to different yet mutually reinforcing colonial dominations in each nation-state, many
Kurds viewed these borders as a mechanism and symbol of their political
and economic suffering. Because smuggling trials were a key context through
which state borders were enforced, security forces' violence was sanctioned,
and Kurdish highlanders across the border were further dispossessed and in-
carcerated, for many of my smuggler and lawyer interlocutors, contesting and
curtailing these trials amounted to challenging colonial domination and the
associated regimes of surveillance and oppression in Kurdistan.

The smuggling trials acquired another layer of political significance in
the background of the counterinsurgency war in which Turkish government
and the judiciary identified Kurdish smuggling economies with the PKK-led
insurgency and thus treated anti-smuggling law enforcement and smuggling
trials in Kurdistan as an extension of the counterinsurgency. Given that the
judiciary took counterinsurgency as a determining yet often undeclared concern in handling the smuggling prosecutions, these prosecutions came to be
incorporated into anti-Kurdish lawfare campaigns in which state authorities
weaponized criminal law against Kurdish rights advocates and prosecuted
them under "political trials" (*siyasi davalar*).[36] To many inhabitants of the
Kurdish borderlands, therefore, smuggling trials constituted another chapter in the Turkish government's anti-Kurdish lawfare campaigns. The traders
and their lawyers made sense of their disruptive borderwork accordingly and
viewed it as another way to contest the Turkish authorities' lawfare campaigns and counterinsurgency warfare in Kurdistan.

Kurdish defendants and their lawyers had long contested the anti-Kurdish lawfare campaigns by turning the criminal prosecutions for allegations
of separatism and terrorism into a site of exposing the crimes of state officials and confronting the legitimacy of the established political and legal
order. Throughout decades of these political trials, Kurdish defendants and
their lawyers developed two main legal defense strategies. The first strategy
was the "legal defense" (*hukuki savunma*), which focused on due process,
challenged the evidence presented to substantiate criminal charges, and articulated rights claims. While the legal defense disputed criminal charges
and aimed at acquittal or alleviating sentences, it accepted the legitimacy
of the courts. In contrast to such a defense strategy, the Kurdish defendants

developed a second strategy, "political defense" (*siyasi savunma*), which refused the courts as legitimate interlocutors and used the trials as a site to symbolically put state authorities on trial for their crimes.[37] Pursuing a strategy of "rupture defense," the Kurdish defendants not only questioned the authority of the courts but also subverted the legal procedures and claimed prosecutorial gaze to symbolically direct such gaze against the state officials in their political defenses.[38] In the political trials of the 1970s and 1980s, for example, Kurdish intellectuals and revolutionaries narrated the officially and publicly denied histories of Kurdish people, Kurdish language, and Kurdistan geography, and articulated the various practices of racism, violence, dispossession, and colonial domination that the state officials deployed against Kurdish communities. By virtue of these defenses inside the courtrooms, the Kurdish defendants repurposed the political trials to publicize otherwise denied (and criminalized) critiques, claims, and knowledge in the official court documents.[39] These political defenses had even become a means of articulating and disseminating new political strategies for Kurdish politicians and revolutionaries. During the decade following his capture in 1999, the PKK leader Abdullah Öcalan, for example, used oral defenses and written defense texts submitted to courts to introduce a new political vision that denied nation-state modalities and prioritized gender-equal, ecological, noncapitalist, and autonomous grassroots democracy. As the oral defenses and defense texts were published and broadly circulated, Öcalan's new political vision came to be discussed within the Kurdish Freedom Movement and other circles worldwide.[40] In this way, Kurdish defendants and their lawyers used political trials for alternative political purposes.

The Kurdish traders and their lawyers' disruptive borderwork also constituted a distinct use of criminal prosecutions, one that sought a political objective of rendering nation-state borders legally unenforceable. To achieve this objective, traders and lawyers practiced a particular form of legal defense strategy that resembled both the political and legal defenses of political trials insofar as it combined the pursuit of legal procedures (from the legal defense) with a political refusal of courts' sovereignty (from the political defense). By following due process and referring to legal rights afforded by the procedural law and evading an open, straight-out rejection of the courts' prosecutorial authority, Kurdish oil traders and their lawyers seemed to undertake a legal defense. Yet, their borderwork differed from other legal defenses in that it impeded the courts' material and legal capacities to adjudicate cross-border mobilities. That is, rather than focus on the rights granted and guaranteed by state legality, the traders and lawyers aimed to curtail the judiciary's authority to enforce state law and sovereignty. In this way, the disruptive borderwork emerged as a legal action that resorted to courts but did not rely on the legal remedies courts provided and, in doing so, transcended rights-based struggles. Even though the defense strategy required traders and lawyers to claim and benefit from particular legal rights, namely the right to a fair trial, the traders and lawyers did not use these rights to establish a particular right (e.g., a right to property, movement, or trade) but instead undercut the state authorities' ability to enforce borders. When sent to court to be prosecuted for smuggling, Kurdish traders did not claim their cross-border trade activities were legitimate through political or legal claims of legal activism. Instead, traders engaged in disruptive borderwork to undermine the court's capacity to prove or disprove an act of smuggling and to render state borders unenforceable.

By undermining the courts' prosecutorial authority, disruptive borderwork bore a resemblance to political defenses. While political defenses strove to expose the state's crimes, symbolically try these crimes, and publicize political causes through political trials and court documents, traders' and lawyers' borderwork achieved a disruption of border enforcement. Although political defenses relied on the upfront and open refusal of courts' prosecutorial authority and legal processes, the disruptive borderwork initially appeared to accept the legitimacy of courts and legal procedures so as to eventually hinder the judicial exercise of sovereign power to sanction mobilities.

SLY LEGALITY IN SMUGGLING TRIALS

By developing technolegal tactics to pursue disruptive borderwork, Kurdish oil traders and their lawyers performed sly legality in criminal courts: They sought to repurpose legal procedures and evidentiary processes, corrode operative logics of the smuggling trials, and eventually hamper the courts' prosecutorial authority to enforce borders and dispossess Kurdish traders of their livelihoods. As illustrated by the nonillegality of contraband oil, sly legality enabled traders and lawyers to resort to state courts without relying on their remedies. In fact, they aimed to curtail these courts' ability to provide such remedies and escape legal sanction.

Given that these traders were caught by law enforcement agencies and sent to criminal courts for allegedly smuggling, as defendants, they did not resort to state law by choice. They were forced to go through criminal prosecutions and defend themselves, as would any other defendant. Yet, the traders' and lawyers' disruptive borderwork and associated technolegal tactics were neither coincidental nor randomly chosen defense strategies, nor were they a last resort. In fact, the oil traders and lawyers could have secured acquittals in other ways, such as misrepresenting contraband oil as legal and misleading the courts into ruling on the legality of the otherwise contraband oil (rather than its nonillegality) and the defendants' innocence (instead of proving neither their guilt nor their innocence). The traders could have also implicated gas station workers or carrier smugglers as the guilty parties by offering them extra cash so as to evade prosecution entirely or be acquitted. Instead, oil traders cooperated with their lawyers to conduct disruptive borderwork, rendering the contraband oil nonillegal by deliberately taking up technolegal arrangements, some of which had to be completed even before the traders were caught, such as chemically "fixing" the contraband oil. In doing so, the traders and their lawyers contested and curtailed the courts' ability to surveil and convict, as well as exonerate and thus co-opt them into the state's legal system. Even when Kurdish smugglers, their families, and their lawyers went to the criminal courts as accusers and filed complaints for smuggler killings, they also practiced sly legality and engaged with the state's legal system to defy and disrupt the redresses it may offer and the co-optation it could entail. The next chapter examines this pursuit of sly legality by the families of the slain smugglers and their lawyers, exploring how they interacted with and repurposed the criminal courts beyond and against their legal and political contours.

FOUR

COUNTERFORENSICS

IN FEBRUARY 2014, I ATTENDED the final hearing for a Turkish soldier who faced charges for killing a Kurdish smuggler. Sinan, the slain smuggler, had been shot in an ambush set by the Turkish army in a mountain pass, near the Turkish-Iranian border in Wan province. In his defense, the soldier claimed he had not shot Sinan intentionally. He had actually fired a warning shot into the ground, but the bullet ricocheted and fatally injured Sinan. The court had already acquitted the soldier of murder and determined that Sinan had been killed as a result of "an inevitable mistake." Yet, during the earlier court hearings, Metin, the lawyer representing Sinan's family, had argued that the crime scene topography contradicted the soldier's statement and instead indicated that the soldier must have directly shot at Sinan. Following this argument, he also appealed the court's acquittal of the soldier. Metin's plea to the Appeals Court succeeded, and the court reversed the criminal court's previous decision and asked it to re-examine the case by considering how the topography had affected the ballistics of the gunshot. The result of that re-examination was to be announced that day.

After explaining how the court had carefully considered the crime scene topography, the judge dismissed the possibility that the accused soldier directly shot at the victim. Instead, he acknowledged that "considering the slope and where the accused stood, the accused must have considered the possibility of a bullet ricocheting." Based on this observation, the judge concluded that the soldier had committed manslaughter. The judge first sentenced the soldier to two years of imprisonment, the minimum sentence for manslaughter. Yet, referring to the "high frequency of terror incidents in the region," which was a mitigating circumstance, the judge expressed his concern that the soldier must have acted under stress. He reduced the sentence to one and a half years and then, as his final decision, suspended the conviction. The soldier did not technically receive any criminal sentence and spent no time in jail.

When we left the courtroom, Metin commented on the decision: "The judge intentionally decreased the sentence to suspend the conviction." Ahmet, Sinan's older brother who was a seasonal construction worker and a former smuggler himself, asked Metin if the decision could be further appealed. Metin said he would object to the decision but doing so would not change the result. He added, "You know the courts protect the state and their men."

"I know, I know," said Ahmet. "Well, at least we proved that my brother was killed by the state's soldier. I will sleep better tonight."

A hardworking man in his early fifties, Metin was one of the few lawyers who had an office in the border district and was one of the founders of the district branch of the İHD, the leading human rights organization in northern Kurdistan (Bakur).[1] He was originally from a border village and had smuggled contraband in his youth. Using his firsthand knowledge of the trade, Metin handled several smuggler killing cases as a human rights lawyer. Ahmet, who was thirty-two at the time, was the main family member who followed Sinan's case. He attended court sessions, visited Metin's office regularly, and accompanied Metin to collect evidence in support of his brother's case.

Each killing or injury of a smuggler needed to be reported to the prosecutor's office, and prosecutors had to investigate these incidents and bring perpetrators to justice. However, identifying the perpetrators was a difficult task because the security forces who conducted the ambushes were known to misreport casualties to protect themselves from criminal liability. As the state forces used heavy combat weaponry, such as Heckler & Koch G3s and HK33s or M16 military rifles, the bullets could penetrate a victim's body and leave them with fatal injuries. This required detailed bullet searches in open and rugged areas. Without the actual bullet that had wounded or killed the smuggler, it was extremely difficult to establish direct and unchallenged ballistic evidence. Even when bullets were recovered, the ballistic evidence collected from them must match the hand and gun swabs. Moreover, security forces often disposed of the smugglers' lifeless bodies in hidden sites far from where the shootings had taken place, which further complicated determining the exact crime scene, collecting meaningful evidence, and identifying the perpetrators.

In addition to the security forces' various strategies to ensure impunity, Kurdish residents in the borderland regions had no trust in the prosecutors' investigations. Two features of these investigations fed their suspicion. First, as members of the Turkish judiciary, prosecutors who conducted the investigations and supervised the evidence collection were state officials who were trained, appointed, and paid by the Turkish government.[2] So, the Kurdish communities suspected these prosecutors of placing the government's and security forces' interests ahead of Kurdish citizens' rights. Second, the gendarmerie, the military force authorized to enforce law in the countryside, helped collect evidence, especially crime scene evidence like bullet cartridges and other ballistic information, even though the perpetrators of such killings were mostly gendarmerie or military units who patrolled the border and ambushed smugglers. Even if the evidence collection was conducted by separate gendarmerie units, the Kurdish communities still worried that these units would protect their colleagues and tamper with the evidence that implicated them.

Suspecting a lack of comprehensive and effective criminal investigations, the families of the murdered smugglers or smugglers who survived armed stings often closely monitored and were involved in the investigations. To do this, they hired lawyers and filed criminal complaints with the prosecutor's offices to pursue the killings as complainants (*müşteki*).[3] To contest the impunity of the perpetrators, the complainants and their lawyers developed their own practices of evidence collection and improvised legal argumentation. In Sinan's case, for example, Metin succeeded in identifying the perpetrator who would have otherwise remained unknown, brought the case to criminal prosecution and even reversed the judge's decision to acquit by appealing to the upper courts. Yet, these legal successes rarely prevented the impunity of the soldiers. As happened in Sinan's case, the criminal courts would eventually generate and maintain perpetrators' impunity. Of the twenty-five criminal prosecutions relating to the killings of Kurdish smugglers that I followed in Wan courts, not a single state officer spent time in jail. The perpetrators' impunity prevailed even when the Kurdish complainants and their lawyers managed to materially prove that the perpetrators had killed the smugglers. Even after Kurdish lawyers legally established the unlawfulness of a killing, as Metin did in Sinan's case, the perpetrators still faced no criminal sentence.

Despite the knowledge and firsthand experience of perpetrators' impunity in Turkish courts, Kurdish complainants and their lawyers continued to engage with the criminal courts and devoted time and resources to collecting evidence that could prove state agents' guilt through the official criminal-legal processes. Ahmet, for example, as a member of the Kurdish borderland community and a former smuggler, was well aware of the likely outcome, yet he still pursued criminal prosecution. In fact, Sinan's case was one of the few instances where Kurdish complainants and lawyers came close to having a soldier imprisoned. Why did Ahmet and Metin, like other complainants and their lawyers, continue to push against the impunity at different criminal-legal stages? If not the legal penalties and sanctions they hoped to achieve, what legal and political meanings did the court processes hold for them?

SMUGGLER KILLINGS IN KURDISH BORDERLANDS

The inhabitants of the Wan borderlands have been the victims of targeted killings and impunity since the establishment of the Turkish Republic. In July 1943, thirty-three border villagers were rounded up from their houses by Turkish forces, detained under smuggling allegations, and then executed without trial in Wan's Qelqelî district.[4] Only one villager survived the execution. The security forces reported that the detained villagers were killed as they attempted to escape arrest. The incident was not investigated until 1950, when the governing party was defeated in the elections and a new inquiry was launched. The regional commander who ordered the shootings was tried, but he died before a verdict was finalized. All other soldiers involved in the shootings were acquitted. Two years later, ten villagers were detained under smuggling allegations from their villages in Wan's Bêgir (Off. Muradiye) district and executed without trial.[5] There was no investigation of that incident either.

The discretionary state killings that targeted Kurdish smugglers, as well as the perpetrators' impunity, were not unique to Wan province. In December 2011, in an incident known as the Roboski massacre, a Turkish F-16 fighter strike killed thirty-four Kurdish smugglers across the Turkish-Iraqi border near Roboski (Off. Ortasu) village. While government officials called the attack an "operation accident," the military blamed the PKK for provoking the attack by using the border region to infiltrate Turkey.[6] More than two years after the air bombardment, in January 2014, a military prosecutor concluded a criminal investigation and decided not to prosecute by calling the attack an "inevitable mistake." The families objected to the prosecutor's decision in a criminal court and eventually brought the case to the Turkish Constitutional Court.[7] After an appeals process lasting a year and a half, the court found the application "inadmissible" because of the overdue submission of a lawyer's power of attorney document. Even the ECtHR confirmed the inadmissibility decision, since the families had failed to exhaust domestic legal means. As with the smuggler killings in Wan, the impunity of the perpetrators in the Roboski massacre prevailed.[8]

The local newspapers in Wan regularly reported anti-smuggling armed stings and smuggler killings. Occasionally, national newspapers covered these killings as well. The local branches of human rights organizations and the Bar Association recorded these incidents, collected eyewitness statements, visited district centers and villages, and published fact-finding reports. Yet, the exact number of smugglers who were killed in the Wan borderlands was unknown. Replying to a parliamentary question, which a pro-Kurdish parliamentarian submitted in December 2012, the Interior Ministry reported that forty-eight people had been killed by border patrols near the Wan border between 2002 and 2012.[9] About three months later, in March 2013, responding to a request by the Van Bar Association's Human Rights Commission, which had initiated a rights advocacy project on the smuggler killings, the Van Governorship stated that forty smugglers had been killed and fifty-two were injured during the same period. As a member of the Bar's Human Rights Commission, I also conducted fact-finding visits in more than forty border villages and recorded sixty-five cases of killing and twenty-nine cases of wounding in addition to the incidents that the governorship reported to the Bar.[10]

Smuggler killings often happened during planned border patrols or armed stings that intercepted smugglers. Despite the mountainous landscape and challenging weather conditions, such as the harsh winters that restricted the military's land and aerial access to region, the Turkish and Iranian governments extensively monitored the border. Under the pretext of counterinsurgency, the Turkish authorities even expanded their surveillance infrastructure and assault capacity through new high-security military stations, watch towers equipped with long-range thermal imagers, remote-controlled weapons, ground sensors, land mines, and aerial drones.[11] While villagers relied on pack animals to navigate the mountains, the security forces in the Wan borderlands resorted to armored four-by-fours to patrol the border and intercept smuggling convoys.[12]

In the context of comprehensive state surveillance, smugglers could bribe lower-ranked gendarmeries to obtain free passage, but bribery did not necessarily spare them from the ambushes and killings.[13] I encountered various incidents in which smugglers were ambushed by the security forces even though they had paid bribes. Against the constant risk of armed stings, the smugglers and border villagers developed several tactics, such as conducting cross-border smuggling journeys in groups or carrying cell phones with both Turkish and Iranian SIM cards so they could notify their relatives and other smugglers of the stings, that allowed them to avoid border patrols or help those who were ambushed and shot by soldiers. In a few cases, the arrival of unattended mules or horses from smuggling convoys signaled to the villagers that an ambush had occurred and that the animals' owners had possibly been shot by soldiers.[14] After learning of an ambush, either by phone or unattended smuggler animals, villagers could then go to the ambush area and help smugglers who were wounded. On several occasions, villagers saved the lives of the injured smugglers left behind by soldiers. Because the smugglers were often ambushed while riding horses that were loaded with contraband, they might also escape by riding toward rocky, muddy, or icy terrain where the security forces' four-by-four trucks could not follow.

For the most part, however, these tactics remained ineffective in protecting Kurdish smugglers from being attacked, injured, or even killed by the security forces. If smugglers did not arrive to their destination or did not contact their family or another villager via phone a few hours after departing—trips usually took three to four hours—families would be left with few options. It was always possible that a convoy had been detained by soldiers, or there was the graver prospect that the smugglers had been injured or killed. If none of the smugglers arrived in the village or called anyone, the villagers would initiate a search party in the nearby mountain passages. In the event that they discovered a body, they were legally required to call the gendarmerie, who would notify the prosecutor's office to launch a criminal investigation.

THE INVESTIGATION AND IMPUNITY

Upon being notified of a smuggler's death, prosecutors began collecting evidence to first determine whether the death was a murder, as opposed to a natural death or suicide, and then identify potential perpetrators or suspects. Without any suspects, the case could not move to trial. As a result, many investigations remained unresolved and fell into a legal category known as "constant search" (*daimi arama*), which meant that, until the statute of limitations expired, the prosecutor's office would continue to search for additional evidence to determine and accuse a perpetrator with sufficient suspicion. Although "constant search" suggests that an active search for evidence would take place, prosecutors often refrained from taking action unless compelled to do so by complainants and their lawyers. If no suspect was formally charged within the statute of limitations, which varied from eight to thirty years depending on the specific charges in question, the case would be permanently closed. In this way, perpetrators' impunity was produced and upheld during the criminal investigation stage, even before a trial began. This pre-trial impunity would have likely been the ending of Sinan's case as well, except that his family, particularly Ahmet, hired a lawyer to monitor and intervene in the criminal investigation.

In November 2006, Sinan and his cousin left their village in the late afternoon to bring diesel from Iran. They had crossed the border and visited the Iranian side a few days prior, when they purchased some fuel and attended the wedding of one of their business partners and tribespeople. They had spent the night in Iran and, the following afternoon, crossed back with the diesel fuel. The second trip, however, was strictly for commercial purposes, and they spent only two hours meeting their partners to pay for diesel fuel and transfer it to plastic containers (*jelikan*).[15] On their way back, they crossed paths with Turkish soldiers who immediately opened fire. Sinan was hit with a deadly shot and fell off his horse, while his cousin, still on horseback, rushed to escape. When the cousin arrived in their village, a group of villagers formed a search party in the mountains to look for Sinan. On their way, they were intercepted by soldiers and ordered to leave the border security zone, where civilian access was banned. Despite the villagers' protest, the soldiers denied that any shooting had occurred and refused to search for Sinan. However, the villagers did not heed their orders and lashed out at the soldiers. The villagers formed small groups and began a more thorough search of the border area. Two hours later, a few villagers discovered Sinan's body a few kilometers from the passage where Sinan's cousin said the soldiers had opened fire. Sinan's body lay a few meters from the border on the Iranian side. The villagers carried the body to the Turkish side and called the gendarmerie to investigate. Ahmet visited Metin's office a few days later to ask him to represent them in the criminal investigation.

The medical examiner at the state's district hospital confirmed that Sinan had died from gunshot wounds. The medical report detailed that his body had been relocated shortly after being shot, before villagers carried it back to Turkey. Yet, there was no specific evidence indicating the initial location of Sinan's body or who had relocated it. To borderland residents and lawyers, postmortem relocation was a well-known strategy that both Turkish and Iranian security forces used to tamper with ballistic evidence and obscure the exact crime scene where critical ballistic evidence could be gathered. Relocating slain bodies also compromised other material evidence that could be collected from those bodies. Moreover, if the bodies were relocated outside of Turkish national territory, Turkish prosecutors might decline the jurisdictional responsibility to investigate the killings because the incidents seemed to have happened in Iran, even though the slain smugglers were citizens of Turkey.

The prosecutor found no ballistic evidence where Sinan's body was discovered. The only material evidence was a bullet cartridge that had remained in Sinan's body. In fact, according to the medical report prepared at the district hospital, the body had three bullet holes. One of two bullets had exited the body, while the other remained inside. This cartridge was, however, partially deformed, and the available ballistic data was insufficient to determine the actual weapon from which the cartridge originated.

Sinan's cousin, who was the last person to see him alive, testified to the prosecutor that Sinan was most probably shot by Turkish soldiers inside Turkey, because they had only encountered Turkish soldiers—not Iranian soldiers—during their smuggling trip, and they had seen the soldiers moments after they entered Turkey through a mountain pass. He also stated that the soldiers patrolling the border region had often asked for bribes, which they refused to pay, thus they may have been targeted on purpose. His testimony, however, did not stand alone as sufficient grounds for prosecuting the Turkish soldiers. Panicking and riding his horse to escape from the soldiers' ambush, the cousin had not seen the specific soldier who fired at and killed Sinan. Yet, even if he had, an eyewitness of the killing would also be ignored if the testimony was not also supported with material, especially ballistic, evidence.

Based on the cousin's testimony though, the district prosecutor asked the nearby Border Security Brigade whether any border patrol had been conducted the day of the killing. Eventually they confirmed that a border patrol had swept the area. The prosecutor then interrogated the soldiers who had been on patrol. When the soldiers mentioned that they heard shootings from the Iranian side of the border, a meeting between the Turkish and Iranian delegations was held. These meetings were called for jurisdictional disputes over the border. Based on a 1937 agreement between Turkey and Iran, Turkish and Iranian authorities would collaborate to investigate killings.[16] If it was proved that security forces from one side had killed or wounded citizens from the other side, the responsible side would compensate the victims or their families. During these meetings, local governors and the higher-ranked military officers represented the border districts. The minutes, recorded in both Turkish and Persian, were confirmed and signed by the head of each side's delegation, and these records were added to the court files. Through these minutes, I examined the meeting held for Sinan's case.

Both Turkish and Iranian security forces denied their involvement in the incident (each claiming not to know about it). The Turkish side mentioned that their soldiers had heard shootings from the Iranian side. In response, the Iranian authorities denied involvement and counterargued that their border patrols had indeed reported shootings from the Turkish side. The Turkish authorities then asked for permission to conduct a crime scene investigation on the Iranian side of the border patrol road. Yet, the Iranians replied that no investigation could be conducted on the Iranian side because of land mines and reiterated that because the Iranian soldiers had heard shootings from the

Turkish side, a crime scene investigation must be conducted in Turkey. They expressed willingness to join the investigation if requested. The Turkish side then responded that the Iranian authorities could participate in the crime scene investigation only if Turkish authorities were allowed to take part in a similar investigation in Iran. The Iranian side once again expressed that this was impossible because of the land mines. After several exchanges of similar arguments, both sides agreed that no crime scene investigation would be conducted in Iran. There was no mechanism for Sinan's family or their lawyer to object to the Iranian authorities' decision. Ultimately, the border, as the territorial limit of Turkish and Iranian jurisdictions and a key means of colonial division and domination of Kurdistan, allowed both state authorities to collectively deny the criminal responsibility. This collaboration between Turkish and Iranian authorities in denying responsibility for the killings of Kurdish smugglers also reflected the inter-coloniality in Kurdistan—how colonial rule and law in one part of Kurdistan reinforced the colonial hold in another.

Metin requested an additional crime scene investigation in the area where Sinan's cousin testified that they had come across the soldiers. This investigation discovered several spent bullet casings. Metin presented these to the prosecutor, who sent them for ballistic assessment at the Regional Police Forensic Laboratory. When the assessment report arrived, Metin and I were both in the courthouse. Metin realized that the cartridges were 7.62x51 mm, the caliber typically used in Heckler & Koch G3 rifles, standard NATO-issued weapons. Only the Turkish military used this rifle in the borderlands. Later that month, Metin asked for a detailed ballistic examination of the chemical content of the bullet cartridge recovered from Sinan's body. The prosecutor could have requested these tests himself, but he did so only after Metin asked him. In other smuggler killing cases, the prosecutors might still have rejected requesting such tests. Yet, by virtue of requesting these tests and putting the requests into the court record, Kurdish lawyers would have documented the prosecutors' noncollection of material evidence.

The chemical content analysis arrived four months later. It indicated that the deformed bullet cartridge had a similar material content to bullets that the Turkish military used. Using this assessment, Metin could reframe the forensic narrative of the killing and show that Sinan was most likely shot by Turkish soldiers. The law still required the prosecutor to identify a suspect, a particular soldier (or a group of soldiers) to accuse to complete the criminal investigation and bring the case to court. The prosecutor requested the border patrol records for the day that Sinan was killed. The records did not mention any ambush or contact with smugglers, which was not surprising because security forces could have easily omitted any killings or skirmishes from their reports. In addition to the postmortem relocation of dead bodies, the "nonrecording" of killings in operation reports was a common strategy for establishing pre-trial impunity for the smuggler killings.[17] The state forces could easily control what was kept on and off the official record and in so doing they produced impunity "not by the absence of documentation but through strategic forms of official writing that anticipate legal interventions in the future."[18] Border patrol records were not the only official report that security forces prepared for their patrols, however. The security forces also reported bullet counts, and soldiers took notes of what they viewed on thermal cameras they used to monitor the border region. Kurdish lawyers could identify potential perpetrators by reading these different reports together and pointing out contradictions across the documents.

Metin realized that the prosecutor had not checked the bullet count reports and asked him to request them from the military. The reports indicated that a soldier had reported missing bullets the week of the attack. The prosecutor then accused that soldier of murder at the criminal court. The case thus escalated from a criminal investigation to a murder prosecution.

Sinan's family, their fellow villagers, and Metin pushed the prosecutor to collect new pieces of evidence, including cartridges collected from the route where Sinan and his cousin encountered the soldiers and bullet counting reports. Thus, they sought to expose not only the state violence but also the deliberate actions of security forces and legal authorities to ensure the perpetrators' impunity. The postmortem relocation of Sinan's body and the nonrecording of the killing by security forces, for example, were also proven tactics used to protect the perpetrators. While Kurdish complainants' and lawyers' own evidence collection led to the identification of the perpetrator in this case, in most of the cases I followed in Wan, no perpetrator was identified. Yet, complainants and their lawyers still documented the legal authorities' efforts to keep the perpetrators unidentified and thus protect them from prosecution. The impunity of the perpetrators, therefore, did not diminish the political and legal significance of Kurdish complainants' and their lawyers' engagement with the criminal courts.

THE TRIAL AND IMPUNITY

During the criminal trial, in part because of the additional evidence that Metin compelled the prosecutor to collect and present, the accused soldier admitted that he had fired his rifle during the ambush, but he denied the allegations that he intended to kill Sinan. He claimed that neither he nor the patrol team had noticed that a smuggler had been shot. The soldier instead blamed the "landscape," and framed the killing as an "accident" because he first shot into the air and then shot in front of the smugglers.[19] He also said that he was at least fifty meters away from the smugglers and had stood on a hill near the pass. The shooting was, he asserted, a lawful and proportionate use of force. The soldier's commander, a member of the Border Security Brigade, also testified that because the ambush was performed in "a terror region (*teröre müzahir bölge*)," they did not get close to the smugglers in case the PKK had planned an attack. However, Sinan's cousin, who survived the shooting, testified that the soldiers did not warn them to stop and instead shot directly at them. He added that the soldiers were standing in the pass, not on a hill. Metin then demanded the arrest of the suspected soldier. Yet, the judge turned down the arrest request and deferred to the commander's and the suspect's testimonies. Thus, Metin began looking for additional evidence to prove the soldier's guilt.

In the following weeks, Metin noticed that the autopsy report showed that the bullet had moved only slightly upward within Sinan's body. Considering the downward slope of the passage, this was an unlikely course for a bullet shot from the top of a nearby hill. Even if the bullet had bounced from the ground and hit the body, it would more likely have been fired by someone standing in the pass. As a former smuggler, Metin was familiar with the specific pass and realized that it was very unlikely that the soldiers had shot at the smugglers from atop a hill. He then thought that the landscape could verify the cousin's testimony that they had come across the soldiers in the pass. The landscape and its topography could serve as new evidence that would reveal the unlawfulness of the killing.

The crime scene investigation report depicted the landscape poorly, with hand drawings that provided no topographic information. Poor drawings were not uncommon in court files for smuggler killings (Figure 2). In several cases, though, I also came across much more sophisticated computer-drawn, three-dimensional topographic maps (Figure 3). These maps made topography appear within what Eyal Weizman, an architect and scholar of spatial and visual cultures, calls the "threshold of detectability" in which topographical features become identifiable and powerful evidence in prosecutions.[20] For this reason, lawyers almost always requested three-dimensional maps, but these requests often went unfulfilled under the pretext of inadequate technical equipment or expertise.

Metin suspected that the crime scene investigation report, autopsy, and testimonies would contradict each other, and decided to examine the

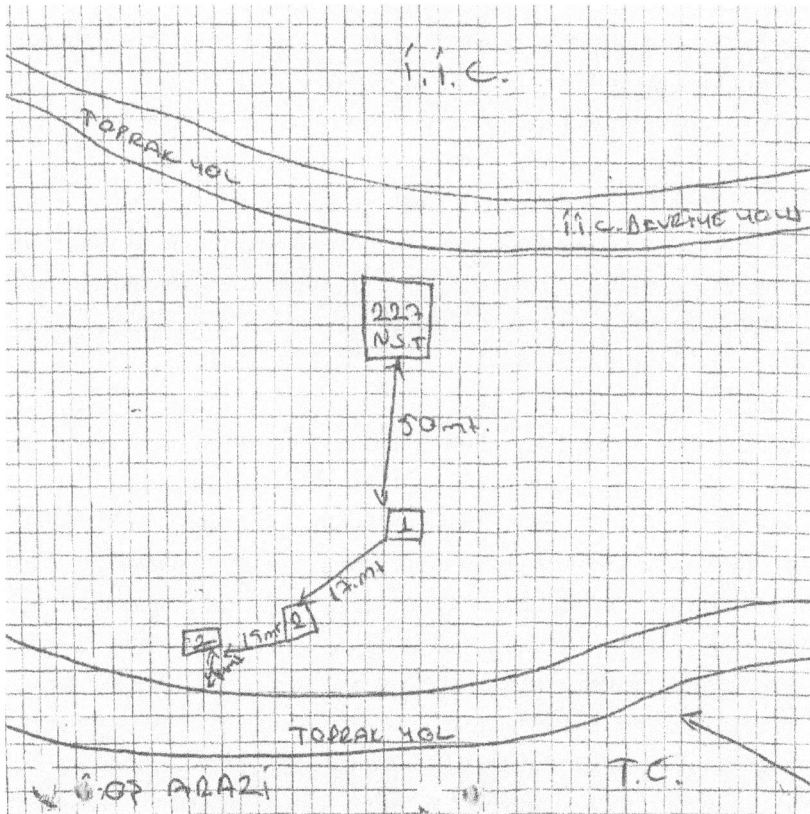

FIGURE 2. A two-dimensional hand-drawn map of a crime scene

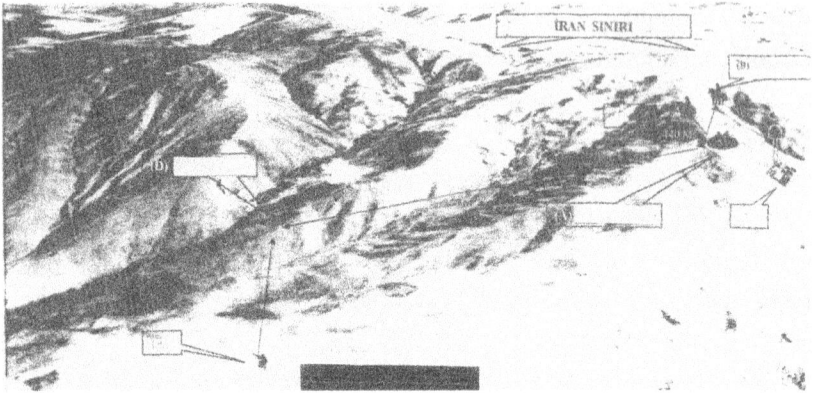

FIGURE 3. A three-dimensional computer-drawn map of a crime scene

landscape himself. When I asked Metin if civilians were allowed to visit the area, which was near the actual border, he said we could visit under the guise of a picnic. The following weekend, Metin, Ahmet, and I had our "picnic." After driving for an hour on a trail, we parked the car and walked ten minutes to reach the area where Sinan and his cousin encountered soldiers. It was clear that no other slope or elevation would have deflected a bullet fired from the hill into Sinan's body from the angle depicted in the autopsy report. We photographed the crime scene. Metin then submitted an official request for an additional crime scene visit to consider the topography alongside the photographs. The judge, however, rejected the request and acquitted the soldier. Metin appealed the decision.

Eight months later, the Appeals Court accepted Metin's request and asked the local court to conduct a follow-up crime scene visit to consider whether the crime scene topography confirmed the soldier's statement. This time, the gendarmerie prepared a three-dimensional crime scene map. Considering the topography in its revised decision, the court agreed that the soldier must have stood in the pass but still rejected the allegation that the Sinan's death was intentional. The accused soldier eventually accepted that he could have also fired his rifle when they entered the pass and admitted that he had forgotten where or when exactly he fired, as he was trying not to lose sight of the smugglers and was worried about a potential PKK ambush. Stressing that the soldier must have considered the bullet's ricocheting as a probable result and thereby should have refrained from shooting, the judge concluded that the soldier committed manslaughter. By reversing his previous decision to acquit, the judge now acknowledged the killing's unlawfulness. Yet, the court repeated its previous designation that the crime scene fell within a "terror region" (*terröre müzahir bölge*), an area that had a high risk for a terrorist attack. Using this risk as an excuse, the judge decreased the soldier's sentence and suspended the conviction.

The judge's decision pointed to another common method by which impunity for the perpetrators of smuggler killings was produced in courts. In this case, the impunity was generated during the trial stage, rather than the investigation. Even when perpetrators were identified as state officers and the unlawfulness of the killings was confirmed in trials, the courts could still produce impunity by legally sanctioning the killings because of extraordinary conditions, a "terror" threat being the most common among them.[21]

Until 2007, the Anti-Smuggling Law (Law 1918), which was first legislated in 1932, had permitted security forces to open fire on smugglers. Under EU-led reforms, this law was replaced by a new anti-smuggling law in 2003, Law 4926, and then another law, Law 5607, in 2007. While prohibiting shooting at smugglers to kill, the new laws still allowed the use of force, but only if proportionate and under certain conditions. The security forces, accordingly, were obligated to order smugglers to stop first before using deadly force. If the order was not followed, they had to shoot in the air as a warning. If the warning was ignored, then the security forces could shoot in front of the smugglers to stop them. However, they were not authorized to directly target the smugglers or shoot to kill, except in self-defense. The security forces' use of violence had to be proportionate to the threat they faced.[22]

Despite these restrictions, the courts continued to fully or partially authorize killings by referring to the 2004 Turkish Criminal Law (Law 5237), which allowed the use of disproportionate force in case of "excusable excitement, fear, or agitation" (Article 27) or as a result of an "inevitable mistake" (Article 30). In the smuggler killing cases, the perpetrators repeatedly referred to the "terror threat" and claimed to have mistaken smugglers for PKK fighters or to have fired warning shots at smugglers from a distance to avoid the risk of a PKK counter-ambush. Deferring to such defense arguments or raising similar arguments themselves, the judges thus treated "the terror threat" as if it were a real and corporeal threat to the state security forces. In this way, the courts effectively sanctioned the killings.

VERNACULAR COUNTERFORENSICS

Sinan's case illustrates how Kurdish complainants and lawyers improvised technolegal tactics to collect, validate, or discredit certain pieces of material evidence; engaged in their own forensic investigations; and contested the forensic knowledge of the smuggler killings that state officials produced. By monopolizing the legitimate use of violence, modern state authorities assume "the ultimate authority to define and govern the dead within their jurisdiction through legislation and institutionalized procedures."[23] This exclusive authority over the dead is facilitated by monopolizing the legitimate means of forensics, namely claiming an exclusive right to either collect evidence or validate such evidence when others collect it. Yet, local communities, independent experts, and human rights defenders may also use or improvise forensic techniques to reveal crimes that state officials and others commit, identify the victims and perpetrators, and provide legal evidence for domestic or international prosecution of these crimes.[24] This civilian use of forensics has been conceptualized as "counterforensics," which Allan Sekula, a photographer and critic, first coined in 1993 when referring to nongovernmental initiatives of "exhumation and identification of the anonymized ('disappeared') bodies of the oppressor state's victims" in Argentina, El Salvador, and southern Kurdistan (Başûr).[25] Weizman has expanded the scope of counterforensics beyond exhumations and describes them as practices that "uncover political violence undertaken by states," which "turns the state's own means against the violence it commits."[26]

My interlocutors also reversed the state authorities' forensic gaze back onto state officials. Yet, the distinctive character of their counterforensic work was in their investigation of the legal authorities' forensic and prosecution processes. In the aftermath of smuggler killings, Kurdish complainants and their lawyers contested the perpetrators' impunity by engaging in "vernacular counterforensics"—a set of technolegal tactics of evidence collection both on smuggler killings and on the criminal investigations and prosecutions of those killings. As a dual forensic examination, vernacular counterforensic practices include everything from organizing unofficial crime scene visits (as Metin, Ahmet, and I had done) and documenting crime scene topography through photographs to collecting bullet cartridges.

Through vernacular counterforensics, Kurdish complainants and lawyers exposed not only state violence but also legal authorities' "impunity work," which operates in two facets: first, the deliberate failure to identify perpetrators through incomplete or misleading evidence collection, and second, when perpetrators could no longer remain unidentified—often due to the counterforensic efforts of the complainants and lawyers—the authorities would sanction the killings by associating the Kurdish borderlands with "terrorism."[27] The judicial impunity work was enacted by multiple agents, including the crime scene investigation team and other members of law enforcement, prosecutors, judges, and court experts, at various stages of the criminal-legal process. At each stage, the production of perpetrators' impunity may require different strategies that compile specific practices of evidence noncollection, deployment (or avoidance) of particular legal procedures, and references to different bodies of law and legal reasonings.

The presence of multiple agents and stages in the production of judicial impunity did not exclude the possibility that individual state officials were sympathetic toward the complainants. In fact, Kurdish complainants and lawyers occasionally encountered such individuals. In one case, an ethnically Kurdish soldier secretly helped villagers find the lifeless body of a smuggler who had been killed during a border patrol. Despite such instances of sympathy and help, my interlocutors knew from previous smuggler killing cases that the legal system as a whole prioritized protecting security forces at all costs. Accordingly, and as my interlocutors often mentioned, if a court acknowledged additional evidence that identified state agents as potential perpetrators, an upper court would almost always dismiss it and vice versa. In some cases, the complainants also mentioned how prosecutors and judges who seemed sympathetic were threatened by the security forces when they intended to investigate the killings. Consequently, individual state officials' efforts of identifying perpetrators and bringing them to justice were routinely undermined by their peers and superiors.

Because the perpetrators' impunity was generated collectively across different phases of criminal investigations and prosecutions, complainants and their lawyers closely monitored the forensic knowledge that judicial authorities produced and aimed to document any contradictions and omissions in officially collected evidence. Vernacular counterforensics thus operated as (people's) forensics of (judicial) forensics and emerged as a particular manifestation of sly legality, the critical engagement with state law that contests and curtails its operative logics. To document a prosecutor's failure or reluctance to collect evidence, for example, lawyers made official requests for additional crime scene visits and evidence collection. Even if these requests were rejected, the rejections were documented in court files and thus became counterforensic evidence of judicial impunity work in their own right. In this way, vernacular counterforensics both concurrently and retroactively documented rights violations by the legal authorities.[28]

In addition to the distinct focus on judicial forensics, the "vernacular" in my interlocutors' counterforensics also highlights the use and knowledge of borderland geography, such as specific border passages and their topographies, and mobilities, for example, how smugglers transported contraband or their specific itineraries. My interlocutors used this local knowledge in combination with their expertise in forensics to closely monitor the legal authorities' criminal-legal accounts of the killings. Metin's knowledge of the specific border passage where Sinan was shot, including its topography, exemplified such use. By combining globally circulated rights advocacy strategies and forensic expertise with the intimate knowledge of local geography and smuggling economies, the Kurdish lawyers and complainants gave these strategies and expertise new purposes, such as recording the judicial impunity work. This approach resonates with what anthropologist Sally Engle Merry calls "vernacularization" in which the global legal norms and rights advocacy strategies are adapted to specific local contexts.[29] In Wan, Kurdish lawyers and rights defenders accessed the global strategies and techniques of rights advocacy through collaborations between the Bar Association or local human rights organizations with other advocacy groups or international NGOs. During my fieldwork, for example, I attended several workshops co-organized by European and Istanbul-based human rights organizations with the Bar Association to train lawyers in forensic techniques for locating and preserving ballistic evidence at crime scenes and exhumation sites. I also observed how Kurdish lawyers, complainants, and other human rights activists refashioned and repurposed (rather than directly employed) this forensic expertise to critically assess and reshape the legal authorities' evidence collection practices. In doing so, they sought to reveal (and challenge) omissions and inconsistencies in these practices.

My interlocutors' vernacular counterforeniscs, however, do not reveal absolute truths that would otherwise be hidden. While identifying state agents as likely perpetrators, counterforensic evidence still operates as a form of knowledge that is not fully available, consistent, or unambiguous. Kurdish lawyers and complainants rather used their counterforensics to understand and contest how judges and prosecutors managed and utilized inconsistencies, uncertainties, and gaps in the official forensic accounts and other legal processes to ensure the impunity of perpetrators. Thus, vernacular counterforensics differs from an act of speaking truth to the courts and urging these courts to recognize the crimes that state officials committed so as to bring perpetrators to justice. Instead, complainants and lawyers revealed the court's role in maintaining the perpetrators' impunity and hence its complicity in the smuggler killings. By doing so, my complainant and lawyer interlocutors rejected the judiciary's claim of being "a producer of impartial and universal justice."[30] As a manifestation of sly legality, vernacular counterforensics, therefore, allowed them to use the criminal courts to defy, rather than envision and trust, the redresses and remedies that the courts could offer.

COUNTERFORENSIC ACCOUNTS OF SMUGGLER KILLINGS

By documenting the judicial attempts to establish soldiers' impunity, vernacular counterforensics provided Kurdish complainants and lawyers with a way of identifying smuggler killings as political killings, rather than individual criminal incidents, that the state authorities systematically committed and collectively authorized. Thus, the lack of effective investigation or the noncollection of crime scene evidence across different incidents of smuggler killings demonstrated the killings' systematic and collective character. In their applications to ECtHR, for example, Kurdish human rights lawyers, including Metin, often cited the "improperly conducted autopsy," "the lack of effective and fair prosecution," and the fact that "the [criminal] investigation remained as a mere formality" to substantiate how the killings became systematic in the Kurdish borderlands. The lawyers further supported these claims with counterforensic evidence, such as their requests for additional ballistic reports and their unanswered calls for follow-up crime scene visits, that they collected and documented during their interactions with judicial authorities in criminal investigations and prosecutions. In Turkish court files and applications to the ECtHR, the lawyers also emphasized the structural aspects of the killings and blamed the Turkish state for "not providing any employment opportunities" and "compelling its citizens to smuggle and risk their lives . . . under arbitrary shooting by soldiers." In doing so, these lawyers and the complainants repurposed criminal courts to reveal and document the systematic, collective, and structural character of the seemingly individual and isolated incidents of smuggler killings.

In addition to revealing and documenting judicial impunity work, Kurdish complainants and lawyers also strove to void these attempts at each stage of the criminal-legal process. Nonetheless, they knew that the perpetrators would ultimately receive impunity. Although the political significance of vernacular counterforensics was not necessarily undermined by their inability to prevent impunity at the early stages of the criminal-legal process, the complainants and lawyers still hoped to curtail judicial impunity work through appeal and retrial phases. By pushing against impunity throughout the process, the complainants and lawyers forced the courts to identify the perpetrators and to use the "terrorism threat" as their last resort to sanction the killings and explicitly state their smuggling-as-terrorism allegations and counterinsurgency concerns in court records. Accordingly, the judges, in their final verdicts, associated the slain smugglers with terrorism by blaming them either for using the same paths as the PKK guerrillas, acting and dressing like them, or even providing them logistical support. In fact, the judiciary mainly prioritized these allegations and concerns when handling smuggling cases in Kurdistan and, as a result, enforced anti-smuggling law more harshly across the Kurdish borderlands. However, they also regularly kept such allegations out of court records. By avoiding an explicit expression of smuggling-as-terrorism allegations or any explicit reference to Kurdishness or Kurdish borderlands, the Turkish judiciary cunningly claimed procedural equality and impartiality in imposing substantive inequality on Kurdish subjects.[31] So, by forcing the judiciary to openly refer to these allegations, my interlocutors' vernacular counterforensics, as a particular mechanism of sly legality, contested this cunning use of law and thus defied the criminal courts' touting itself as an impartial arbiter of justice.

In doing so, Kurdish complainants and lawyers also exposed the anti-Kurdish "state racism" in which the Turkish state authorities viewed Kurdish people as a subordinate group and thus as expendable.[32] By associating smuggling with terrorism in Kurdish borderlands and thus sanctioning smuggler killings, the Turkish courts identified the slain smugglers as well as the entire borderland population with terrorism, which thereby sanctioned their deaths.

Michel Foucault has suggested the analytic of state racism to explicate how the state's biopower to "make live and let die"—the management of population using systematically collected demographic knowledge such as birth, death, or disease rates—operates together with its sovereign power to "take life or let live."[33] For criminal trials of smuggler killings, the Foucauldian analytic is particularly useful since the state authorities' monopolization of the legitimate means of forensics and legal evidence facilitated its sovereign exercise of the power to kill by virtue of generating and sustaining impunity.[34] Through such monopolization, the judges treated particular locations and people who lived in or crossed through the borderlands as representing terrorism or its threat. The courts used this perceived risk as legal evidence that there were mitigating circumstances or as justification for the noncollection of crime scene evidence. Modern state authorities, including self-proclaimed liberal democracies, have increasingly used the threat of terrorism to legally justify the criminalization of dissent and imposition of state violence on certain individuals and population groups.[35] Similarly, in Turkish courts, judges identified Kurdish borderlands as "terror regions" (*teröre müzahir bölgeler*) and designated those who lived in or happened to cross these regions as expendable, which justified denying them legal protection. A routine encounter between a lawyer and a prosecutor that I witnessed in a district courthouse revealed to me the judiciary's view of the whole borderland population as expendable.

I was accompanying a Kurdish lawyer to the prosecutor's office to submit an official request for a new crime scene visit. When the lawyer submitted the paperwork, the prosecutor rejected the request by referring to the "terror threat" in the region: "I could not endanger the lives of our soldiers, and your clients must know that their relative was smuggling and he was not supposed to enter that region anyway."

"But my clients live in that region, the crime scene is a few kilometers outside of the village, and the soldiers patrol the area every other day," the lawyer said, implying that the PKK guerrillas did not pose a security risk. In fact, the security forces, especially land forces, could ambush smugglers in the areas where the guerrillas had limited or no access and control.[36] So, the military and the courts' designation of ambush areas as terror regions hardly reflected the reality on the ground. In this way, the lawyer's objection underlined that the security risk was not the PKK guerrillas but the border residents themselves. Kurdish residents came to be identified as supporters of terrorism or potential terrorists and thus were rendered killable. This identification was also reflected in the legal phrase *teröre müzahir bölge*, which legal authorities used to sanction the smuggler killings. Although the phrase can simply be translated as "terror region," it may also denote that the region in its entirety supports terrorism. When used in courts, the term was understood to have both meanings: A region that was designated as a terror region (*terröre müzahir*) thus meant to the court that those who lived in the region all supported terrorism and thus were potential terrorists.

THE INJUSTICE OF DOMESTIC AND INTERNATIONAL LAW

Court files in smuggler killing trials became a means of recording the criminal court's complicity in the killings and a basis for refusing these courts as legitimate sources of justice for Kurdish people. Through these court files, the injustice that Turkish courts imposed on Kurdish smugglers became observable to other actors, including fellow villagers and other legal authorities such as the ECtHR. In fact, the European Court's judicial review and requirement that domestic legal means be exhausted as its main criterion for admissibility contributed to the emergence of vernacular counterforensics. This criterion led human rights lawyers in Kurdistan and elsewhere under the court's jurisdiction to strategically engage with local courts to not only fulfill admissibility requirements but also produce "evidence [that] would later be legible to Strasbourg as the kind of procedural (rather than fact-based) body of material on which it could justify jurisdiction and issue violations."[37] Partly anticipating the ECtHR process, therefore, Kurdish lawyers engaged with the domestic courts to generate evidence that corroborated both the killings committed by state officials and judicial impunity work. Yet, my interlocutors valued the political significance of this evidence over any of the redresses that ECtHR might provide. For instance, consider a conversation I had with Ferhat, whose twenty-two-year-old brother was killed by Turkish gendarmeries while smuggling cigarettes from Iran.

I met Ferhat nearly ten years after his brother's death. He stopped by Metin's office to ask about his brother's case in the ECtHR. In his late forties, Ferhat now worked as a construction subcontractor and lived between Wan and Istanbul. I visited him the following day in his village in Wan. Unlike most village houses where people sit on the ground, his had comfortable sofas and a china cabinet. After Ferhat's cousin had served us tea and before I even had the chance to inquire about the case, Ferhat stood up and retrieved something from the cabinet. He handed me a neatly organized folder; each page of the document was in a sheet protector. It was his brother's case file.

"How can one prove the absence of a gun? How can one prove the fact that something does not exist?" Ferhat asked ironically. The first document in the folder was the final court decision. The questions referred to the accused gendarmerie's claim that the smugglers, including Ferhat's brother, had fired at him first and, after he shot back at them, the smugglers retreated across the border into Iran. Just one smuggler, Ferhat's brother, was shot and fell off his horse. The smugglers denied the allegation that they had been carrying firearms and had fired at the gendarmeries. However, the gendarmerie insisted that the smugglers must have hidden their firearms on the Iranian side, where Turkish patrols could not conduct a crime scene investigation. Deferring to the gendarmerie's testimony, the court asked the surviving smugglers to prove that they had not been carrying firearms, and eventually the court acquitted the gendarmerie. The court counterfactually designated the smugglers as armed subjects and used a legally constructed "myth of a civilian-combatant distinction" to authorize state violence.[38] Ferhat continued: "That decision itself shows how the courts protect soldiers. . . . I am also a citizen of this state. Yet, the decision tells me that I am not a real citizen. There is no justice for Kurds in Turkish courts. And it is not something that I just say. It is in their [court] documents."

According to Ferhat, by making an impossible demand on the smug-glers—to prove the absence of a nonexistent gun—the court protected the perpetrator and produced impunity, despite there being material evidence of unlawful state violence. For Ferhat, the court file became proof of the injustice that Turkish courts imposed on Kurdish citizens. Rather than use the juridical authority to hold security forces accountable and rely on the ju-diciary's promise of justice, Ferhat framed his engagement with the criminal courts as a work of proving the court-imposed injustice.

Ferhat further explained how these documents allowed him to shame the Turkish courts before "European" courts: "Our case is now in the European court [ECtHR], so the Europeans would also see how the [Turkish] court had asked for the impossible." In this way, Ferhat called upon ECtHR judges to witness the injustice that Turkish state courts imposed. Human rights defenders have long shamed state authorities before international publics to force them to redress rights violations. Yet, as anthropologist Tobias Kelly has astutely noted, shaming strategies also "hide as much as [they] reveal" in the context of state-committed rights violations, such as torture, since "the tech-nical ways in which human rights obligations are interpreted, the shame of torture is dispersed into arguments about procedure."[39] For my interlocutors, however, legal procedures and forensic processes became a way to reveal the partiality and complicity, rather than impartiality, of the Turkish judiciary as well as the international human rights institutions. Kurdish complain-ants and lawyers, in that sense, extended their vernacular-counterforensic attention to international institutions and courts, primarily the ECtHR. In documenting the Turkish judiciary's impunity work in their applications to the European court, they also put the ECtHR's claims of universal justice under scrutiny.

Accordingly, Ferhat did not necessarily expect that the ECtHR would acknowledge the injustice he faced: "They [the ECtHR judges] must see the injustice if they really care about justice." In fact, his engagement with the court provided him with an opportunity to question the court's commitment to human rights and possibly shame the ECtHR as well. In his view, the Eu-ropean court's operation was shaped by international politics. In that sense, it was not much different from the Turkish courts. When I asked whether he thought the European court's judges cared about justice, Ferhat said, "It is about politics; the Europeans know all about the oppression against the Kurds, but Turkey is a strong state, and they may prefer working with the strong rather than siding with the oppressed."

"Siding with the oppressor is not justice, though," I said.

"This is why I said if they actually cared about justice, they would decide on behalf of us." He thought that the Turkish courts or the ECtHR did not necessarily pursue justice because politics shaped how these legal institutions act.

By engaging with the ECtHR, Ferhat and various other Kurdish complainants whom I had met were prepared to face and document injustice instead of justice. Nonetheless, the European Court did acknowledge some of the injustices that people faced and decided on behalf of them. Regarding smuggling killings and other issues, such as forced village evacuations, the ECtHR decided that the Turkish authorities violated the European Convention on Human Rights (EConHR). Yet, for my interlocutors, especially Kurdish human rights lawyers like Metin, such decisions did not necessarily produce legitimacy of the liberal rule of law and rights. Rather than accept and act on liberal arguments of universal justice, impartiality, or equality before the law that the EConHR presented, Kurdish lawyers often expressed how the ECtHR decisions were already always political, regardless of whether they won or lost their cases.

Since the 2000s, Kurdish lawyers have accused the ECtHR of favoring Turkish authorities for political, rather than legal, reasons. In the 1990s, the ECtHR acted as a first-instance court and processed Kurdish complainants' applications without requiring them to exhaust domestic legal means. Yet, in the 2000s, the court diverged from its earlier case law and recognized Turkish legal authorities as effective means of justice by citing Turkey's EU-led reforms and appropriation of human rights discourse.[40] Kurdish human rights lawyers have heavily criticized the ECtHR for considering the Turkish courts as effective means of justice and for encouraging Turkish authorities to legally justify their anti-Kurdish oppression through strictly imposed legal procedures.

One source of this criticism was how the European Court handled the 2011 Roboski massacre. The government claimed that the bombardment was an accident in their "legitimate" struggle against "terrorism" and unilaterally offered monetary compensation to the families of the slain smugglers.[41] Citing this claim, the military prosecutor decided not to pursue a criminal prosecution.[42] The Roboski families objected to this decision and, after their objection was rejected, they brought the case before the Constitutional Court. Shortly after receiving the application, the court noticed missing documents and asked the applicants to complete these documents in fifteen days. One of the lawyers, who represented only three of the fifty-three applicants, submitted the power of attorney document two days after the deadline. The lawyer also submitted a health report to explain the delay in his submission. In February 2016, one and a half years after the submission of the medical report, the court decided that it would not accept the health report as a legitimate reason for the delay and rejected the application on procedural grounds.[43] The Roboski families then brought the decision to the ECtHR, which found the application inadmissible because it did not exhaust domestic legal remedies, particularly those of the Constitutional Court.[44] In their inadmissibility decisions, both the Constitutional Court and ECtHR justified the smuggler killings under the pretext of procedural mistakes made by the complainants' lawyers. For Kurdish complainants and lawyers, however, these procedural arguments and related legal reasonings served as evidence of the courts' impunity work and complicity in the killings. In that sense, the decisions highlighted the hollowness of liberal arguments for equality before the law and universal justice.

JUSTICE BEYOND COURTS

The families of the slain smugglers filed complaints with the Turkish criminal courts to demonstrate that the seemingly individual or isolated incidents of smuggler killings were systematically committed by security forces and collectively sanctioned by the judiciary. Rather than anticipate the courts' ability to identify perpetrators and bring them to justice, the families and their lawyers sought to document the judiciary's impunity work and thus their complicity in the killings. Kurdish complainants viewed this vernacular-counterforensic work as seeking justice for their slain relatives and fulfilling a political and moral responsibility toward them and the broader borderland community. This sense of responsibility was illustrated when Ahmet said that he would sleep better after proving his younger brother was killed by a Turkish solider and contesting the soldier's impunity throughout the appeal and retrial stages despite the soldier not serving prison time. In doing so, Ahmet, with the help of his lawyer Metin, proved that Turkish courts imposed injustice on Kurdish residents, as did many other complainants and lawyers.

By documenting the systematic injustices against Kurds, the complainants and their lawyers came to articulate an alternative understanding of justice, one based on collective accountability, that contested systematic and institutional injustices imposed by the undeclared colonial rule in Kurdistan rather than establish individual rights, responsibilities, or redresses. In rejecting the liberal legal assumption that procedural equality ensures substantive equality and demonstrating that the opposite was the case for Kurdish people, they envisioned a form of justice that was not tied to the impartiality that a supreme legal authority that exercised sovereignty over citizens and noncitizens could guarantee. Instead of being interpellated through various forms of legal recognition—such as legal rights, protections, or redresses—by such an authority and thereby being incorporated into its sovereign supremacy, the complainants and lawyers sought recognition among equals. Thus, given their vernacular counterforensics, court documents that exposed injustices became crucial tools for seeking justice in virtue of inviting others to recognize these injustices and show solidarity.

By seeking and formulating an alternative understanding of justice, the complainants and their lawyers positioned themselves as part of a distinct political community of noncollaborators—those who resisted and refused Turkish state authorities' colonial domination in Kurdistan, particularly the counterinsurgency war and its associated regimes of violence and dispossession. The families of the slain smugglers and their lawyers expressed their noncollaboration through vernacular counterforensics, the leading techno-legal mechanism by which they practiced sly legality in the killing prosecutions. Similarly, Kurdish smugglers, traders, and their lawyers enacted noncollaboration in smuggling trials through disruptive borderwork, the primary means by which sly legality was practiced in these cases. The next chapter explores how Kurdish smugglers and their lawyers practiced noncollaboration through the pursuit of sly legality both in and outside of court and how they construed its significance within the broader context of Kurdish freedom politics.

FIVE

NONCOLLABORATION

ON A FREEZING MORNING IN March 2013, Mahmut and I were seated waiting for Metin in his law office. Almost a year before, Turkish soldiers had intercepted Mahmut and several other smugglers shortly after they crossed a valley, as they were transporting contraband diesel fuel and cigarettes. All six smugglers were on horseback, guiding several mules carrying contraband cargo. When they crossed the Turkish border, they were met with gunfire by the patrolling soldiers, even though they had bribed the soldiers before their trip. In response, the smugglers scattered, but Mahmut was shot and fell off his horse. The soldiers next moved to block the way of another escaping smuggler, whom they also shot, though he remained mounted on his horse. Mahmut and the other smuggler were detained, while the others successfully escaped to the village.

A few weeks after the incident, the district prosecutor brought smuggling charges against Mahmut and the second wounded smuggler. The prosecutor, however, did not immediately open a criminal investigation against the soldiers for wounding the smugglers. Only after Metin, on behalf of Mahmut, filed petitions against the soldiers did the prosecutor launch an investigation into the shootings as a crime of wounding with intent. In the first investigation, Mahmut and the other smuggler faced smuggling charges. In the second, they appeared as complainants who accused the soldiers of disproportionate use of force. Both investigations unfolded at the same time and were adjudicated by the same prosecutor.

At first glance, the incident did not seem much different from any other anti-smuggling ambush in the borderlands. Nor was it exceptional that the security forces had shot at the smugglers after they had bribed them for safe passage. The case was distinct because the second wounded smuggler was reluctant to pursue a criminal case against the soldiers. The smuggler even testified in court that the soldiers had asked them to surrender first and that he had heard gunfire from a direction other than the one the soldiers were in—which implied that other people might have been shooting at them. His testimony contradicted that of Mahmut, who identified the soldiers as the only possible perpetrators. Not unexpectedly, their contradictory testimonies would make it much more difficult to prove the soldiers had unlawfully targeted them.

Mahmut's visit to Metin's office, in fact, was about the second smuggler's "act of betrayal." Mahmut heard that the smuggler had recently started a job at a construction company with the help of the district governor's office. This made him conjecture that the smuggler might be "collaborating" with the soldiers. Mahmut thought that the job might have been offered as "hush money" in exchange for fabricated testimony because Mahmut himself had been approached by a military commander with such an offer several weeks after the incident. The commander also promised Mahmut that if he were to accept the offer, he would only receive a minor sentence from the smuggling charges and that his sentencing would be postponed.

Despite the commander's attempts to "collaborate" with him, Mahmut was determined to pursue his case but was also concerned that the second smuggler's testimony would harm it. His family also feared that the commander would influence the court's decision about the smuggling charges and that Mahmut would receive a harsher criminal sentence than the one he was already facing. Metin confirmed such fears during our conversation.

After Mahmut left the office and I stayed with Metin, I asked about the second smuggler and his family. Metin, who knew the family well, explained that the smuggler had relatives who were both guerrillas and village guards—state-recruited paramilitaries. Given the decades of conflict in the borderlands, having family members in both groups was not uncommon, so the family was not particularly known as "collaborators." Although Metin understood the importance of having a stable job to support one's family, he was also disturbed by the smuggler's testimony, which would significantly undermine the vernacular counterforensics that Mahmut and Metin were pursuing and which would contribute to the impunity of the soldiers. For Metin, this act of sabotaging their counterforensic work constituted "collaborationism" (*işbirlikçilik*). When I asked his opinion on the hypothetical situation in which the smuggler had been working alone and had accepted the job in exchange for abandoning the prosecution, Metin said his stance would depend on whether the family needed the money for a pressing issue—such as someone's health-related emergency—in which case he might not consider it collaboration. However, he noted that he was unaware of any pressing issue burdening the smuggler's family and that some other smugglers continued their cases in court despite their financial desperation. Even if the second smuggler had been alone, Metin believed that his abandonment of the prosecution and sabotaging of the counterforensic work still raised doubts about collaborationism.

Kurdish borderland communities employed the phrases "collaborationism" and "collaborators" to politico-morally designate and denounce borderland residents who were perceived to be working for state security forces and/or contributing to the counterinsurgency efforts in Kurdistan. Since the late 1980s, security forces had been appropriating particular smuggling networks in Kurdistan to recruit and finance paramilitary forces, thereby transforming smuggling into a crucial site of collaborationism. While Kurdish borderland communities viewed smuggling as a politically and socially legitimate economic activity—especially in defying state borders that divided Kurdistan from within—they also disapproved of smuggling activities performed by those who they believed were collaborating with the state security forces, whether through providing paramilitary services or intelligence on guerrillas in exchange for the forces' condonation of their smuggling. In the Kurdish borderlands, therefore, smugglers' noncollaboration, namely, their evasion of collaboration with counterinsurgency forces, became a key rationale in justifying one's smuggling activities.

As the counterinsurgency war became entrenched, however, the means of claiming noncollaboration became more varied and contested. Since the state security forces had established surveillance infrastructure in the Kurdish highlands but were unable to completely end the guerrilla presence, smuggling economies operated across both state-controlled and guerrilla-controlled areas. As a result, smugglers had to engage with security forces to arrange free passage through offering bribes, but in so doing, they became prime targets for recruitment as sources of intelligence on the guerrillas' whereabouts and interactions with the local population. To refrain from the security forces' constant recruitment demands and avoid the risk of being co-opted into their paramilitary efforts, smugglers often offered to pay higher bribes. However, this sort of evasion of collaboration still involved the constant risk of facing anti-smuggling operations or armed stings, even the loss of their livelihoods, limbs, or lives. Kurdish smugglers therefore were "forced constantly to negotiate the shifting boundaries of permissible and impermissible complicity" and claimed the politico-moral legitimacy of their smuggling activities by evading collaboration and maintaining their noncollaboration.[1]

Mahmut's case further illustrates that one's noncollaboration—and thus the legitimacy of one's smuggling activities—also depended on whether and how one pursued criminal prosecution against the security forces' use of violence during anti-smuggling ambushes. Other smugglers could claim noncollaboration by engaging in technolegal tactics of fixing contraband oil, repackaging smuggled sugar, procuring authentic-yet-false trade documents in anticipation of anti-smuggling operations, or conducting disruptive borderwork in smuggling trials. Smugglers, thus, substantiated their noncollaboration through their engagement with criminal courts before, during, or after prosecutions that involved smuggling allegations or the security forces' attacks. This chapter probes how specific articulations of collaboration and noncollaboration among smugglers shaped their interactions with state authorities, including the courts, and turned these interactions into a means of performing noncollaboration while smuggling. Ultimately, these forms of noncollaboration enabled smugglers and their lawyers to develop and pursue sly legality tactics. This chapter further interrogates how smugglers' and lawyers' pursuit of sly legality in

Turkish courts—through disruptive borderwork or vernacular counterfo-rensics—expanded the political scope of noncollaboration in smuggling. It does this by reframing noncollaboration as active work that curtailed the judicial authorities' capacity to legally enforce borders or to act as the supreme arbiters of impartial justice.

MONEY IN BLACK OR BLOOD

I entered Ayfer's office in Wan city center which, like many other lawyers' offices in Wan, had been converted from a residential three-bedroom apart-ment. I was visiting Ayfer to discuss a recent cigarette smuggling case file that she had shared with me. For more than twenty years, she had been a defense lawyer for various smuggling cases, predominantly those that involved heroin trafficking. She was one of the few women "smuggler lawyers" (*kaçakçı avu-katı*) in the region. Ayfer was originally from a border district known for heroin trafficking and had family members who had been accused of smug-gling heroin and had faced prison sentences in the 1980s and 1990s. These family connections made her a credible defense lawyer for many smugglers, particularly heroin traffickers. After discussing the cigarette smuggling case with her for about an hour, I changed the topic and asked her about the public's perception of smuggling in the Kurdish borderlands, particularly the social legitimacy of heroin smuggling. She confirmed that smuggling activ-ities, which ranged from smuggling a few liters of diesel fuel to heroin traf-ficking, could all be framed as socially legitimate in the Kurdish borderlands: "Yes, it is black money, but it is still legitimate." Yet, she also noted that not all smuggling activities were socially and politically licit: "If you work with the state, especially with the deep state, then your money gets bloody."

While asserting that smuggling became politically and morally reprehen-sible when smugglers collaborated with state officials, she notably referred to the state as "the deep state"—a phrase commonly used to refer to an alleged coalition among the Turkish civilian, judiciary, and military bureaucracy.[2] In the Kurdish context, "deep state" took on a further meaning to denote the state counterinsurgency forces, particularly the death squads and other paramilitary forces. I asked Ayfer if she had used the phrase in that way. She confirmed:

[Working with the deep state is] like smuggling heroin or any other contraband good with high-ranking commanders and special forces. For example, some [village] guards (*korucular*) have engaged in smuggling business with the deep state, and even some became [village] guards for the sake of engaging in such businesses with the state. They not only smuggled with the help of the state but also provided intelligence and military services against the Kurdish guerrillas. But the money that they earn from smuggling is bloody money. It is not legitimate.

In describing what she called "working with the state," Ayfer clearly did not mean a mere business partnership. Whether smugglers joined and contributed to the counterinsurgency efforts mattered most to her. Providing intelligence on the smugglers—as well as offering paramilitary services and fighting against the guerrillas—was considered particularly reprimandable and worthy of politico-moral condemnation. She mentioned village guards who engaged in actual fighting with PKK guerrillas as an example of smugglers who "worked with the deep state." However, and given that some villagers accepted the guard postings to avoid the evacuation of their villages, becoming a village guard did not necessarily mean that one pledged political loyalty to the Turkish state.[3] Hence, Ayfer specified that she was talking about guards who worked with the state officials in their smuggling activities or who fought against Kurdish guerrillas by providing intelligence or direct operational support.

Ayfer thus suggested that neither the material specificity of the contraband— whether diesel fuel, cigarettes, or heroin—nor the amount of money involved in smuggling transactions, by itself, determined the social legitimacy of smuggling. Rather, the nature of the smuggler's relationship with state officials, particularly with the security forces, determined if the smuggling activity could be claimed as socially legitimate.[4] Yet, Ayfer's was not the only defense of smuggling I came across in my fieldwork. I met Kurdish traders and smugglers who defended the moral uprightness of their smuggling activities because they were trading staples, such as diesel fuel, tea, sugar, and cigarettes, and not heroin, hash, or guns. So, a discourse that morally dismissed heroin smuggling was also prevalent in the Kurdish borderlands. Ayfer must have been aware of such discourse, and perhaps this is why she referred to the money generated from smuggling as "black money," which implied that some smuggling activities, such as heroin trafficking, were politically tolerated if not socially or morally endorsed. But those traders and smugglers who refrained from heroin smuggling also denied collaboration with the counterinsurgency forces and used their noncollaboration to claim the political and social legitimacy of their smuggling.

While smugglers' collaboration typically involved providing intelligence on guerrillas or paramilitary labor for the state's counterinsurgency efforts, collaborators could also work as carrier smugglers in smuggling operations organized by certain members of the security forces. For example, in the 1990s, a few high-ranking military commanders were tried for establishing their own smuggling syndicates where collaborator smugglers, recruited as paramilitaries, were employed to procure and transport contraband items— such as heroin—and were even allowed to use the army's armored vehicles for these operations.[5] During my fieldwork, I also occasionally heard rumors about smugglers who traded with state officers and used military or law enforcement vehicles in their activities. I was curious to know whether these rumors were true. One day, while visiting another defense lawyer who specialized in smuggling cases, I asked if he knew of any court cases in which state officials were charged with smuggling or, more generally, of state officers who were active in the smuggling trade. The lawyer smiled and handed me a local newspaper. I had not had the chance to check the news that day.

The front page featured a news report about two prosecutors based in Wan province who had been using the district courthouse's minibus to transport heroin that the gendarmerie had confiscated.[6] The prosecutors had been in a traffic accident close to a central Anatolian city. When their vehicle broke down, their behavior raised suspicion from the mechanics who came to their aid, and they decided to notify the police. Once the police arrived, the prosecutors showed documents indicating that they had been tasked with transporting fifty six kilograms of confiscated heroin to the criminal laboratory in Ankara. In searching the vehicle, however, the police discovered that they were actually carrying seventy six kilograms of heroin. A day later, the district gendarmerie station sent to the police a document stating that they had made a mistake—the original amount should have been recorded as seventy-six kilograms. What made the incident even more suspicious was the fact that the gendarmerie station had failed to notify the other stations along the route about the transfer. Moreover, according to regulations, transporting confiscated heroin to central criminal laboratories was not listed among the prosecutors' duties. When I finished reading the news story, the lawyer said:

> Maybe it was a mundane bureaucratic mistake that the actual amount of heroin was written wrong, but it was also possible that the prosecutors were actually smuggling that extra twenty kilograms of heroin. And if that was the case, how did they find it? Maybe some professional smugglers supplied it, and by abusing their legal immunities, the prosecutors were just transporting the heroin to the West. Or maybe, the heroin was indeed confiscated during an anti-smuggling operation, and it was never recorded. Still, the prosecutors would have needed some smugglers to sell it in Ankara or Istanbul. There was still the possibility of a smuggler-prosecutor collaboration.

Neither the lawyer nor I knew much about the prosecutors. There was no way of confirming whether this was a bureaucratic error or an inside job. Yet the prosecutors' smuggling heroin was broadly viewed as plausible. Following that incident, and at different times in my fieldwork, I came across various smugglers and lawyers who mentioned that incident as an example of how Turkish state officers engaged in smuggling. Many of these smugglers and lawyers claimed that the state's counterinsurgency facilitated and even promoted such collaborations. In their view, the officers saw clear advantages in cooperating with village guards or repentants in order to engage in smuggling for their personal enrichment and to further counterinsurgency efforts. In the context of generalized efforts to entice smugglers to contribute to the counterinsurgency, many residents of the borderlands framed evasion of such collaborations (i.e., noncollaboration) as the main political and moral justification for smuggling activities in Kurdistan.

NONCOLLABORATIVE ENGAGEMENTS

On the face of it, the most reliable way to secure one's moral reputation as a smuggler was to avoid any relationship whatsoever with state officials. Yet, in the context of the counterinsurgency war and accompanying regimes of surveillance and control, Kurdish smugglers rarely operated far from the purview of the security forces. It was almost impossible to avoid them. For part-time or occasional smugglers, the use of joker cars or back roads could be helpful in bypassing security forces' surveillance. However, the carrier smugglers who engaged in frequent smuggling journeys—a few journeys every month—or those who owned contraband-selling retail stores—such as gas stations or trade companies—often bribed military and gendarmerie officers for free passage or for "tip-offs" about upcoming anti-smuggling operations. Such bribery was not necessarily seen as support for the counterinsurgency war in Kurdistan or as a betrayal of the guerrillas. As long as the smugglers did not provide intelligence on the guerrillas or directly join clashes on behalf of the military, the bribery did not signify a "deeper" engagement with security forces. Instead, these smugglers claimed to forge a noncollaborative engagement with the security officials and framed bribery as a necessary evil.

For some smugglers, however, bribery was more than a necessary evil and even became an opportunity to patronize—rather than be patronized by—security forces. Resul, a Kurdish smuggler who identified himself as a Kurdish patriot and supporter of the PKK, framed his bribery of Turkish soldiers in this manner.

Resul and I were driving to his village near the Turkish-Iranian border. Once we exited the inter-city roadway and turned onto the gravel trails that led to his village, Resul offered to drive, given his familiarity with the road's narrow curves and deep holes. We spent more than two hours driving on these trails. Resul's village was located far away from the district center in a unique geographical location that interconnected several key mountainous border passes. Its location meant that Resul's family frequently encountered guerrillas and provided them with logistical and financial support. In fact, Resul and his family were known to be Kurdish patriots (*welatparez*) and committed supporters of the PKK. Resul also had brothers and cousins who joined the PKK ranks.

Besides being pro-PKK, Resul was also a smuggler who dealt in all kinds of goods, from diesel fuel to historical artifacts. In response to my question as to whether he had ever bribed soldiers, he told me how he used to gather all the commanders of nearby military stations and negotiate a bribe with each of them in order to secure his enterprise. As he complained about how cumbersome it was to negotiate with each commander separately, he seemed very proud of himself for buying Turkish commanders off and, in doing so, patronizing them.

> I told them that I do not have time to deal with them individually and asked them for a common price for each passage. I told them they would share the payment with each other. Turkish soldiers are all like this, they all have a particular price.

Suspicious of his rather boastful story, I slightly challenged Resul and asked him whether he saw any contradiction in supporting the guerrilla fight and cooperating with the Turkish soldiers for smuggling. Resul replied that

> Everyone in this town knows us, we have neither become [village] guards nor smuggled with soldiers. The party [PKK] also knows us. Also, who is that [military station] commander, especially the lower-ranking ones instead of the high-ranking regional commanders . . . he is a peasant from the Black Sea region or western Anatolia.

Resul's reply makes a clear differentiation between the act of bribing security forces to facilitate one's own smuggling activities and smuggling as a way of collaborating with the forces in their counterinsurgency. He further explained how his bribery negotiations strategically allowed him to patronize the Turkish military officers—through bribing, he could buy the Turkish military rather than sell off his political loyalty. In mocking the military commanders for having "a particular price," he was deriding their susceptibility to his manipulation. Instead of providing intelligence on the guerrillas or participating in paramilitary services, he offered money to the nearby military and gendarmerie stations, thereby avoiding having to compromise his political and ethical allegiances. Resul's strategy seemed even more relevant given that he had faced arbitrary detention and torture at the hands of these commanders on several occasions. For him, bribery turned smuggling into a political negotiation through which he could redefine the power differential between himself as a smuggler and the commanders and even use them to his advantage.

Against the background of the state violence in the borderlands, however, Kurdish smugglers' noncollaboration with the security forces often entailed more than evading paramilitary services or refusing to collect intelligence.

After stings in which smugglers were wounded or killed, for instance, other smugglers reaffirmed their noncollaboration by actively showing their support and solidarity with those who were attacked and their bereaved families. Furthermore, and as shown in Mahmut's case, the attacked smugglers expected other smugglers to support them during criminal prosecutions against the military by providing eyewitness testimonies, assisting lawyers in the collection of evidence, or submitting their own criminal complaints and pursuing their own criminal cases if they also had been involved in the targeted convoy. Another way of showing solidarity with the attacked and their families was to temporarily pause smuggling journeys and to seek the bereaved family's approval before recommencing. This gesture of solidarity allowed smugglers to signal their loyalty to the broader community, even in cases when they needed to continue to bribe military officers, some of whom might have been involved in the killings. I witnessed such solidarity gestures while working with Metin on another case.

A Turkish soldier had been charged with allegedly killing a sixteen-year-old boy who was smuggling cigarettes from Iran. Metin and I visited the boy's father in his village to interview him and to update him on the prosecutor's investigation. I asked the father to tell me everything that happened, especially the legal procedures that had been pursued, to gain a better understanding of the incident. He meticulously described the events, including the investigation of the crime scene, the collection of testimonies, and the funeral that followed the boy's autopsy. He added: "Our neighbors and other villagers visited me a week after the incident and asked for my permission to resume their smuggling campaigns." With surprise, I asked, "Did they stop their campaigns after the incident [in which his son was killed]?" "Of course they did," he replied. "There is blood between the state and me because of this smuggling work, and without my permission, the money they make from this work would be bloody because my son was killed by the state while smuggling."

On our way back to Metin's office in the district center, I thought about the grieving father's testimony. The visit from the fellow villagers and their request for permission to resume their smuggling activities clearly seemed a thoughtful way to show solidarity with the family while condemning the security forces' use of violence. As I shared this initial reading of that symbolic gesture with Metin, he added a new aspect that had not occurred to me. Once they continued their smuggling operations, Metin emphasized, the fellow villagers would still need to bribe the security forces who patrolled the region where the father's son had been killed. Even though the villagers would not necessarily bribe the security officers who were directly involved in the killing, the borderland communities considered the state authorities as a whole—rather than individual security officers—responsible for the killings. Given that the villagers would, at a minimum, financially contribute to the armed forces responsible for the killing of a neighbor's son, their visit and request for the father's permission to resume their smuggling can be seen not only as a symbolic expression of solidarity, but as a political act of non-collaboration. In a way, the neighboring villagers had indirectly asked the father's permission to maintain their smuggling by bribing—and, therefore, by financially benefiting—the security forces who killed his son. The father gave his permission, knowing that bribery was necessary—however unpleasant—for the villagers to continue the smuggling operations without being co-opted to the state's counterinsurgency efforts while continuing to earn their daily subsistence.

SMUGGLERS' TARGETABILITY

The price of a smugglers' noncollaboration could be more onerous than any bribe. Even those smugglers who paid off security forces remained vulnerable to criminal punishment or violent confrontation with these forces. Bribes, in this sense, offered no guarantee of protection. Yet because the security forces did not target every smuggling convoy or smuggling activity, it was difficult to assess when and where violence might occur. Noncollaboration, therefore, placed smugglers in a peculiar position in which their targetability by the security forces was always expected but the actual timing, location, or intensity of the attacks was impossible to predict. The unpredictability of these attacks gave the state officials' execution of the sovereign power to kill, maim, or wound an "aleatory" character that made individual attacks seem random, obscuring their potential systematicity or rationale.[7]

The state security forces could have randomly targeted noncollaborative smugglers as part of the ongoing push and pull with guerrillas. The guerrillas carried out random attacks on different military stations to maintain their shifting yet insistent territorial control in the highlands. This dynamic stalemate between the Turkish military and the Kurdish guerrillas could un-expectedly activate the military surveillance of smugglers and lead to their arrest. I encountered such a case through one of my neighbors, whose son was caught transporting twenty kilograms of hashish in his car. A surprise guerrilla attack on a gendarmerie station on an inter-city road network acti-vated—instead of disabling as expected—the station's checkpoint and led to the arrest of my neighbor's son. My neighbor, who was in his late sixties and a recent retiree from the General Directorate of Highways, knew about my research and, after his son was arrested, asked me to refer him to an afford-able lawyer.

I eventually referred the neighbor to a lawyer who did not ask for extra payment from the family.[8] I also followed the son's trial. The neighbor's son was arrested near the Bedlîs city center in September 2012, shortly after a period of heightened guerrilla activity in a time when the PKK forces held territorial control in the Şemzînan district of Colemêrg province.[9] I learned more about the case from my neighbor. There were actually two cars involved. The first was the "joker" car, which was supposed to scout ahead and check whether the security forces were occupying the road checkpoints. The second car, which carried the twenty kilos of hash, was supposed to be roughly ten minutes behind the joker car. If the first car came upon an attended check-point, the driver would signal to the second car to avoid the checkpoint by returning, waiting, and hiding until the soldiers left. A second option was to bypass the checkpoint using back roads.

Both cars approached a military station next to the Wan-Bedlîs land road at around 3 a.m. The driver of the second car, the neighbor's son, was at ease since the first car had not signaled. There were no signs of any checkpoints or ambushes. In fact, I attended the court session in which he described the moment he was caught: "I was driving and everything seemed fine but all of a sudden I saw a moving light, almost like lightning, which was followed by an explosion." Without mentioning the first car, he went on: "Then, I heard machine gun fire and saw a few people waving their rifles. . . . I stopped the car, got out of it and told them that I was smuggling hash; I was scared of being mistaken for a suicide bomber and being killed." The neighbor's son had approached the military base during a surprise attack by PKK guerrillas.

Somehow, he managed to convince the soldiers and village guards that he was merely a smuggler—and not a guerrilla. He showed them the hash packages in the trunk and offered to bring them to the owners of the packages who were supposed to meet him in the Diyarbekir/Amed city center. They detained him and confiscated the car along with the hash. Yet, since the military base was still under attack by the guerrillas, they kept the driver and the car inside the base and waited until the following day to report the smuggling and jail the driver.

As the first car did, the second could have just gone through the gendarmerie station if the guerrillas had not attacked at that precise moment. According to my neighbor, it was his son's "bad luck" that the guerrillas' attack had not occurred five minutes later. Yet, since his son was scared of being mistaken for a guerrilla and executed extrajudicially, he surrendered himself and the hash packages before the security forces searched the car. As a result, he benefited from the penitence regulations, and the court decreased his criminal punishment by a third. He was sentenced to three years of imprisonment.

The surprise attack was part of the PKK's struggle for territorial control in the region. Yet, ironically, for my neighbor's son, the attack activated and thus unexpectedly re-instigated the state's security efforts over the official land-road network. The counterinsurgency war and the dynamic stalemate between the state forces and the PKK rendered smuggling fraught with added unpredictable dangers of lethal violence, incarceration, or dispossession. Moreover, the stalemate gave the state's territorial control and sovereign power an aleatory character, literally ruled by luck—or "bad luck," in my neighbor's words.[10]

The security forces' attacks against noncollaborating smugglers were also aleatory because the smugglers could never be sure of why they were targeted. Noncollaborating smugglers often came up with different interpretations of the rationale behind a particular ambush. Most of the smugglers viewed these ambushes as a strategy that individual security forces deployed to increase the price of bribes. The carrier smugglers based in mountain villages also identified particular security officials as notorious for their greedy and ruthless behavior. In Wan's Çaldêran/Ebex district, for example, I often heard the name of a sergeant whom the smugglers blamed for conducting violent ambushes as a strategy to intimidate smugglers and to compel higher bribes. At the time of my fieldwork, there were two different criminal prosecutions in which the accused sergeant was charged, one with killing a smuggler and another with wounding a smuggler.

The smugglers also mentioned that random anti-smuggling operations could be conducted by the security forces merely to fend off allegations of corruption from specific state officials. After such operations, according to smugglers, the security officials who had promised free passage would blame their upper-ranking officers for having forced them to ambush the smugglers. While the smugglers generally found these explanations unconvincing, the exact reason(s) for a particular anti-smuggling operation typically remained unclear. A trader smuggler, Bekir, complained to me about a gendarmerie station commander who had blamed an anti-smuggling ambush—in which the trader lost contraband cigarettes—on a surprise visit from a higher-ranking commander. I had learned of the case earlier that day when Bekir's lawyer, Servet, brought it to my attention.

After the lawyer handed me the court file, I quickly glanced over the documents and found the crime scene investigation report (*olay yeri görgü tespit tutanağı*). Three vehicles loaded with contraband cigarettes had been intercepted on a village road near the district center. Bekir, the trader smuggler, had not been involved in the case directly. Servet explained that the defendant, whom he was representing, was not the actual owner of the cigarettes but a carrier smuggler who was working for Bekir. So, the contraband cigarettes belonged to Bekir, who had organized for their transportation. Neither Bekir nor the carrier smuggler was aware of the other two vehicles. Bekir had bribed the station commander in exchange for safe passage, and accordingly, the commander requested that the cigarettes be transported on that road at that hour.

"They were caught at night on the side road," said the lawyer. I quickly checked the crime scene report and realized that the defendant, using village roads to bypass checkpoints blocking his entry into town, had veered off the main road before reaching the town center. Despite the safe passage that Bekir had prearranged, the vehicle was ambushed on the village road. As Servet explained, an upper-ranking commander from Wan had apparently visited the town gendarmerie station without notice and wanted to patrol the countryside. The crime scene report indeed mentioned the inspection by the upper-ranking commander. The surprise visit seemed to have suspended the unofficial arrangements between the smugglers and the local gendarmerie commander.

The gendarmerie patrol headed directly to the village road that bypassed the district center entrances. The crime scene report also used the term "bypass roads" and provided an official definition: "the side roads which are considered as being constructed by smugglers in order to circumvent the checkpoints." The document assured that the local gendarmerie was aware of the smugglers' back roads, so when a higher commander visited the station and asked to target smugglers, the station commander knew where they were.

The crime scene report stated that the visiting commanding officer left the station with a group of gendarmeries on a rainy night at 2:00 a.m. Shortly after the patrol left the station, at 2:30 a.m., the gendarmeries became suspicious of three vehicles that had left the main road and turned onto the village road. When the drivers saw the gendarmerie, they sped up and tried to escape. In their attempt to outpace the officers, one of the vehicles got stuck in the mud from the rain. The drivers proceeded to abandon their vehicles, but the gendarmeries eventually caught up with them. Not long after, the gendarmeries noticed another vehicle's headlights a quarter mile away on the same village road and decided to move toward the vehicle. When they reached it, they found it abandoned and loaded with contraband cigarettes. As they continued their search of the area, the gendarmeries found another vehicle loaded with more contraband. In less than half an hour the gendarmerie patrol had intercepted three different convoys. It is likely that other convoys were using the village road that night. After hearing of the ambush, these other convoys probably changed their route or did not move at all.

Bekir—and possibly the other smugglers who were caught—had bribed the security forces at the local gendarmerie station for safe passage on that night and were instructed to use the back roads. If the gendarmeries in the local station were surveilling both the inter-city land road and the village roads, why had the commander not directed them to use the main road? And if the commander was aware of the smuggling convoys, why did he not redirect the visiting commander's patrol? Perhaps the commander was setting a trap for the smugglers. Yet, there were other instances in which Bekir had bribed the commander and the smugglers had securely transported contraband cargo on that village road. Why would the commander want to conspire against Bekir? And why on this particular occasion? Neither Bekir nor Servet knew why. They had several guesses based on piecemeal information but nothing they could confirm. Referring to this uncertainty and unknowability, Servet claimed that the ambush suggested Bekir's targetability despite the bribery and, therefore, his refusal to assist the security forces and, potentially, his status as noncollaborator.

According to Servet, the commander's reason for calling an ambush did not matter much, whether he had intended to make an example of Bekir, to raise his bribes, or to achieve some other aim. The noncollaborating smugglers—those who did not "work with the deep state"—remained within the zone of targetability and would eventually be singled out, no matter what they did. In Servet's account, Bekir and other smugglers could always be targeted by the security forces for their noncollaboration, even if they could never confirm why they were targeted at a particular place and time.

Later that day, Bekir confirmed the background story that I had heard from Servet and further emphasized that he did not trust the local commander, who he suspected of lying. Bekir speculated, "[The commander] either wanted to raise the bribery amount, or he just wanted to pretend that he was performing his duty, or both."

"But," he added, "I already knew that bribery alone would not stop them from setting an ambush on us." When I asked Bekir whether, as a Kurdish smuggler, he could completely avoid the anti-smuggling ambushes, he assuredly answered no. After pausing for a minute or so, he added, "Unless you are working for the state." His answer resonated with what I had repeatedly heard from other smugglers and criminal lawyers when I asked about targetability.

WHEN NONCOLLABORATION MATTERS

Kurdish smugglers substantiated their politico-moral legitimacy by avoiding collaboration with the state's counterinsurgency. Yet, why did the political morality of smuggling matter so much to the smugglers? And why was it so frequently discussed as a matter of great importance?

One could argue that smugglers feared social pressure, judgment, or exclusion. As Ayfer and many other Kurdish lawyers asserted, they would not provide legal services to collaborators. Almost all smugglers I met also claimed that they would avoid working with collaborating smugglers and that they would refrain from sharing their networks of accountants, money launderers, warehouse owners, car dealers, and other key actors essential to conducting smuggling activities. In this way, a smuggler's negative reputation could result in dire economic isolation and an almost total severance from the networks that made smuggling possible. These claims indicate a moral—or even a politico-moral—economy of smuggling in the borderlands.[11] Under such moral economy, the smugglers' noncollaboration became a constitutive and constituting aspect of the existing social norms and mutual obligations sustaining the operations of Kurdish smuggling economies. If they did not substantiate their noncollaboration, Kurdish smugglers risked being cast out from the overall smuggling networks and would face challenges to finding business partners and service providers. Still, the broad geographical, economic, and social scales of smuggling economies, which connected various Kurdish regions and different parts of Turkey to the global economy, made me question the long-term effectiveness of social exclusion mechanisms. Indeed, and despite these politico-moral expectations, the collaborator smugglers could still deliver their contraband goods to other smuggler networks in central or western Turkey.

Collaborator smugglers might have risked being targeted by the guerrillas for offering intelligence or military service against the PKK, however. The fear of the PKK or of lethal retaliation may thus explain why smugglers were so invested in the political and moral legitimacy of their work. Yet, such an explanation would be limited given the power asymmetry between the security forces and the PKK. Based on such asymmetry, avoiding collaborating with security forces created broader lethal, criminal, and financial risks for the smugglers. Noncollaborating smugglers were more likely to face violent anti-smuggling ambushes, confiscation of their contraband, and criminal charges. In this sense, the fear of potential retaliation from the PKK does not exhaustively explain smugglers' motivation to avoid a deeper collaboration with the state forces.

Moreover, PKK forces did not have a record of targeting smugglers, including those who also served as village guards, in the Kurdish borderlands. While the guerrillas occasionally attacked village guards for their military collaboration, these attacks did not imply that every guard was a target.

Moreover, the PKK carefully avoided targeting guards who agreed not to participate in the army's military operations and, on a few occasions, declared amnesty for those who had actively fought against the guerrillas. During my fieldwork, guerrillas kidnapped and killed village guard leaders in two separate incidents, both connected to the same counterinsurgency operations the guards had supported. When the soldiers located one of the guard's dead bodies near a village road in October 2014, they found paper money stuck in his mouth. A few days later, the PKK claimed the killing and, in a public statement, announced that the village guard was executed for participating in anti-guerrilla military operations, including an operation in which fifteen women guerrillas had been killed in March 2012.[12] The guerrillas blamed the guard for providing intelligence on the whereabouts of the women guerrillas and therefore held him directly responsible for their lives.

As with other revolutionary or liberation movements, the PKK operated on the basis of a "moral contract" where both the movement and the Kurdish people mutually agreed that the goals of the revolution would take precedence over the private pursuits of individuals or groups.[13] In framing such a moral contract that rearticulated otherwise personal, intimate, or familial issues as matters of political or ideological loyalty and betrayal, Kurdish people also engaged in "a moral bargain" with the Kurdish movement to claim and negotiate the politico-moral legitimacy of their actions.[14] By avoiding deeper collaborations with the security forces, Kurdish smugglers and their lawyers could be understood as negotiating the politico-moral legitimacy of particular smuggling activities through a moral bargain with the PKK and Kurdish borderland communities. Accordingly, the smugglers rendered their smuggling politically and morally licit by not supporting the ongoing counterinsurgency war and, as a result, faced anti-smuggling operations in which they were arrested and imprisoned, lost their contraband goods, or even were injured or killed. Thus, one could suggest that Kurdish smugglers prioritized the movement's goals over their personal or familial interests.

The notion of a moral contract or a moral bargain often frames morality as a collectively or centrally structured and enforced set of rules and norms. Yet, the manners in which Kurdish smugglers, their families, and lawyers articulated and reflected upon the politico-moral legitimacy of smuggling exceeded centrally imposed norms or social pressure. In claiming their evasion from collaborating with the counterinsurgency forces and the politico-moral legitimacy of their smuggling activities, Kurdish smugglers also claimed and forged particular sets of values and positions. These positions ranged from explicitly supporting the Kurdish political cause to prioritizing fairness and care in their dealings with business partners and coworkers. In practicing their noncollaboration, the smugglers could further reflect upon the moral implications of the many inequalities within the smuggling economies and inflect their behavior in considering its potential effects on other smugglers.

These inequalities were grounded in an uneven distribution of risks and profits among the smugglers. While trader and investor smugglers received the largest profits and risked greater financial loss, carrier smugglers faced criminal sentences, fines, and much greater dangers to their physical safety— such as being wounded or killed—during anti-smuggling stings. Despite these grave risks, carrier smugglers earned only a small share of the overall profit. The claims and performances of noncollaboration with pro-Kurdish political standing allowed the trader or investor smugglers, who benefited most from these inequalities, to criticize such inequalities while justifying their work and revenue. By blaming both the colonial domination of Kurdistan on nation-state authorities and the ongoing counterinsurgency war for these inequalities, these smugglers often framed their role in smuggling as a politically and morally justifiable—if not preferable—choice.

Bekir shared similar politico-moral reflections with me. The case described above was not the only anti-smuggling prosecution he was facing. To my knowledge, he was connected to three other cases—one involving contraband oil and two related to cigarette smuggling. Yet, he was not officially implicated in any of them. In each case, the carrier smugglers were transporting the contraband cargo that Bekir owned. After attending a few meetings with Bekir in the law office and visiting his gas station, I felt comfortable enough to ask him, in non-accusatory language, about the inequalities of the smuggling economies and whether he benefited from these inequalities. Despite my initial fear of upsetting him, Bekir responded to my question calmly. After describing his support for the Kurdish Freedom Movement and noncollaboration, he also explained how he fulfilled his responsibilities to the carrier smugglers working for him in cases of ambushes or raids: by sending his lawyer to assist them during criminal prosecutions and providing financial support to their families. Furthermore, he did not deny the uneven distribution of risks and profits between himself and the carrier smugglers under his employment.

Bekir ultimately blamed the Turkish authorities for these contradictions and inequalities. He held them responsible for imposing anti-smuggling ambushes, criminal charges, and the confiscation of trade items, and for enforcing "the border dividing the [Kurdish] homeland." In his view, all these conditions jointly accounted for the predicament that carrier smugglers systematically faced. Yet, Bekir still received the lion's share of the profits from smuggling journeys. Moreover, in prosecutions where contraband cargo was seized, his name was not mentioned in the indictments, so he faced no criminal penalties. When law enforcement discovered his contraband cigarettes, for example, he did not surrender himself as the owner. Instead, he continued to arrange new smuggling journeys, secured larger profit shares, and left carrier smugglers to bear the greater risks. In this way, Bekir's claims to the social legitimacy of his smuggling activities were not free from contradiction. Nevertheless, his political and moral reflections on the contraband commerce, from which he primarily benefited, were neither disingenuous nor dishonest. According to him, his and other trader smugglers' noncollaboration allowed them to navigate the inequalities of the smuggling economies and their inherently problematic ethical implications, framing the benefits they gained politically and morally tolerable—to many, if not to all, smugglers or borderland residents.

DOUBTS OF COLLABORATION

As smugglers' noncollaboration was closely linked to their targetability, one might assume that being targeted by security forces—whether through ambushes at border crossings, inspections on inter-city or village roads, raids on retail stores or warehouses, arrests, or criminal prosecutions—would effectively "safeguard" a smuggler's reputation. Conversely, smugglers who had never been arrested, never been subjected to sting operations, or never had their contraband goods confiscated often aroused suspicion, which led others to accuse them of collaborating with the counterinsurgency forces. On one occasion, Servet speculated: "If a smuggler has never been caught while frequently engaging in smuggling activities, he would be seen as one of those smugglers who sold his people out. . . . In Kurdistan, having never been caught is the worst."

In the context of the ongoing counterinsurgency war, however, claims and suspicions of noncollaboration were not without challenges, even for those whose smuggling activities were targeted by security forces. Accusations of collaboration, whether tied to past or present actions, often provoked counteraccusations against the denouncing smuggler. These claims were frequently entangled with competition over land, shares of contraband commerce, or political repositioning among individuals, families, villages, or tribes. In this atmosphere of constant accusations and counteraccusations, even the smugglers who faced ambushes, raids, or trials could still be accused of collaboration. Other smugglers and borderland residents might question the authenticity of such targetings and whether being targeted truly indicated a smuggler's noncollaboration. I encountered such suspicions regarding an anti-smuggling raid on a gas station.

In May of 2013, I was staying with Selahattin in his village, Sterik, in Wan's Mehmûdî district, located at the Turkish-Iranian border. Selahattin earned his livelihood by ferrying passengers from his village to the Mehmûdî and Qelqelî district centers. In the early morning, we left the village to go to the pro-Kurdish party building. It would be an exciting day since the co-chairperson of the leading pro-Kurdish party—the BDP, at the time of my fieldwork—would visit the neighboring districts of Qelqelî and Mehmûdî. The visit would be also anxiety-producing for party members because of the upcoming municipal elections. There was intense competition among the potential candidates within the BDP, the party favored to win.

Qelqelî and Mehmûdî were very close—in fact, Mehmûdî used to be a town in Qelqelî district. In 1988, Mehmûdî was declared an independent district that would host the border gate of Kapıköy—one of the three land border passages between Turkey and Iran.[15] When we first met, Selahattin proudly told me how he had been among the founders of the party's branch in Mehmûdî shortly after it became a separate district, and how he had faced arbitrary beatings, insults, and death threats from, as well as arrests by, state security officers during the 1990s. He further explained how the pro-Kurdish BDP was particularly strong in the villages, while the district center tended to support right-wing parties. For ten years, it was the AKP that the town center had supported. In the previous election, the pro-Kurdish party won the mayor's office in Qelqelî but lost in Mehmûdî. This time things could be different, though. New legislation had extended municipal zones into the villages, which had been consistently voting for pro-Kurdish parties.[16] Thus, the BDP would likely win the elections. According to Selahattin, this newly favorable situation for the BDP prompted many new candidates to join the party to bolster their campaigns.

Then, we received a phone call—the chairperson's convoy was approaching Qelqelî. We left the party building to welcome it. We got into Selahattin's minibus with a few other party members. He started the engine but quickly realized that we were running out of fuel. As an active member of the party's district branch, he had been overwhelmed with the preparations to host the chairperson in recent days, so he had forgotten to check the fuel in his minibus, even after we had driven from his village to the district center. Selahattin called a friend who was selling contraband diesel from his village house, but unfortunately the friend did not have any fuel for sale. After that, he contacted another friend who also drove a minibus to ferry passengers between district centers and Wan city. He did not have any diesel either.

I suggested that we go to the gas station to refuel. Selahattin did not respond and kept driving. Initially, I thought my suggestion to purchase legal fuel was naïve. I thought that, as a patriotic Kurd, Selahattin may have been reluctant to pay the Turkish state fuel taxes—which made up to 70 percent of the fuel cost at the time. A short time later, I realized why my comment had come off poorly. Selahattin informed me that the former mayor's brother owned the gas station; this was why he did not want to go there. I knew that the former mayor wanted to join the pro-Kurdish party, and it was speculated that, during his visit, the BDP chairperson would declare his participation. Such an act would publicly honor the former mayor. However, many party members, including Selahattin, did not like the former mayor or his brother. Recently, Selahattin had expressed disapproval about them joining the party and mentioned that, during his term in office back in the 1990s, the former major provided the municipality's bulldozer to the military to display the tortured and dead bodies of PKK guerrillas in the town center.[17] Given the frequent torture, kidnappings, and killings publicly carried out by counterinsurgency forces during that period, the mayor might have had no other option, and it was likely that the forces used the bulldozer without asking for his permission. Yet, Selahattin still believed that the former mayor should have resisted or at least resigned rather than facilitate the public display of the tortured bodies of killed guerrilla members. Accusing the former mayor of "collaborationism," Selahattin believed that the two brothers were pretending to support the pro-Kurdish party only because it had been gaining power. With the party's support, he suspected, the brothers were hoping to benefit from the political and financial opportunities, such as public work contracts, that the municipality might provide.

We did not have much time to search for fuel because the chairperson's convoy was rapidly approaching. Escorting the chairperson's convoy into Qelqelî was a very important performance of one's party membership, especially before and during election campaigns. With the upcoming elections and the tight competition for the municipal candidacy, Selahattin—as one of the founders of the party's district branch and a potential municipal assembly candidate—did not want to miss the chance to demonstrate his commitment to the party by showing off his minibus decorated with party flags.

Another party member in the minibus interrupted our conversation to explain that, a couple of days earlier, the police had actually shut down the mayor's brother's station for selling smuggled oil, so we could not go there either. Selahattin was incredulous:

> They must have been putting on an act; they would never smuggle oil or sell smuggled oil. They have always worked with the state. Now they are just pretending in order to gain prestige, to help their transition to the party for their own benefits. They want to present themselves as smugglers to convince people of their [Kurdish] patriotism.

For Selahattin, the mere fact that they were targeted by anti-smuggling law enforcement did not necessarily establish the brothers' noncollaboration. Instead, he questioned the motives behind the raid. We could not buy any additional diesel fuel, but luckily the remaining fuel was just enough to reach Qelqelî and to escort the party bus to Mehmûdî. Selahattin met the party chairperson. However, during his talk in Mehmûdî, the chairperson also welcomed the former mayor to join the BDP and helped him pin the party badge on his suit. The party entered the elections with a different candidate, though, who was elected mayor, and Selahattin joined the municipal assembly under the party's list.[18]

SLY LEGALITY AND NONCOLLABORATION IN COURTS

Amid accusations of smuggler collaboration and doubts about the authenticity of anti-smuggling raids, pursuing sly legality—through disruptive borderwork or vernacular counterforensics—emerged as a key strategy to substantiate smugglers' noncollaboration. Kurdish oil traders—trader smugglers—for instance, employed specific technolegal tactics, such as chemically fixing the contraband oil and procuring authentic-yet-false trade documents, to disrupt border enforcement during smuggling trials. These traders often engaged in such tactics in anticipation of anti-smuggling raids, as well as of the criminal investigations and prosecutions that would follow. Even though they had frequently bribed state officials, the traders still conducted these technolegal preparations because they knew that, as noncollaborating smugglers, the bribery alone did not guarantee immunity and, therefore, they remained at risk of becoming targets at any time. In this way, these pre-trial technolegal preparations and the subsequent practice of disruptive borderwork during the trials functioned as evidence of these trader smugglers' targetability and, therefore, of their noncollaboration, both before and after being subjected to anti-smuggling raids, investigations, and criminal charges.

In instances of anti-smuggling ambushes, filing criminal complaints against the security forces' use of violence and pursuing vernacular counterforensics also came to demonstrate the noncollaboration of smugglers and their families. As illustrated in Mahmut's case, not even the fact of being wounded in an ambush necessarily established the smugglers' noncollaboration—such proof depended, rather, on whether they pursued counterforensics in criminal courts. Just as disruptive borderwork necessitated trader smugglers to work with different experts and actors, including their lawyers, accountants, and chemists, vernacular counterforensics also relied on the involvement of various other actors, such as fellow smugglers or villagers who could provide eyewitness testimonies about a smuggling trip and an anti-smuggling sting, or lawyers and family members who visited and photographed crime scenes or provided previous court files to be used as legal precedents. By participating in these counterforensic practices, these actors both showed solidarity with wounded or slain smugglers and established their noncollaboration.

Importantly, in addition to demonstrating the smugglers' noncollaboration in contraband commerce, the pursuit of sly legality enabled smugglers and their lawyers to practice another form of noncollaboration within and through the courts: by transforming criminal-legal processes into a critical site of resistance and refusal. This court-based noncollaboration relied on the rejection and evasion of legal surveillance, sanctioning, and redress. Along with concretely defying state-enforced borders through smuggling across dividing lines, for example, Kurdish smugglers—with the help of their lawyers and other actors involved in technolegal practices—also rendered these borders legally unenforceable by obscuring the provenance of contraband goods in courts. Instead of seeking legal recognition for their cross-border trade—which would reinforce nation-state borders and lead to co-optation into the colonial division of Kurdistan—the smugglers aimed to disrupt the authorities' ability to grant such recognition and to enforce borders and law. Through their vernacular counterforensics, Kurdish complainants and their lawyers used criminal courts not to seek redress, but to expose the legal authorities' complicity in the killings committed by security forces, thereby avoiding legitimizing the state legal system as the supreme arbiter of universal justice. By repurposing legal processes to carve out pockets of escape from legal regimes of surveillance, containment, and co-optation, sly legality thus allowed Kurdish smugglers to practice noncollaboration in courts. This court-based noncollaboration was distinct yet interconnected with the noncollaboration these smugglers performed through their contraband commerce, each reinforcing one another.

NONCOLLABORATION AS EVASIVE ENGAGEMENT

For Kurdish smugglers, noncollaboration required a constant effort to evade cooperation with the security forces in their counterinsurgency efforts. However, this evasion did not mean avoiding all encounters or interactions with the state authorities, particularly security forces. Since the smuggling economies had to operate through areas monitored by these forces, smugglers needed to engage with them. In fact, complete evasion—having no contact with security forces or never being subjected to anti-smuggling raids or ambushes—came to signal the smugglers' collaborationism in the border-lands. Instead, noncollaborating smugglers interacted with security forces, offering bribes to evade potential demands of collaboration and to resist being co-opted into counterinsurgency efforts. Thus, their noncollaboration emerged as an evasive engagement—a tactical engagement with oppressive actors aimed at escaping their practices of control and containment.

The noncollaborating smugglers also pursued sly legality—another form of evasive engagement with state authorities, particularly courts and legal processes—to both preemptively and retroactively mitigate and respond to the criminal-legal and physical targetability that came as a cost of their non-collaboration. Through their sly legality, these smugglers performed a distinct practice of noncollaboration in courts, using legal processes to interrupt the state authorities' ability to enforce borders, sanction state-sponsored unlawful killings, or claim to deliver impartial justice. Like their noncollaboration in smuggling, this court-based noncollaboration unfolded as evasive engagement which, rather than enacting strict disengagement or outright defiance, relied on specific ways of interacting with legal authorities and processes aimed at corroding their operative logics and procedures. In linking together their court-based and smuggling-related practices of noncollaboration through sly legality, Kurdish smugglers, their lawyers, and other actors involved in the technolegal tactics of disruptive borderwork and vernacular counterforensics formed a distinct political community of noncollaborators dedicated to op-posing the colonial domination of Kurdish lives and livelihoods.

CONCLUSION

IN FEBRUARY 2019, METIN AND I met via video conference to discuss updates on his ongoing smuggler-killing cases. He did not have much to share. "It has gotten worse," he said, "the courts directly dismiss our requests for evidence collection or assessment." Metin was referring to how the political situation in Kurdistan and Turkey had become increasingly oppressive after I completed my fieldwork and left Wan at the end of summer 2014. In the subsequent years, the Turkish government resumed its counterinsurgency war in Kurdistan, conducted military operations in more than thirty Kurdish towns and cities, and forcibly displaced half a million people. Moreover, Turkey faced an attempted military coup and a two-year-long emergency rule in its aftermath. President Recep Tayyip Erdoğan eventually solidified his autocratic rule by implementing an executive presidency equipped with exceptional powers.

I last visited Wan province a few weeks after the parliamentary elections in June 2015. In the elections, the pro-Kurdish HDP, a leading coalition of leftist parties, gained eighty seats and ended the governing AKP's thirteen-year parliamentary majority.[1] HDP had run on a platform that opposed an executive presidency—a regime change agenda that Erdoğan, who was elected president in August 2014, was pursuing.[2] Yet, hopes of preventing the regime change were shattered shortly after the June elections. On July 20, a suicide bomber attacked a press conference and killed thirty-three socialist activists in Pirsûs (Off. Suruç)—a Kurdish town of Turkey located on the Syrian border and a key access node to the regions governed by a Kurdish-led coalition in North and East Syria.[3] ISIS (the Islamic State of Iraq and Syria) claimed responsibility for the attack.[4] On July 22, two days following the suicide attack, two police officers were found dead in their apartments in Serê Kanî (Off. Ceylanpınar), another Kurdish-majority town of Turkey on the Syrian border. Turkish officials blamed the PKK for killing the officers. Even though the PKK denied involvement and dismissed the government's allegations as a provocation, the AKP-led interim government cited the murders as an excuse to reinstate the counterinsurgency war in Kurdistan, ending the Peace Process, during which the PKK had declared a ceasefire in March 2013. The Turkish military conducted at least fourteen waves of airstrikes against the PKK forces in the Kurdish highlands of Turkey and Iraq in the following weeks. In less than two months, the Turkish police had arrested more than eight hundred party supporters.

The counterinsurgency operations and arrest campaigns conducted in northern Kurdistan (Bakur) during the summer of 2015 only aggravated the Kurdish people's sense of insecurity and distrust of the government. On August 7, during a police operation in the district center of Silopî/Girkê Emo (Off. Silopi) in Şirnex (Off. Şırnak), a Kurdish province near the Iraqi border, police officers randomly fired at civilians, killing three. To protest this incident and the escalating state oppression, the Şirnex People's Assembly—a civilian platform that various nongovernmental organizations and local branches of pro-Kurdish political parties joined—declared self-rule on August 10, 2015.[5] The following week, in seventeen Kurdish neighborhoods and towns, other peoples' assemblies followed suit, and Kurdish youth militias built barricades and dug trenches to block the security forces' access.[6] In Wan, self-rule was also declared in four districts: Rêya Ermûşê (Off. İpekyolu) and Artemêtan (Off. Edremit) in August, and Tûşba (Off. Tuşba) and Erdîş (Off. Erçiş) in October 2015. In response, the government launched military operations in various Kurdish cities and towns and imposed round-the-clock curfews. From July 2015 to June 2016, a period that was also known as *şehir savaşları* (urban warfare) in Kurdistan, more than two thousand people were killed and over a hundred thousand homes were destroyed.[7] After coalition negotiations failed, the AKP-led interim government called for early elections.

Against the background of the heavy clashes with the Kurdish youth militia in Kurdistan, elections were held in November 2015. Framing the clashes as a threat to national security, the AKP managed to garner robust electoral support and regain its recently compromised parliamentary majority.

On July 15, 2016, the country witnessed a coup attempt in which more than three hundred people were killed. The AKP government blamed the Gülenists, followers of the influential preacher Fethullah Gülen, who had moved to the U.S. in 1999 and passed away there in 2024.[8] In the 2000s and early 2010s, Erdoğan and AKP circles had allied with Gülen to fight against military tutelage. During this period, AKP hired thousands of Gülenists and replaced secularist bureaucrats in governmental positions, particularly in the police, the military, and the judiciary. Following the coup attempt, the AKP government declared a state of emergency, targeted the Gülenist bureaucracy, and commenced an unprecedented purge of high-ranking bureaucrats, including judges, prosecutors, as well as police and gendarmerie commanders. Because Wan is a regional administrative center, the anti-Gülenist purge also hit the province's judiciary. During the first week following the coup attempt, the lead prosecutor of Wan ordered the arrest of fifty-five judges and prosecutors, almost half of the judiciary staff in Wan courts.[9] From July 2016 to February 2024, over four thousand judges and prosecutors were dismissed across the country—nearly a third of all judges and prosecutors who had been active in 2016 prior to the coup attempt.[10] In the same period, the government hired around twelve thousand new judges and prosecutors among pro-government loyalists. As of 2023, these newly recruited judiciary members constituted half of all judges and prosecutors in the country.[11]

The anti-coup investigations also targeted a wide array of dissidents, including human rights activists, leftist circles, and members of the Kurdish Freedom Movement. Through emergency rule decrees (*olağanüstü hal kanun hükmünde kararnameleri*), the government closed more than a hundred civil society organizations, labor unions, and media outlets; dismissed more than one hundred and twenty-five thousand state officers; and investigated around half a million people and revoked nearly two hundred thousand passports. In particular, the government used the emergency rule to weaken Kurdish electoral politics. In September 2016, the government began removing democratically elected Kurdish mayors and members of the municipal assemblies and appointed governors as trustees to control the municipalities. In November, parliamentarians from the pro-Kurdish HDP, including the party co-chairs, were imprisoned. Many pro-Kurdish party members, supporters, and elected politicians were arrested and tried for terrorism. In April 2017, while emergency rule was still in effect, President Erdoğan, with the backing of the ultranationalist MHP, passed constitutional changes that established his autocratic presidency in a snap referendum, despite credible accusations of election fraud. The persecution of Kurdish politicians, rights defenders, journalists, and activists expanded in the following years.

As with the residents of other Kurdish provinces, residents of Wan, from the city center as well as from border towns and villages, experienced the heightened oppression. Taking advantage of the already established surveillance and assault infrastructure, which had been quietly strengthened during the Peace Process, state security forces were able to further restrict smugglers' mobility and to target smuggling convoys in Wan and neighboring provinces more frequently and effectively. While deepening anti-Kurdish lawfare through terror trials, state criminal courts maintained the legal protection of security forces who had committed rights violations, including in cases of smuggler killings, and upheld their impunity. Yet, the intensified state oppression in Kurdistan, the expanding authoritarianism, and the extralegal violation of rights and freedoms during and following the emergency rule were neither new nor unexpected developments for Kurdish people, including my lawyer and smuggler interlocutors in Wan. My conversation with Metin in February 2019 mirrored this feeling of déjà vu. After describing how judges and prosecutors had become increasingly dismissive of Kurdish rights and lives, he said, "But this is not something we cannot handle; we know it from the 1990s."

During the decades-long counterinsurgency war in Kurdistan and multiple anti-Kurdish lawfare campaigns, Kurdish lawyers and their clients had become familiar with the state officials' legal and illegal practices of repression. In response to these practices, they pursued—among other strategies— what I have theorized as sly legality: a political-legal tactic of engaging with the state's legal institutions, rules, and procedures to undermine their operations from within. As a political-legal strategy of curtailing official persecution and the oppressive use of law, sly legality became even more relevant in Turkey and Kurdistan during the late 2010s and early 2020s—a period marked by an autocratic presidency and intensified anti-Kurdish warfare and lawfare campaigns. The lawyers and smugglers with whom I maintained contact during this period shared how they continued to employ what I have referred to as tactics of technolegal politics—that is, "disruptive borderwork" that manipulates the material content and documentation of contraband items and renders these items nonillegal in smuggling trials. They also continued to employ "vernacular counterforensics" to substantiate the judiciary's methods of selectively collecting and assessing legal evidence to ensure the impunity of the perpetrators in smuggler killing cases. In a FaceTime call in 2018, one lawyer expressed how it had become "even easier" to document the judiciary's complicity because the courts grew increasingly careless in concealing their protection of state officials who committed smuggler killings and other crimes. For my interlocutors, therefore, sly legality emerged as a crucial strategy to contest the coarse regimes of oppression unleashed through courts, as well as the more subtle and insidious oppressive legal schemes of liberal recognition and co-optation, both of which serve as distinct yet related features of the undeclared colonial rule in Kurdistan in the late 2000s and onward.[12]

USING THE LAW TO REFUSE

When seen in the broader context of rising authoritarianism and right-wing populist politics across Eastern Europe, Turkey, and South and North America, the concept of sly legality has worldwide political and analytical relevance. Since the 2010s, Turkey and Erdoğan's autocratic presidency has been called out as a leading example of the rise of authoritarianism as a global phenomenon. Some scholars have referred to Erdoğan's tactical use and abuse of EU-driven liberal reforms and existing liberal institutions, such as elections and courts—as is also the case with Victor Orbán in Hungary—as "democratic backsliding."[13] In such analyses, Erdoğan's executive presidency is viewed as a sharp deviation from the trajectory toward a fully established liberal rule of law, under the EU accession process, and as an exceptional phase in a process through which the government has achieved complete control of the judiciary.[14] Yet, approaching the emergency rule or Erdoğan's autocratic presidency as a period of exceptional departure from the rule of law presumes that a truly functioning liberal law would necessarily guarantee rights, freedoms, and equality before the law.[15] As this book has shown, liberal law, legal proceduralism, and evidentiary processes are rather central to legal violence and to the channeling of this violence against marginalized groups. In the same stroke, however, the law should not be seen as completely subsumed under the ruling authorities' control, even in the context of entrenched authoritarian regimes.[16] Indeed, disenfranchised actors may occasionally challenge state power and undermine regimes of coercion and dispossession through domestic courts, turning the law into a contingent field of rights advocacy. Operating as both a tool of domination and a means for seeking rights and protections against oppression, the law features paradoxical affordances, reflecting what anthropologist Mark Goodale calls "the Janus-faced logics of law."[17] The liberal law, accordingly, moderates the rulers' domination to strengthen their authority and, in so doing, facilitates dominated groups' pursuit of freedoms and protections. It also moderates the oppressed populations' deployment of the law for rights advocacy by filtering out demands for structural changes to ruling systems.

Against the backdrop of the law's Janus-faced logics, some disenfranchised groups still engage with courts to safeguard already won rights and protections, to build new advocacy alliances both domestically and globally, or to advance political goals set independently from specific legal remedies.[18] Others have grown increasingly skeptical of liberal legal forums, withdrawing from or avoiding participation in them and actively seeking to build new relationalities and justice practices. Anthropologist Charles Hale calls these two approaches "use" (or "struggle from within") and "refusal," identifying them as key currents in the counterhegemonic struggles of Indigenous and other marginalized groups within the context of "neoliberal multiculturalism," where broader rights advocacy and the formal recognition of collective rights intersect with neoliberal reforms that ultimately work to contain or undermine those very rights and advocacy efforts.[19] While the use approach dominates the counterhegemonic politics in the era of neoliberal multiculturalism, the refusal approach has been rearticulated as a struggle that pursues the development and practice of alternative forms of governance alongside a sharp critique of the first approach's reliance on, and subjection to, the sovereignty of liberal law and nation-state authorities.[20] As the era of neoliberal multiculturalism gives way to one marked by intensified attacks and the reversal of rights and other hard-won gains beginning in the mid-2010s, Hale observes the rise of a new mode of political struggle—which he broadly calls "use-and-refuse strategies/sensibilities," or more specifically "using and refusing the law" regarding the context of national or international courts—in which the newly articulated refusal approach takes prominence, while the use approach can still offer crucial space and protection for refusal struggles against the regimes of oppression and containment imposed by liberal law and state authorities.[21] Yet, the use and refusal approaches still require distinct, and at times opposing, sets of tactics, knowledges, and practices. The first approach involves the counterhegemonic use of domestic or international courts, frequently drawing on liberal legal discourses and running the risk of accepting or endorsing the liberal law's and nation-state authorities' claims to sovereign supremacy. In contrast, the second approach centers on a strict refusal to participate in the institutions and procedures of national and international law in order to reject any form of subjugation to them or their claims to sovereign supremacy, and instead turns toward constructing and enacting alternative political structures and futures grounded in Indigenous or other alternate ways of knowing and living. Some disenfranchised actors may strategically mobilize both approaches to respond in contextually situated ways to shifting needs and circumstances. For instance, in their land rights struggle in Chiapas, Mexico, the Indigenous Ch'ol community initially adopted the first approach by filing legal rights claims with the Mexican courts. However, after years without a verdict from the Supreme Court, the community ended their legal engagement with the state and adopted a strategy of refusing the law by taking direct action and occupying the land that settlers had illegally taken.[22] Despite their potential to be adopted by the same actors at different points of struggle, these approaches remain to be fraught and thus pose "new challenges in articulating the 'use' with the 'refuse' in the realm of both sensibilities and strategies."[23] My interlocutors' practice of sly legality can be understood as answering such challenges by integrating the approaches under the same political-legal objective of using—and abusing— liberal law to refuse it.

By using liberal law, my interlocutors exercised political refusal, which consisted of, on the one hand, acts that interrupted the criminal courts' capacity to legally enforce state borders and exercise sovereignty, and, on the other, acts that repurposed the courts as potential spaces where alternative solidarities and alternative Kurdish political communities could be built and enacted. Membership in these political communities was based on noncollaboration—or on an active evasion of collaboration—with the state authorities' counterinsurgency and with the broader colonial domination of Kurdistan. Sly legality enables its practitioners to use the state's legal system to engage in a strategic refusal because the tactic is predicated on resorting to law, but not because of the legal remedies it offers. In fact, my interlocutors engaged with criminal courts to undermine or counteract, rather than bank on, legal redresses and other ways in which the courts may interpellate them as atomized rights-bearing subjects, defendants, or criminals. What made it possible for my interlocutors to turn to state law, without necessarily seeking its remedies and other interpellations and at times even frustrating them, was their use of technolegal tactics and the practice of technolegal politics in courts. In developing and deploying specific technolegal practices, they brought together seemingly unrelated legal knowledge and technical-scientific expertise in novel ways to manipulate legal proceedings and seek out political objectives that surpassed what was achievable in existing legal frameworks. One such political objective is illustrated by how Kurdish smugglers and their lawyers engaged with criminal courts to curtail the authorities' ability to declare a particular trade item or livelihood activity illegal or legal and to refuse the sovereign enforcement of borders by rending such borders technolegally unenforceable.

Sly legality and the associated practice of technolegal politics also provide insights into how marginalized actors use liberal law and the judicial system to challenge crimes committed by state officials without relying on formal legal remedies, precisely because such reliance could paradoxically allow state authorities to reclaim political legitimacy by positioning themselves as enforcers of the law. For instance, Kurdish complainants and their lawyers interacted with domestic and international courts not only to identify the perpetrators of smuggler killings and to establish the unlawfulness of such killings but also to document how the courts established—or reaffirmed— the impunity of state officials. They repurposed the criminal-legal processes to demonstrate the hollowness of liberal law's promise of impartiality and to disavow its self-positioning as the ultimate arbiter of justice.

Another political objective that sly legality may enable marginalized actors to pursue is the documentation of systematic, collective, and structural aspects of rights violations and the resulting collective suffering through criminal courts, even though the primary operative logic of criminal law and forensics is to individualize such violations and suffering. This objective is illustrated by how my interlocutors repurposed the legal-criminal processes to frame smuggler killings as political killings—killings that were committed and sanctioned by state authorities in an organized and collective manner—despite the fact that the authorities, including the judiciary, officially framed the killings as isolated and infrequent incidents. As criminal law and forensics remain critical forums for disputing rights violations across various contexts—from authoritarianism and counterinsurgency to racialized policing, border enforcement, and climate change—sly legality may thus offer rights advocates a novel approach: using—and eventually refusing—these forums to expose and contest the routinized, organized, or structural nature of crimes that state authorities—or corporate actors—commit, as well as the legal systems' structured efforts to obscure both the systematic execution and systemic embeddedness of such crimes.[24]

EVASIVE ENGAGEMENT

This book has introduced the concept of sly legality to formulate a particular mode of engaging state law. It further expands the notion of sly legality to theorize evasive engagement—a broader political strategy that enables marginalized actors to contest and corrode oppressive institutional practices. Even while sly legality has been used in state courts and other legal institutions as a type of evasive engagement, alternative forms of evasive engagement can also be deployed in other governmental or corporate institutional settings, albeit in customized ways, to interrupt and frustrate the specific operative logics and processes characteristic of these particular institutions. As my interlocutors' practices of sly legality exemplify, evasive engagement strategies pursue political refusal of the ruling authorities and their assertions of sovereign supremacy through persistently interacting with these authorities. Thus, evasive engagement resonates with refusal practices observed in other contexts, such as the "cooperation without submission" that Hopi Tribes and several other Indigenous nations in Turtle Island (North America) practiced.[25]

These Indigenous nations continue to interact with U.S. authorities to re-lentlessly perform their refusal of subjugation and to enact a horizontal sov-ereign-to-sovereign—government-to-government—relationship even though their counterparts deliberately—or unintentionally—fail to recognize such refusals and continue to act as a supreme sovereign. In addition to rejecting the supremacy claims of ruling authorities, those practicing evasive engage-ment also actively work to thwart the execution of such claims, thereby inte-grating the practices of political refusal and resistance politics. The political strategy of evasive engagement, thus, echoes resistance practices that contest and counteract the dominant systems of surveillance and containment. In this way, evasive engagement rehearses what sociologist Simone Browne has theorized as "dark sousveillance"—tactics that Black people have developed, in both the historical context of slavery and contemporary settings of racial-ization, to monitor and generate knowledge of how surveillance technologies operate ("sousveillance"), as well as to use this knowledge to make themselves illegible to such technologies ("anti-surveillance").[26] In performing evasive engagement, disenfranchised actors develop and deploy different sousveil-lance and anti-surveillance practices to curtail and, when possible, disrupt the ability of dominating authorities to monitor and control. In so doing, they create critical pockets of evasion within regimes of surveillance and con-tainment. These pockets also serve as spaces in which these actors cultivate new forms of relating with each other and other human and more-than-hu-man actors, as well as to imagine alternatives to the nation-state, capitalism, liberal law, or other prevailing modalities of governance.

Evasive engagement coexists and complements other forms of contentious politics—from street protests and strikes to civil disobedience, direct action, and armed struggle—that, with various degrees of success, contest schemes of coercion, exploitation, and confinement. Depending on specific historical and political contexts, different forms of contentious politics facilitate and are facilitated by evasive engagement. As a type of politics that works in tandem with other forms of contentious politics, evasive engagement allows us to move beyond reified logics of opposition between different political dispo-sitions and actions—such as the rigid contrast between armed rebellion or civil disobedience and electoral politics or legal activism. As reflected in my interlocutors' exercise of evasive engagement in Turkish courts (i.e., their sly legality), acts of legal or human rights activism may simultaneously serve as political refusal of and resistance to state law. Their evasive engagement thus furthers an anti-colonial and decolonial political vision, which the armed rebellion in Kurdistan also shared and advanced. In this way, the lens of evasive engagement helps us identify and theorize acts of political resistance and refusal that might otherwise be missed or misread as moments of compliance or co-optation. In this sense, evasive engagement serves as a key framework for understanding the coexistence, association, or integration of diverse types of politics.

Evasive engagement holds profound analytical and political relevance for today's world in which individuals and communities are increasingly subjected to ever-expanding and insidious regimes of surveillance and oppression, sharpened by the advance of digital computing technologies within the broader context of the global war on terror, "militarized global apartheid," and data-driven capitalism.[27] This mode of engagement with governing actors and institutions—without succumbing to submission or facilitating their surveillance and control—might offer a path for inhabiting and navigating geographies of state violence and other zones of oppression. By carving out spaces of evasion within the systems of rule and containment, evasive engagement can ultimately offer sly and impactful ways of resisting, refusing, and escaping, and serve as a basis for cultivating alternative relationalities both within and beyond these systems.

NOTES

Note on Naming

1. For the undeclared colonial rule in Kurdistan, see the Introduction. For a detailed analysis of racialization without naming, see Chapter 2.

2. I adopted and slightly adjusted this approach of referring to place names from anthropologist Marlene Schäfers, *Voices That Matter.*

Introduction

1. *Qaçax* is a Kurdified version of the Turkish *kaçak* (smuggled or illegal). In the Wan borderlands, *qaçax* was widely and colloquially used to refer to Kurdish smuggling economies, while *qaçaxçî*, a Kurdified version of Turkish expression *kaçakçı*, denoted smuggler. The Kurdish *qaçax* and the Turkish *kaçak* also refer to the illegal, the outlawed, and the fugitive in addition to smuggling and the smuggled, while the Kurdish *qaçaxçî* and the Turkish *kaçakçı* are used for smugglers. Elsewhere I define *kaçak/qaçax* as "inexhaustible capacity to escape" (Bozçalı, "Partners in Crime"). For an articulation of *kaçak* as political fugitivity that escapes state, capital, and family, see Ustundag, "Kaçak as a Mode."

2. For a detailed analysis of distinguishing between what states consider legitimate/illegitimate ("legal/illegal") and what certain social groups consider legitimate/illegitimate ("licit/illicit"), see Abraham and van Schendel, "Introduction."

3. For a discussion on political trials, see Ertür, *Spectacles and Specters.*

4. In political trials, Kurdish defendants (and lawyers) also developed a particular style of defense, "political defense" (*siyasi savunma*), similar to what Jacques Vergès (*Savunma Saldırıyor*) has called "rupture defense," in which defendants contest and reverse the state court's prosecutorial role, treating it as expressing state crimes in political defenses (see Hakyemez, "Margins of the Archive"; Chapter 3). Although Metin and other interlocutors used the terms "political crime" and "political trials" to refer to smuggling and smuggling court cases, none of them defined their defense as a political defense. For a

detailed discussion on Kurdish political groups and individuals' defenses in the Turkish courts, see Gündoğan, *Kawa Davası Savunması*.

5. *Partiya Karkerên Kurdistan*.

6. Bhabha, *The Location of Culture*.

7. Bhabha, *The Location of Culture*, 141.

8. Scholars have also read the discursive ambiguity that sly civility creates as a hidden transcript and suggest that sly civility resembles what Jim Scott (*Weapons of the Weak*; *Domination and the Arts of Resistance*) calls everyday resistance (see Jones, "It's Not [Just] Cricket"). I diverge from these readings because Scott's analysis relies on strict binaries between sites of domination and resistance that do not consider symbolic, cultural, or linguistic mediation across these sites (Gal, "Language and the 'Arts of Resistance'"). Sly civility, however, hinges on such mediations and thus involves mutual appropriations across the sites and actors of domination and resistance. Thus, the analytical lens of the hidden transcript and everyday resistance is limited in explicating sly civility and my articulation of sly legality.

9. Comaroff and Comaroff, "Law and Disorder in the Postcolony."

10. In the U.S., for example, labor and social movements turned to specific litigation campaigns to obtain new social rights, recruit new members, garner financial support, or raise public awareness about their cause (Scheingold, *The Politics of Rights*; Handler, *Lawyers and the Pursuit*; McCann, *Rights at Work*). For recent studies showing how rights advocacy groups engage with state courts to raise public awareness regarding their cause, even if they lose those legal cases, see Chua, "Collective Litigation," on China, and Narrain and Thiruvengadam, "Social Justice Lawyering," on India.

11. Anti-impunity activism views the lack of criminal prosecutions of individual perpetrators as the main reason for the continuation of human rights violations and so prioritizes individual criminal responsibility to reveal past violations, achieve the right to truth, and deter future violations (Sikkink, *The Justice Cascade*). A leading context in which anti-impunity activism emerged is the post-military-rule democracies in Latin America, where human rights lawyers and activists used foreign (European or American) courts to prosecute perpetrators of rights violations because the amnesties imposed by previous military governments blocked the prosecutions in domestic courts (Lutz and Sikkink, "International Human Rights Law"; Sikkink, *The Justice Cascade*). By using foreign and international courts to pressure domestic courts, these activists legally and politically contested the amnesties and eventually prosecuted rights violations in countries where they were committed, a phenomenon called the "boomerang effect" (Lutz and Sikkink, "International Human Rights Law").

However, anti-impunity activism has been criticized for viewing rights violations as isolated incidents committed by individual perpetrators and ignoring how state crimes have often been systemically conducted by various actors officially or unofficially affiliated with states, as well as for ignoring the broader political and economic conditions that perpetuate these crimes (Clarke, "Affective Justice"; Engle, "A Genealogy of the Criminal Turn").

12. Even if individuals or groups may successfully try state crimes in domestic or international courts, the court cases, which seem to be triumphs of human rights law, may

lead to what anthropologist Jessica Greenberg ("Counterpedagogy, Sovereignty, and Migration") calls "counterpedagogy," in which state authorities learn how to preemptively manipulate court procedures and evidence-making processes to render future crimes or human rights violations non-prosecutable.

13. For the deradicalization of political demands in the court, see Leachman, "From Protest to Perry." The deradicalization of political demands through litigation may also lead to the rearticulation of central matters of contention as if they required legal-technical solutions rather than political-structural changes—a phenomenon that resonates with what James Ferguson (*The Anti-Politics Machine*) calls "depoliticization," in the context of development projects: the process by which political inequalities demanding political solutions are understood as being technical problems that are solved through technical (nonpolitical) expertise and interventions (for a similar point, see Li, *The Will to Improve*). Thus, depoliticization depends on a division that the ruling authorities strategically claim and maintain between technical and political issues. Yet, conceptualizing technopolitics, other scholarly accounts (including this book) have shown that the political and the technical are not disparate sites of action and knowledge.

14. For analyses on how state (or liberal) legalities individualize otherwise collective sufferings and rights demands, see Engle, "A Genealogy of the Criminal Turn"; Kesselring, *Bodies of Truth*; Mamdani, "Amnesty or Impunity." When recognizing collective rights, such as Indigenous land rights claims, liberal state law takes reified and ahistorical cultural differences to base such rights recognitions, which may lead Indigenous groups to strategically essentialize otherwise contingent cultural practices and identities. For a critique of liberal legal articulation of culture as ahistorical and homogenized, see Hale, "Activist Research v. Cultural Critique"; Povinelli, *The Cunning of Recognition*.

15. De León, *The Land of Open Graves*; Sundberg, "Diabolic *Caminos* in the Desert"; Vogt, *Lives in Transit*.

16. Gallien and Weigand, *The Routledge Handbook of Smuggling*; McMurray, *In and Out of Morocco*.

17. Anthropologist Andrew Ong (*Stalemate*) has also articulated a form of (state) evasion through engagement in the context of Wa polity and its practice of regional autonomy, which avoided claiming independent statehood while rejecting full incorporation in Burmese statehood. Ong argues that there is no contradiction between evasion and negotiation; the evading actor can engage with the evaded and negotiate its level of engagement. In this articulation, the difference between evasion and negotiation seems to disappear and the acts of evasion may come to refer to the terms or compromises that are simply rejected (or renegotiated) in a negotiation. My articulation of evasive engagement, however, maintains a difference between evasion and negotiation and associates the former with an act of political refusal. Rather than negotiating or compromising to maintain certain smuggling activities in exchange for accepting the state authorities' restrictions on other activities, the smugglers and lawyers aimed to curtail the authorities' exercise of sovereign power over certain mobilities, lives, and livelihoods by engaging with the legal processes to corrode how these processes operate.

18. The implementation of colonization policies in Kurdistan dates back to the nineteenth century, during which the Ottoman imperial authorities deployed such policies in

the empire's peripheries and borderlands as part of their attempts to centralize and modernize the empire into a nation-state (Deringil, *The Well-Protected Domains*; Klein, *The Margins of Empire*; Kühn, "An Imperial Borderland as Colony"). Historian Janet Klein (*The Margins of Empire*) has identified the Hamidiye Light Cavalry Regiments as a site of such colonial policies in 1890s Ottoman Kurdistan.

19. Beşikçi, *Devletler Arası Sömürge Kürdistan*. İsmail Beşikçi is one of the first Turkish sociologists to conduct ethnographic fieldwork in Kurdistan and contest the denial of Kurdish people, Kurdistan, and its colonization. In doing so, he violated what sociologist Barış Ünlü ("The Kurdish Struggle") calls the "Turkishness contract" and lost his academic position and was imprisoned for more than seventeen years. Beşikçi first published his book *International Colony Kurdistan* (*Devletler Arası Sömürge Kürdistan*) in 1990. Although the book was banned shortly after its publication, it was printed clandestinely and reached a broader readership in leftist and Kurdish circles.

20. Comparing the colonial condition in Kurdistan to colonies in Africa, Asia, and Latin America, Beşikçi (*Devletler Arası Sömürge Kürdistan*) underlines that the colonizers of Kurdistan have denied the existence of Kurdish people and their homeland as distinct political and social entities and thus have avoided granting any political status to Kurdistan, including an official status as a colony. For this reason, Beşikçi calls Kurdistan, "a country that could not even be a colony" (*Devletler Arası Sömürge Kürdistan*, 14). Yet, while emphasizing the "statusless" (*statüsüz*) character of Kurdistan, Beşikçi seems to identify political status, even the status of being a colony, with nation-statehood, or at least the delineation of a bordered political entity. This approach ignores the cases of colonization that lack the creation of colonized or mandated states, such as the settler-colonialism that Indigenous peoples of North and South America, South African Black communities, or Palestinian people faced; the approach thus fails to draw similarities across the colonial condition in Kurdistan and these settler-colonial settings. For a discussion of settler-colonialism and colonized Kurdistan, see Yarkın, "İnkâr Edilen Hakikat Sömürge."

Other scholars have also suggested the concept of an "internal colony" to describe the colonial situation in Kurdistan, as the Kurdish population in each non-Kurdish nation-state has been colonized by the dominant national-ethnic group within the borders of the same country rather than by a separate, geographically distant state (Kurt, "My Muslim Kurdish Brother"; Salih, "Internal Cultural Imperialism"; Soleimani and Mohammadpour, "Life and Labor on the Internal Colonial"). In doing so, however, these works fall into methodological nationalism and reproduce the colonial borders dividing Kurdistan (for a similar critique, see Göner, "Rightful Recognition of Kurdistan"). For a genealogy of the Kurdistan as colony thesis, see Duruiz, "Tracing the Conceptual Genealogy"; Kurt and Özok-Gündoğan, "The Decolonial Turn in Kurdish Studies."

21. Beşikçi, *Devletler Arası Sömürge Kürdistan*.

22. The hostilities among the governments colonizing Kurdistan are exemplified by the Iran-Iraq War (1980–1988) and most recently the Turkish military's invasion of northern Syrian regions in 2018 and 2019. As part of such hostilities, these governments may even support Kurdish liberation movements within another's jurisdiction while continuing to oppress the Kurdish people under their own rule. For instance, the Iranian

government supported the Mullah Mustafa Barzani–led Kurdish revolt in Iraq during the 1960s and 1970s and, throughout the Iran-Iraq war, each government supported and recruited Kurdish armed groups that contested the other government (van Bruinessen, "The Kurds Between Iran and Iraq"). Similarly, in the 1980s and 1990s, the Syrian government condoned the PKK militants' use of Syrian lands to access the PKK camp in Lebanon's Beqaa Valley and the PKK leader Abdullah Öcalan's residence in Damascus. Yet, the governments colonizing Kurdistan often ensured that their support for Kurdish movements in rival states remained mostly provisional and never threatened the international colonization of Kurdistan.

The ultimate collaboration among the colonizing governments to maintain colonial rule in each part of Kurdistan geography has been recently illustrated by how the Turkish and Iranian governments strongly joined the Iraqi central government's rejection of the 2017 Kurdish Independence Referendum, which was unilaterally held in areas controlled by the Kurdistan Regional Government (KRG) in Iraq. Despite the close political and economic partnership that the Turkish government developed with the KRG, particularly the Kurdistan Democratic Party (*Partiya Demokrat a Kurdistanê*, PDK) at the expense of the Iraqi central government, Turkish authorities swiftly left the partnership, which included economic interests tied to the Iraqi Kurdish oil sector, and supported the Iraqi central government by launching a military operation with the Iraqi central army on the Turkey–KRG border a few days before the referendum; they threatened the KRG with a military invasion and halted land border crossings and civilian flights after the referendum. Because the 2017 Referendum appeared as a step toward Kurdish assertion and execution of self-determination and therefore a clear contestation of the international colonization of Kurdistan, it led to a swift, radical policy change from the Turkish government.

23. My articulation of inter-coloniality builds on Aníbal Quijano's ("Coloniality and Modernity/Rationality") concept of coloniality, which highlights the persistence of power, oppression, and exploitation beyond the formal end of colonial rule. In the Kurdish context, however, colonial rule has neither ended nor been officially declared. Therefore, inter-coloniality in Kurdistan should be understood as undeclared yet powerful systems of colonial domination.

24. The undeclared character of the Turkish government's colonial rule in Kurdistan is exemplified by secret governmental policy papers and reports prepared on Kurdistan. In these documents, which were discovered in the 1990s, state officials recommended the implementation of "colonial" policies in Kurdistan (Yarkın, "İnkâr Edilen Hakikat Sömürge"). Despite these secret reports and exchanges between state officials, the colonial character of the implemented policies has never been declared or accepted by the Turkish government.

25. Zeydanlıoğlu, "Turkey's Kurdish Language Policy"; Derince, "A Break or Continuity?"

26. Veli Yadirgi (*The Political Economy of the Kurds*) suggests de-development, rather than underdevelopment, as a conceptual framework for describing how state policies toward Kurdistan from the first quarter of the twentieth century to the 2010s. These policies not only excluded Kurdish lands from the state's development schemes and

investments but actively undermined the conditions for any independent economic dynamic to thrive in the region.

27. Kurdish communities led by tribal and religious leaders and other provincial notables forged an alliance with the Grand National Assembly government (or Ankara government) led by Mustafa Kemal during the War of Independence and fought against Greek and French forces in Western and Southern Turkey. In addition to the Kemalist regime's denial of Kurdish autonomy, the end of the Kurdish-Kemalist alliance could also be attributed to the abolition of the caliphate and, despite Mustafa Kemal's early promises to the Kurdish leaders, the new regime's inaction in liberating southern Kurdistan (Başûr) from the British forces (Bozarslan, "Kurds and the Turkish State").

28. In secret governmental policy papers, Turkish officials addressed that Kurdish lands must not be governed through Turkish laws but through a set of separate (mostly martial) laws and regulations, thereby illustrating the colonial character of special laws imposed in Kurdistan (Yarkın, "İnkâr Edilen Hakikat Sömürge").

29. Hamit Bozarslan ("Kurds and the Turkish State") describes Kurdish resistance in the early Republican period (1923–1938) as "years of revolt" and the following absence of political mobilization (1938–1961) as "the period of silence." In greater Kurdistan, a period of silence, in the sense of the lack of organized Kurdish political resistance, prevailed from the defeat of the Kurdistan Republic in Mahabad in December 1946 to 1961, when Mullah Mustafa Barzani, who had returned to Iraq from exile following the 1958 military coup, launched a rebellion in southern Kurdistan (Garapon and Çelik, "From Tribal Chiefs to Marxist Activists"). For the Kurdish Republic in Mahabad, a Kurdish state that existed for eleven months in 1946 before it was ended by the Iranian forces, see Vali, *Kurds and the State in Iran*.

30. As part of the Kurdish political revival among the urban elite in this period, the PDK/Bakur (Kurdistan Democratic Party/North, *Partiya Demokrat a Kurdistan/Bakur*), a pro-Kurdish political party, was illegally founded in 1965.

31. The protest meetings, known as Eastern Meetings (*Doğu Mitingleri*), were organized by Kurdish activists who were involved with TİP (Workers' Party of Turkey, *Türkiye İşçi Partisi*), a legal left-wing political party, and evolved into the foundation of a network of Kurdish youth clubs. These clubs were organized under the name of DDKO (Revolutionary Eastern Culture Hearts, *Devrimci Doğu Kültür Ocakları*).

32. Jean Comaroff and John Comaroff define lawfare as "the resort to legal instruments, to the violence inherent in the law, to commit acts of political coercion, even erasure" ("Law and Disorder in the Postcolony," 30).

33. Bayir, *Minorities and Nationalism in Turkish Law*. The anti-Kurdish lawfare campaigns can be tracked back to 1959 and the prosecutions known as the trial of the 49'ers (*49'lar davası*) that began in 1961. After three Kurdish intellectuals published a poem in Kurdish, these three and forty-seven other Kurdish intellectuals, including writers, journalists, artists, and lawyers, were detained in September 1959. Because one of them died under detention, these Kurdish intellectuals were called the 49'ers. More than six months after the detentions, in May 1960, there was a military coup. The intellectuals spent fourteen months in detainment and their prosecution began in January 1961 under the military rule. The prosecutions ended in 1965, and fifteen intellectuals received prison sentences.

34. For the articulation of the Kurdistan as colony thesis among Kurdish student and political movements, see Jongerden and Akkaya, *PKK Üzerine Yazılar*. The Kurdistan as colony thesis was not welcomed by a majority of Turkish leftist groups. A leading Turkish leftist group in the second half of the 1970s, Dev-Yol (Revolutionary-Path), for example, contested this thesis by arguing that Turkey was a semi-colony, which was formally an independent state but economically and politically colonized by Western imperialist powers, and suggesting that only a capitalist state can be a colonizer; therefore Turkey, as a semi-colony, could not be considered as a colonizer of Kurdistan (Jongerden, "Colonialism, Self-determination and Independence"). For the emergence of competing Kurdish leftist groups in the latter half of the 1970s, see Güneş, *The Kurdish National Movement*; Jongerden and Akkaya, *PKK Üzerine Yazılar*.

35. In the 1977 local elections, socialist Kurdish candidate Mehdi Zana won the city municipality of Diyarbekir/Amed as an independent candidate. In the municipal elections held following the resignation of the elected mayors, independent Kurdish candidates supported by Kurdish revolutionaries led by Abdullah Öcalan—Edip Solmaz in Sêrt (Off. Siirt)'s Êlih (Off. Batman) district and Nadir Temel in Riha (Off. Urfa)'s Curnê Reş (Off. Hilvan) district—won their respective municipalities in 1979. Twenty-eight days after his election, Edip Solmaz was killed by an unknown assailant in November 1979, while Nadir Temel was removed from office in April 1980 and later arrested. Mehdi Zana was also removed from office and arrested following the military coup of September 1980.

36. The political group that evolved into the PKK was first known as the Kurdistan Revolutionaries (*Kürdistan Devrimcileri*) and was led by Abdullah Öcalan. The group decided to establish a new revolutionary party in November 1978 in a hamlet in Diyarbekir/Amed's Licê (Off. Lice) district, but the name of the new party, the PKK, was determined later in April 1979. For the accounts of PKK's foundation and its ideology, see Güneş, *The Kurdish National Movement*; Jongerden and Akkaya, *PKK Üzerine Yazılar*.

37. The military junta detained over 650,000 people, prosecuted more than 240,000 detainees, revoked the citizenship of 14,000 individuals, tortured thousands of detainees, and executed over 50.

38. The military authorities also removed and imprisoned the independently elected mayor of Diyarbekir/Amed alongside thousands of Kurdish revolutionaries.

39. The Emergency Rule Regional Governorship (*Olağanüstü Hal Bölge Valiliği*, OHAL) had jurisdiction over Çewlîk (Off. Bingöl), Diyarbekir/Amed, Xarpêt (Off. Elazığ), Colemêrg, Mêrdîn, Sêrt, Dersim (Off. Tunceli), Wan, and Şirnex (Off. Şırnak) and Êlih, two provinces that had been part of Sêrt province and were declared as new provinces in May 1990. While these provinces covered most of Turkey's conditions, the OHAL jurisdiction could also be extended to "neighboring" (*mücavir*) provinces of Semsûr (Off. Adıyaman), Mûş and Bedlîs, which were either predominantly or partially Kurdish-populated. Consequently, the OHAL region ruled most of the northern Kurdistan. The OHAL governors, or super-governors, were granted extraordinary authority; for instance, they could ban any media outlet or exile individuals or settlements.

40. Marking Kurds/Kurdishness/Kurdistan without naming them/it can be considered a specific form of racialization that the Turkish officials developed against the Kurds

under the undeclared colonial domination of Kurdistan. For a discussion on this mode of racialization, see Koğacıoğlu, "Knowledge, Practice, and Political Community"; and Chapter 2.

41. After a key party member was captured by the Turkish police, the PKK's leader Abdullah Öcalan left Turkey for Syria in the summer of 1979 with the help of Kurdish smugglers with whom Öcalan connected via another party member from the borderland region. In Syria, Öcalan secured the PKK's cooperation with the Palestinian revolutionary organizations, mainly the Democratic Front for the Liberation of Palestine and to a lesser extent the Popular Front for the Liberation of Palestine, and transferred almost three hundred militants to Lebanon before the devastating 1980 military coup in Turkey (Akkaya, "The Palestinian Dream"). While the Palestinian organization procured Palestinian refugee ID cards for PKK members and thus facilitated their mobility in Syria and Lebanon, the PKK cadres cooperated with local Kurdish smuggling networks to transfer party members from Turkey to Syria (Akkaya, "The Palestinian Dream").

42. The PKK forces resisted Israel's 1982 invasion of Lebanon, losing ten fighters in the clashes while fifteen PKK members were captured by Israeli military and spent time in Israeli prisons. Based on its participation in defending Lebanon against the invasion, in 1983, the PKK obtained its own camp place, the Helweh camp in the Beqaa Valley, which it held until September 1992 (Akkaya, "The Palestinian Dream"). In July 1983, the PKK also reached an agreement with the PDK to station its forces along the Turkish-Iraqi border (Gunter, "A de Facto Kurdish State"). Although the PDK withdrew from such agreement at the end of 1987, the PKK has since maintained its military presence across the Iraqi-Turkish borderlands and southern Kurdistan within the borders of Iraq (Gunter, "A de Facto Kurdish State").

43. Between 1990 and 1993, popular uprisings, known as *serhildan* in Kurdish, erupted in several Kurdish cities and towns. These uprisings could last for several days and were supported by various sectors of the urban population, who joined street protests, clashed with security forces, shuttered their stores in protest, and boycotted schools. The first uprising occurred in Nusaybin during the funeral of PKK guerrillas in 1990, which was one of the first public funerals held by the families of the slain guerrillas in Kurdistan (Marcus, *Blood and Belief*). For more on urban uprisings and their role in Kurdish liberation politics, see Westrheim, "Taking to the Streets"; O'Connor, *Understanding Insurgency*. For the use of Newroz (the Northern Hemisphere's vernal equinox) celebrations and related mythologies as a means of political mobilization, see Aydın, "Mobilising the Kurds in Turkey"; Rudi, "The PKK's Newroz."

44. O'Connor, *Understanding Insurgency*.

45. For a detailed analysis of the state's counterinsurgency war and how it reshaped smuggling in Kurdistan, see Chapter 1.

46. *Halkın Emek Partisi*.

47. The leading central-left party at the time was the Social Democratic Populist Party (*Sosyal Demokrat Halkçı Parti*, SHP).

48. Because of the difficulty of receiving 10 percent of the national vote required for gaining seats in the parliament, the HEP-supported pro-Kurdish candidates entered elections in the SHP's lists. As the SHP failed to go beyond the mainstream political position

regarding Kurdish political demands, the pro-Kurdish deputies left the SHP and joined the HEP in July 1992.

49. Güneş, *The Kurdish National Movement.*

50. *Halkların Demokratik Partisi.*

51. *Barış ve Demokrasi Partisi.*

52. Babül, *Bureaucratic Intimacies*; Can, "Human Rights, Humanitarianism, and State Violence." Before the 1980 coup, human rights organizations were established or supported by some leftist circles, yet these organizations did not last long and disappeared after a few years because organizing political movements and parties were thought to be more urgent than human rights advocacy (Çalı, "Human Rights Organizations in Turkey").

53. *İnsan Hakları Derneği.*

54. Kurban, *Limits of the Supranational Justice.*

55. In June 1991, a bomb was denoted in Diyarbekir/Amed İHD's office. In February 1993, human rights lawyer Metin Can and Hasan Kaya, a medical doctor from Xarpêt İHD branch, were kidnapped and killed.

56. Kurban, *Limits of the Supranational Justice*; Watts, "Institutionalizing Virtual Kurdistan West."

57. A few human rights lawyers who became politicians with leading roles in pro-Kurdish electoral politics in the 2000s and onward include the former co-chair of pro-Kurdish HDP Selahattin Demirtaş; the former mayor of Diyarbekir/Amed and a former HDP parliamentarian Osman Baydemir; and another HDP parliamentarian, Meral Danış Beştaş, who had all been former members of the board of İHD's Diyarbekir/Amed branch.

However, some lawyers who took prominent roles in Kurdish electoral politics and were elected as mayors or members of parliament faced criticism for adopting a utilitarian approach to their rights advocacy work and turning it into a means of pursuing a political career. In addition to these complaints, some lawyers were criticized for requesting significant portions, sometimes as much as half, of the settlements their clients received as compensation for state-committed rights abuses. In my research, I encountered lawyers who charged up to one third of the compensation awarded to their clients and those who offered pro bono or reduced-fee legal services.

58. Akarsu, "We're Tired of This Weber Guy!"; Babül, *Bureaucratic Intimacies*; Babül, "Radical Once More."

59. Hakyemez, *Lives and Times of Militancy*; Yonucu, "The Absent Present Law"; Yonucu, *Police, Provocation, Politics.*

60. Le Ray, "Experiencing Justice and Imagining State"; Biner, "Documenting 'Truth' in the Margins"; Biner, *States of Dispossession.*

61. *Koma Civakên Kurdistanê.*

62. While local and international human rights advocates accused the Turkish police of the killing, a Diyarbekir/Amed-based criminal court acquitted the accused police officers. For a comprehensive analysis of Elçi's murder, see the report prepared by the international human rights research agency Forensic Architecture ("The Killing of Tahir Elçi"), which suggests that the police officers at the scene were the most likely perpetrators.

63. Jasanoff, *Science at the Bar*; Lynch and Cole, "Science and Technology Studies on Trial." Richard Wilson ("Expert Evidence on Trial") also discusses how a similar "clash-of-epistemologies" approach has been suggested to explain the law's encounter with anthropological knowledge and other social sciences. For examples of this approach, see Anders, "Testifying about 'Uncivilized Events'"; Good, "Cultural Evidence in Courts of Law"; Kelsall, *Culture under Cross-examination*.

64. Although scientific epistemology denies universal decisiveness and accepts the irreducible possibility of negation of scientific truth claims, legal authorities may treat technoscientific knowledge as stable, certain, and definitive (Lynch and Cole, "Science and Technology Studies on Trial").

65. Legal decisions and legal truth claims must not be understood as being absolute. Instead, courts decide based on standards, such as "beyond a reasonable doubt," that also acknowledge an irreducible level of uncertainty (Kruse, *The Social Life of Forensic Evidence*). Also, for a discussion on how technoscientific evidence needs to be construed and thus constructed within specific legal contexts, see Clarke and Kendall, ""The Beauty Is That It Speaks for Itself.'"

66. Latour, *The Making of Law*; Bergen and Solan, "The Uneasy Relationship."

67. Examining the development of nuclear weapon technologies in the context of the Cold War, historian Gabrielle Hecht has defined technopolitics as the "strategic practice of designing or using technology to constitute, embody, or enact political goals" (Hecht, *The Radiance of France*, 15). Timothy Mitchell (*Rule of Experts*) has shifted the analytical focus on state authorities' use of technology to how technopolitical processes create connections across apparently unrelated processes and thus lead to unintended consequences.

68. Technopolitics may have unintended consequences and connections as well as enable disenfranchised groups to bypass states' regimes of control or obtain illegal or informal forms of access to natural or public resources (Anand, *Hydraulic City*; Björkman, *Pipe Politics, Contested Waters*; Degani, *The City Electric*; Gupta, "An Anthropology of Electricity"; Mitchell, *Rule of Experts*; Mitchell, *Carbon Democracy*; Schnitzler, "Citizenship Prepaid"; Schnitzler, *Democracy's Infrastructure*). Taking advantage of the governments' search of popular legitimacy, these groups might negotiate semi-legal guarantees for their illegal or informal gains (Anand, *Hydraulic City*; Björkman, *Pipe Politics, Contested Waters*). In this manner, these population groups performed what Partha Chatterjee calls the "politics of the governed" (*Politics of the Governed*). Given that the specific technopolitical arrangements that enable illegal/informal gains can be further secured in exchange for electoral support or another means of popular legitimacy, this form of politics could also be called "technopolitics of the governed."

69. As a sub-regional administrative center, the city of Wan hosted regional appeals courts. While district courts in Wan and neighboring provinces were the initial judicial authorities that processed smuggling allegations, the appeal processes brought various cases to Wan's central courts.

70. The Grand National Assembly of Turkey, "Akaryakıt Kaçakçılığının Ekonomiye, İnsan ve Çevre Sağlığına."

71. Türkiye Büyük Millet Meclisi [The Grand National Assembly of Turkey]. "TBMM İnsan Haklarını İnceleme Komisyonu Faaliyet Raporu 23. Dönem 4. Yasama Yılı Ekim

2009–Ekim 2010 [Activity Report of the Parliamentary Investigation Commission on Human Rights, October 2009–October 2010]." November 2010, https://www5.tbmm .gov.tr/ihtisas_komisyonlari_dosyalari/fr_23_4_et.pdf.

72. See Akad, *Hudutların Kanunu*; Gören, *Katırcılar*; Ghobadi, *A Time for Drunken Horses*.

73. In transporting contraband cargos across rocky and icy borderlands, Kurdish smugglers relied on pack animals, mules, and horses. Acknowledging the indispensable role that the horses and mules play, I refer to these animals as smuggler animals (see also Bozçalı, "Partners in Crime").

74. The minimum monthly income at the time of my fieldwork was $400.

75. Arbitrage is often defined in relation to financial arbitrage, which refers to the simultaneous purchasing and selling of financial assets in two distinct markets to profit from a price differential (Miyazaki, *Arbitraging Japan*). Arbitrage in the sense of value creation and capture through price differentials can happen in various other contexts, such as everyday cash economies (Guyer, *Marginal Gains*) and corporate employment strategies (Ong, *Neoliberalism as Exception*; Mannov, "Maritime Piracy and the Ambiguous Art of Existential Arbitrage"). Because arbitrage requires price differences across the commodities that present similar qualities or functions, other scholars have examined the material and discursive practices that make or pretend to make otherwise different commodities have similar functions or qualities that enable pharmaceutical or chemical arbitrage (Peterson, *Speculative Markets*) or contraband commerce of coffee (Donovan, "Magendo").

76. For a similar point, see Özcan, "Yüksekova'da Sınır Deneyimleri."

77. To carry a few hundred liters of diesel fuel, a modified passenger car, minibus, or pickup truck was used. For bulkier items, such as tea, sugar, or cigarettes, or a large volume of oil products, carrier smugglers used cargo vans, mini-size trucks, or cargo trucks and semitrailer trucks.

78. For a critique of studies of smuggling and other illegal economies that systematically ignore the role and agency of women, see Schuster, "Gender and Smuggling."

79. While my analysis focuses on state sovereignty, forms of sovereignty claimed and exercised by state authorities, it relies on anthropological approaches that do not equate sovereignty solely with statehood—particularly the nation-state and the Westphalian inter-state order—but instead understand it as the "exercise of authority within regimes of power," claimed, performed, and contested by various actors in different institutional, relational, or spatial contexts (Bryant, "Sovereignty," 1). Based on these insights, I demonstrate how legal proceduralism becomes a key site not just for claiming and performing state sovereignty but also for unsettling it, in the sense of contesting sovereignty claims without making counterclaims for sovereign supremacy or equality. For a discussion on unsettling sovereignty, see Bonilla, "Unsettling Sovereignty."

80. For an example of such articulation of legal procedures, see Burns, *A Theory of the Trial*.

81. Lazarus-Black, "The Rites of Domination"; Kelly, *This Side of Silence*; Chatterjee, "The Impunity Effect"; Chatterjee, *Composing Violence*; Akarsu, "We're Tired of This Weber Guy!"

82. Schmitt, *Political Theology*; Agamben, *Homo Sacer*; Agamben, *State of Exception*.

83. Hansen and Stepputat, "Sovereignty Revisited."

84. For a historical account of the legal-procedural notion of "reasonable doubt," see Whitman, *The Origins of Reasonable Doubt*.

85. Whitman, *The Origins of Reasonable Doubt*.

86. For a similar discussion of legal procedures in modern law, see Cover, "Violence and the Word."

87. Nasser Hussain ("Hyperlegality") has conceptualizes "hyperlegality" to denote to the phenomenon of increasing bureaucratization manifested through the creation of additional regulations, procedures, and institutions that govern legal exceptions in the context of the global war on terror and antiterrorism legislation.

88. Benjamin, "Critique of Violence." The German *gewalt* can be translated in different ways that range from "violence" to "(legitimate) authority," "power," "order," or "force" (Lloyd, "From the Critique of Violence to the Critique of Rights"; Derrida, "Force of Law").

89. Agamben, *State of Exception*.

90. To break this cycle, Benjamin ("Critique of Violence") formulates "divine violence," an act that aims to refuse and destroy the existing legal system without creating yet another legal order, by considering a general strike, rather than strikes that aim at specific demands from specific employers, as an exemplary of such acts.

91. Hansen, "Performers of Sovereignty."

92. Campt, "Black Visuality and the Practice of Refusal"; McGranahan, "Theorizing Refusal"; McGranahan, "Refusal as Political Practice"; Prasse-Freeman, "Resistance/Refusal"; Prasse-Freeman, *Rights Refused*; Shange, "Black Girl Ordinary"; Simpson, *Mohawk Interruptus*; Simpson, "The Ruse of Consent and the Anatomy of 'Refusal'"; Sojoyner, "Another Life Is Possible"; Weiss, "Refusal as Act, Refusal as Abstention."

93. For a formulation of refusal as a critique and response to liberal politics of recognition, see Simpson, *Mohawk Interruptus*; Coulthard, *Red Skin, White Masks*.

94. McGranahan, "Theorizing Refusal"; McGranahan, "Refusal as Political Practice."

95. For a discussion of how Indigenous peoples interacted with the U.S. authorities to express their refusal of the latter's sovereign supremacy (even though the U.S. counterparts did not register such refusals) and tried to enact sovereign-to-sovereign interactions with the U.S., see Richland, *Cooperation without Submission*. Sarah Wright ("When Dialogue Means Refusal") has also stated that dialogue can be an act of political refusal as long as it facilitates expression and performance of refusal to the superiority-claiming authorities.

96. McGranahan, "Refusal as Political Practice"; Prasse-Freeman, "Resistance/Refusal."

97. Anthropologist Elliot Prasse-Freeman (*Rights Refused*) offers a similar critique and suggests that refusal politics leaves the trajectory of political action to the sovereign superiority-claiming party's initiative and hence can lead to political passivism.

98. For another articulation of political refusal as an act of resistance, see Prasse-Freeman, *Rights Refused*.

99. *Toplum ve Hukuk Araştırmaları Vakfı*.

100. A group of Kurdish lawyers founded a law office to represent Abdullah Öcalan, monitored his health and whether he was exposed to any rights violations, and shared Öcalan's thoughts and statements with the outside world. However, the state authorities heavily restricted Öcalan's meetings with his lawyers and relatives. For example, since July 2011, his lawyers had visited Öcalan only once, in May 2019.

101. Only one temporary first-degree criminal court judge asked me not to attend hearings. To avoid conflict, I skipped this judge's court proceedings.

102. See note 16 above.

103. In addition to family names and affiliations, I was mindful of other types of information, such as specific disputes in which families were involved, unique smuggling techniques, or specific smuggled goods, that may make it possible for community insiders to identify my interlocutors.

104. For ethnographic refusal, see Simpson, *Mohawk Interruptus*; Shange, "Black Girl Ordinary." For a formulation of (Black) fugitivity as method and "knowledge-making" that aims at "becoming undisciplined," see Gross-Wyrtzen and Moulton, "Toward 'Fugitivity as Method,'" as well as Harney and Moten, *The Undercommons*; Kelley, "Black Study, Black Struggle."

Chapter One

1. The Armenian resistance began on April 19, 1915, amid the arrival of Armenian refugees fleeing mass massacres in the countryside and attacks on the Armenian neighborhoods in the old city (Hovannissian, *Armenian Van/Vaspurakan*; Akçam, *A Shameful Act*). The resistance secured control of the old city and neighborhoods around the Wan citadel, declared self-government, and created a safe haven for the refugees fleeing from the genocide committed in the countryside. The Ottoman forces regained control of the city center twice before the Russian army expelled them in September 1915. Following the withdrawal of the Russian army in the wake of the Bolshevik revolution in the summer of 1917, Wan Armenians established a second self-government, which survived until the Ottoman military recaptured the city center in April 1918.

2. These monopolies were established in capitulated, bilateral trade agreements that the Empire made with European states, primarily France (Birdal, *The Political Economy of Ottoman Public Debt*).

3. In 1879, tobacco monopolies were first given to the Ottoman Public Debt Administration, which had been established to collect payments owed to European creditors who sent representatives to its governing council (Birdal, *The Political Economy of Ottoman Public Debt*).

4. Birdal, *The Political Economy of Ottoman Public Debt*.

5. The republican authorities claimed monopolies of tobacco, alcohol beverages, salt, match gunpowder, and explosives in the 1930s and 1940s. In 1983, the State Monopoly Directorate, which operated under the Ministry of Customs and Monopolies, became a state-owned Public Economic Enterprise (*Kamu İktisadi Teşebbüsü*) known as TEKEL A.Ş. The alcoholic beverages division of TEKEL was privatized in 2004, while the tobacco division followed in 2008.

6. Öztan, "The Great Depression and the Making of Turkish-Syrian Border."

7. In the nineteenth century, China emerged as a leading market for opium consumption as a result of the British East India Company's policy of maintaining the trade. Despite the eventual prohibition of opium in China, the British merchants continued to supply it illegally—even after Chinese authorities destroyed British-owned opium cargo in the Opium Wars between the Qing dynasty and the British Empire. The British victory in the war opened the Chinese domestic market to Indian and Ottoman opium traded by British merchants (Gingeras, *Heroin, Organized Crime*).

8. Gingeras, *Heroin, Organized Crime*; Erdinç, *Overdose Türkiye*.

9. The first factory was owned by a consortium that included four (two Muslim and two Armenian) citizens of Turkey and a Belgian-Mexican citizen who was a known, key actor in global heroin smuggling; an Armenian-Turkish citizen and a Japanese citizen owned the second factory; and the third was run by a Jewish family of Turkish nationality (Gingeras, *Heroin, Organized Crime*).

10. Öztan, "The Great Depression and the Making of Turkish-Syrian Border."

11. Öztan, "The Great Depression and the Making of Turkish-Syrian Border."

12. Gingeras, *Heroin, Organized Crime*.

13. The rebellion was led by the Naqshbandi Shaikh Said of Piran, and Turkish forces suppressed the rebellion in April 1925 (see Olson, *The Emergence of Kurdish Nationalism*; van Bruinessen, *Agha, Sheikh, and State*).

14. Çelik, "Challenging State Borders"; Öztan "The Great Depression and the Making of Turkish-Syrian Border."

15. While Kurdish insurgents escaped persecution from Turkey by migrating to Syria in the 1920s and 1930s, Turkish authorities pressed the French authorities to disarm and surveil these refugees and relocate them (initially at least thirty kilometers and later fifty kilometers) away from the border (Altuğ, "The Turkish-Syrian Border and Politics of Difference"; White, *The Emergence of Minorities in the Middle East*).

16. Altuğ, "The Turkish-Syrian Border and Politics of Difference."

17. The 1931 report could be considered as "the founding text in the construction of smuggling as 'national problem'" (Çelik, "Challenging State Borders," 166).

18. Çelik, "Challenging State Borders."

19. For the period between 1938 and 1952, Neşe Özgen ("Sınırın İktisadi Antropolojisi") has noted that oil, salt, roll paper, paper, bulbs, and lamp mantles were smuggled from Syria to Turkey, while tobacco, fish, molasses, and cut and trimmed wood were smuggled out of Turkey. For the same period, across Turkey's borders with Syria, Iraq, and Iran, İsmail Beşikçi (*Doğu Anadolu'nun Düzeni*) lists textiles, fabrics, oil products, lamps, glassware, and carpet as the main items smuggled into Turkey, while sheep were mainly smuggled out of the country.

20. Aras, *The Wall*; Özgen, "Sınırın İktisadi Antropolojisi."

21. Aras, *The Wall*; Özgen, "Sınırın İktisadi Antropolojisi"; Beşikçi, *Doğu Anadolu'nun Düzeni*.

22. Şenoğuz, "Ahlaki Ekonominin Sınırları."

23. Beşikci, *Doğu Anadolu'nun Düzeni*.

24. In explicating the surprisingly central role of Licê in Turkey's smuggling economies, Adnan Çelik ("Challenging State Borders") stresses that the province was at a

crossroads of trade routes that linked Syria, Iran, and western and northern Anatolia, and families in the province had engaged in long-distance caravan trade in the Ottoman, pre-Republican era.

25. Gingeras, *Heroin, Organized Crime.*

26. Çelik, "Challenging State Borders"; Gingeras, *Heroin, Organized Crime.*

27. The business partnership between Behçet Cantürk, a leading opium/heroin smuggler from Licê and of Kurdish-Armenian descent, and Avni Karadurmuş (known as Sarı Avni, Avni the Blonde), an Istanbul-based smuggler originally from the Black Sea region, illustrated the connections between the Kurdish and Black Sea smugglers in the 1970s (Yalçın, *Behçet Cantürk'ün Anıları*). Following the coup d'état of 1980, Karadurmuş relocated to Zurich, Switzerland, to protect himself from the military junta and maintain relations with his Italian smuggling contacts. Cantürk was also accused of supporting Armenian and Kurdish insurgents in the early 1980s and eventually was kidnapped and executed by a state paramilitary group in January 1994 (Bozarslan, *Network-Building, Ethnicity and Violence in Turkey*; Çelik, "Challenging State Borders").

28. Yalçın, *Behçet Cantürk'ün Anıları.*

29. The leading figures of the racketeers of the time were Dündar Kılıç and İdris Özbir (İdris the Kurd), and the smugglers were Uğurlu family, Bülent Çelenk, Mihri family, Avni Karadurmuş, and İsmail Hacısüleymanoğlu, Kılıç's brother-in-law (Yurdakul, *Abi*). Having been based in Istanbul, these smugglers were originally from the Black Sea region and northern Kurdistan.

30. *Milliyetçi Hareket Partisi.*

31. Among those smuggler bosses, Abuzer Uğurlu was a key figure. Coming from a family of Kurdish smugglers from Malatya, Uğurlu had right-wing political affiliations and helped Abdullah Çatlı, a notorious ultranationalist militant, who received counterguerrilla training and engaged in killing seven leftist students in Ankara on October 8, 1978 (the Bahçelievler Massacre), to leave Turkey illegally after the 1980 military coup and be stationed in Europe. Uğurlu also helped another ultranationalist militant who attempted to assassinate the pope in 1981. Through Uğurlu's smuggling network in Europe, Çatlı engaged in arms and drug smuggling while conducting counterguerrilla operations against leftist, pro-Armenian, and pro-Kurdish circles in and outside of Turkey. Uğurlu also worked as an informant for MİT (National Intelligence Organization) as early as 1974 (Gingeras, *Heroin, Organized Crime*).

32. These militants were blamed for various attacks and assassinations, including killing seven leftist students in Ankara (the Bahçelievler Massacre) and killing more than a hundred people during the seven-day-long attacks on Alevi neighborhoods in Kahramanmaraş city center (Söyler, *The Turkish Deep State*; Üngör, *Paramilitarism*). As anthropologist Deniz Yonucu (*Police, Provocation, Politics*) has noted, these counterguerrilla attacks mainly aimed to provoke further right-wing violence and the involvement of the military. Before the Kahramanmaraş Massacre, for example, a bomb attack on a movie theater owned by a right-wing figure was organized by counterguerrilla right-wing militants to provoke right-wing retaliation against leftist and Alevi groups in the city. Following the massacre, martial law was imposed in thirteen provinces, including the Kurdish provinces along the Turkish-Syrian border and Diyarbekir/Amed.

33. Bozarslan, *Network-Building, Ethnicity and Violence in Turkey*.

34. One such case was shared with me by my father, Hikmet Bozçalı, who was a Kurdish student leader in the 1970s. Together with another Kurdish student, he received twelve handguns financed by Kurdish filmmaker and actor Yılmaz Güney and supplied by two established figures of the Istanbul underworld, Dündar Kılıç and Kürt İdris (Özbir).

35. The Grand National Assembly of Turkey, "Akaryakıt Kaçakçılığının Ekonomiye, İnsan ve Çevre Sağlığına."

36. Accurately determining the actual economic cost of the armed conflict between the Turkish military and Kurdish guerrillas is difficult in part because the war expenses were provided through both budgetary and non-budgetary funds, such as Saving Incentive Fund (*Tassaruf Teşvik Fonu*), and confidential or slush funds allocated for national security expenses, such as covert appropriation (*örtülü ödenek*), that were available to the government and certain state agencies (Doğan, *Savaş Ekonomisi*). Moreover, the cost of the war cannot be reduced to military expenditures. As Servet Mutlu ("The Economic Cost of Civil Conflict in Turkey") emphasizes, there were significant indirect economic costs, such as the opportunity cost of foregone investments or the financial cost of domestic and external borrowing. Considering different forms of expenses, Mutlu estimates the cost of the conflict ranged from $147.79 billion to $169.17 billion between 1990 and 2008. Moreover, Mutlu suggests that the military expenses increased the annual budget deficits at different rates, from 4.32 percent to 24.55 percent, between 1990 and 2005.

37. An interview with a PKK executive council member and guerrilla commander Duran Kalkan, "Büyük kazandık [We won big]." *ANF News*, August 13, 2018, available at https://firatnews.com/kadin/bueyuek-kazandik-111972.

38. The reason for the cancellation was controversial. While Ali Ömürcan (known as Terzi Cemal), the commander of the guerrilla group who was supposed to conduct the attack, claimed that he had received the attack order late, PKK leadership denied the commander's assertions and later accused him of treason for intentionally canceling the attack (Karayılan, *Bir Savaşın Anatomisi*). The commander was executed by the PKK in 1992.

39. O'Connor, *Understanding Insurgency*.

40. Cemal, *Kürtler*, 162.

41. Kurdish guerrillas approached and made use of the highlands as three-dimensional volumes rather than two-dimensional zones to uphold a recalcitrant armed presence despite the Turkish military and, in doing so, constituted a counter "politics of verticality" (Weizman, *Hollow Land*). The understanding and use of territories as three-dimensional volumes have been recently theorized by geographers and anthropologists (Billé, *Voluminous States*; Elden, "Secure the Volume").

42. For a similar point about how the mountainous terrain enabled armed resistance against technologically advanced militaries in various contexts, from Afghanistan to Colombia and China, see Gordillo, "Terrain as Insurgent Weapon"; Gordillo, "Hostile Terrain"; Otero-Bahamon et al., "Seeing Like a Guerrilla"; White, "Sparks from the Friction of Terrain."

43. The documentary film *Bakur: Inside the PKK* (dir. Demirel and Mavioğlu, *Bakur*) depicts the guerrillas' use of deep caves and bases at three guerrilla camps established in

northern Kurdistan. The documentary was the first independent documentary film that covered the PKK guerrillas' daily lives and permanent guerrilla camps inside Turkey, camps that were officially denied and publicly unknown or ignored. The Turkish authorities have also viewed the guerrillas' use of caves as a state security issue; for the authorities' view of caves as obstacles to national development, state security, and energy sovereignty, see Oğuz, "Cavernous Politics."

44. For a detailed analysis of political symbolism around mountains and being on the mountains in Kurdistan, see Düzel, "Fragile Goddesses." Salih Can Açıksöz (*Sacrificial Limbs*) also discusses how this Kurdish patriotic and revolutionary symbol has been mimicked and reversed by Turkish soldiers.

45. Joost Jongerden (*The Settlement Issue in Turkey and the Kurds*) observes that the Turkish security authorities' counterinsurgency resembled most of the British counterinsurgency campaigns in Malaya in the 1950s. For Turkey's adoption of counterguerrilla and counterinsurgency tactics developed by the British forces in Malaya and the U.S. military in Vietnam and Afghanistan, see also Üngör, *Paramilitarism*; Yonucu, *Police, Provocation, Politics*.

46. Açıksöz, *Sacrificial Limbs*.

47. The post of village guard already existed in Village Law, yet the authorities created two new posts as paramilitary forces to fight the PKK in 1985, the temporary (*geçiçi*) and voluntary (*gönüllü*) village guards. The voluntary guards were given arms and tasked with protecting their villages and nearby regions, while the temporary guards received arms and monthly salaries and joined the military operations under the command of the gendarmerie, the rural law enforcement agency.

48. Beşe, "Geçici Köy Korucuları."

49. The Law on the Provisions to be Applied to Some Criminal Perpetrators (Law No. 3419) was ratified on March 25, 1988.

50. *Jandarma İstihbarat ve Terörle Mücadele Grup Komutanlığı.*

51. Beşe, "Özel Harekat."

52. Cem Ersever, a former gendarmerie major who claimed that he was among the founders and commanders of JİTEM, was a leading example of guerrilla-like soldiers (Yalçın, *Binbaşı Ersever'in İtirafları*). Dressed like a Kurdish villager (or guerrilla) and speaking Kurdish, Ersever conducted secret and special operations in northern Kurdistan and southern Kurdistan (Başûr) during the late 1980s and early 1990s. Criticizing the state authorities for being light-handed against the PKK, Ersever resigned and, in interviews with journalists, confirmed the presence of JİTEM in March 1992. His lifeless body was found in November 1993.

53. *Milli İstihbarat Teşkilatı.*

54. The Turkish police had already established its own Special Operations Office. In the summer of 1993, police special forces were reorganized under the Special Operations Department and were used in anti-PKK operations (Beşe, "Özel Harekat").

55. In the early 1980s, the security forces mobilized ultranationalist militants abroad, such as Abdullah Çatlı, against the leftist and pro-Armenian circles that the state associated with the ASALA (the Armenian Secret Army for the Liberation of Armenia); see Yonucu, *Police, Provocation, Politics*.

56. To emphasize the state's support and manipulation of Hizbullah, particularly its informal paramilitary role, locals called it "Hizbu-Kontra" (Işık, *Turkish Paramilitarism in Northern Kurdistan*; Kurt, *Kurdish Hizbullah in Turkey*).

57. Işık, *Turkish Paramilitarism in Northern Kurdistan*; Üngör, *Paramilitarism*.

58. Green, *Fear as a Way of Life*.

59. I borrow the notion of rhythmanalysis from Henri Lefebvre (*Rhythmanalysis*), who introduces it as a systematic analysis of daily rhythms in urban contexts to emphasize how urban space and temporality are not given but are constantly produced, and how this spatiotemporal production is central to the capitalist mode of production. I used this articulation to understand rural Kurdistan, specifically the Kurdish highlands, not as a given entity but as a site that needs to be produced and maintained. By attending to the spatiotemporal production of the Kurdish highlands through shifts in rhythms that reorganize how people experience (or navigate) the land during day, night, or a specific season, I note that the production of rural space and time was key for the reproduction of the state's colonial regimes of domination and dispossession in Kurdistan. For a broader analysis of how the Turkish state's counterinsurgency reproduced and reshaped rural Kurdistan, see Jongerden and Gambetti, *The Kurdish Issue in Turkey*.

60. During the 1990s in the Kurdish highlands and nearby city centers, residents became used to the sounds of different weapons and could recognize specific rifles, bombs, and other weapons by their sound (Özcan, "Curfew 'until Further Notice'").

61. The Turkish military acquired its first drone systems, which were used as training targets, in 1989 and deployed reconnaissance drones to support its counterinsurgency operations in 1994. Because these earlier drone systems were prone to crashes, especially in severe weather conditions, the military stopped using drones until the late 2000s. The Turkish government procured more advanced reconnaissance drones from Israel in 2007 and 2010, and deployed them again in its counterinsurgency war in Kurdistan. By the mid-2010s, Turkish state-owned and private military industry companies began manufacturing reconnaissance and assault drones in Turkey.

62. For a similar point, see Gusterson, "Drone Warfare in Waziristan."

63. Jongerden, *The Settlement Issue in Turkey and the Kurds*.

64. The exact number of people who endured this treatment is controversial. While Ankara-based Hacettepe University researchers, who collaborated with the state authorities, estimated that between 950,000 and 1,200,000 individuals were forcibly evacuated, the London-based Kurdish Human Rights Project (KHRP) estimated the number of forcibly displaced Kurds to be between three and four million (Jongerden, *The Settlement Issue in Turkey and the Kurds*). The TESEV (*Türkiye Ekonomik ve Sosyal Etütler Vakfı*, Turkish Economic and Social Studies Foundations), an Istanbul-based liberal research institute, calculated the approximate number of internally displaced individuals to be 1.5 million (Aker et al., *Türkiye'de Ülke İçinde Yerinden Edilme Sorunu*).

65. Özar et al., *From Past to Present a Paramilitary Organization in Turkey*.

66. Yadirgi, *The Political Economy of the Kurds of Turkey*.

67. Doğan, *Savaş Ekonomisi*.

68. On January 7, 1993, in international waters in the Mediterranean Sea, Turkish authorities intercepted an ocean freighter operated by a Turkey-based company; authorities

revealed contraband cargos of cannabis and morphine base. One of the owners of the contraband cargo was claimed to be Hüseyin Baybaşin, a Kurdish smuggler boss who identified himself as a Kurdish nationalist. Baybaşin left the country following the death squad killings of Kurdish heroin smugglers in 1994.

69. In a parliamentary investigation, Tansu Çiller, then the prime minister, accepted the existence of such lists and that she had discussed these lists with high-ranking military officers; see Türkiye Büyük Millet Meclisi [The Grand National Assembly of Turkey], "Darbe ve Muhtıraları Araştırma Komisyonu Tutanakları [Minutes of the Commission on Investigating Coups and Memorandums]," November 7, 2012, https://www.tbmm.gov.tr/Files/MeclisArastirmasiKomisyonlari/DarbeMuhtira/tutanak_son/28_subat_alt_komisyonu/28_subat_alt_komisyonu/07.11.2012/Tansu%20%C3%87%C4%BoLLER-07.11.2012.pdf.

70. Yöndem and Bakacak, "Bu Terör Bitmez."

71. *"PKK'yla olduğu gibi, PKK'ya mali destek sağlayanlarla da her biçimde mücadele edecektir,"* cited in Göksedef, "90'larda Öldürülen Kürt İş Adamları."

72. "İşadamlarına Terör Uyarısı [Terror Warning to the Businessmen]," *Milliyet*, November 12, 1993.

73. Cantürk was arrested in 1984 and interrogated about allegations of providing financial support to ASALA (Armenian Secret Army of Liberation of Armenia) and pro-Kurdish organizations, such as DDKD (Revolutionary Eastern Culture Associations) (Yalçın, *Behçet Cantürk'ün Anıları*).

74. The journalist Cengiz Erdinç (*Overdose Türkiye*) argues that the killings of Kurdish businesspeople and smuggling bosses as part of the state's counterinsurgency strategy began much earlier than 1994. According to him, the state authorities launched what he called "the anti-Kurdish operation (*Kürtlere operasyon*)" as early as 1988 by manipulating Kurdish smuggling networks and setting rival Kurdish smugglers against each other (*Overdose Türkiye*, 285). Erdinç notes that from 1988 to the end of 1993, forty-two people who were allegedly involved with heroin smuggling were killed, most of them Kurdish.

75. Baksi, *Teyrê Baz, ya da, Hüseyin Baybaşin.*

76. Işık, *Turkish Paramilitarism in Northern Kurdistan.*

77. The Human Rights Association recorded 42 killings in 1989 to 1991, 210 killings in 1992, 510 killings in 1993, 292 killings in 1994, 321 killings in 1995, 78 killings in 1996, 109 killings in 1997, 192 killings in 1998, and 210 killings in 1999. These numbers are provided in a press release published on January 24, 2000. See İnsan Hakları Derneği [Human Rights Association], "Faili meçhul siyasal cinayetler [Political killings by unknown perpetrators]," January 24, 2000, https://www.ihd.org.tr/faili-mel-siyasal-cinayetler/.

78. See Türkiye Büyük Millet Meclisi [The Grand National Assembly of Turkey], "Ülkemizin Çeşitli Yörelerinde İşlenmiş Faili Meçhul Siyasal Cinayetler Konusunda 10/90 Esas Numaralı Meclis Araştırma Komisyonu Raporu [Report of the Parliamentary Research Commission with Reference Number 10/90 on Unsolved Political Murders Committed in Various Regions of Our Country]," The Grand National Assembly of Turkey, October 12, 1995, https://www5.tbmm.gov.tr/sirasayi/donem19/yilo1/ss897.pdf.

79. The incident is known as the "Susurluk incident," or "Susurluk scandal," and the paramilitary death squads organized around the Turkish police special forces came to be called the Susurluk gang.

80. One of these reports was prepared by Kutlu Savaş, the head of the Prime Ministry Inspectorate in 1997. When the report was distributed publicly, several pages were classified and removed from the version that was publicly available. In 2008, in criminal prosecutions against military coup plots known as the Ergenekon trials, a prosecutor added the allegedly classified sections of the report. According to these sections, the report blamed Turkish police for planning and executing the killing of Behçet Cantürk; see "Susurluk'un 'sırları' da iddianamede [The indictment includes the Susurluk 'secrets']," *Cumhuriyet*, August 8, 2008.

81. For Turkey, see Bovenkerk and Yesilgöz, *The Turkish Mafia*; Erdinç, *Overdose Türkiye*; Darıcı, "Negotiating Smuggling"; Gingeras, *Heroin, Organized Crime*; Işık, *Turkish Paramilitarism in Northern* Kurdistan; Özar et al., *From Past to Present a Paramilitary Organization in Turkey*; Üngör, *Paramilitarism*. For other contexts, see Andreas, *Blue Helmets and Black Markets*; Andreas, *Smuggler Nation*; Heyman, *States and Illegal Practices*.

82. Erdinç, *Overdose Türkiye*.

83. "Askeri Araçlarla Uyuşturucu Kaçırıldı [Drugs Were Smuggled Using Military Vehicles]," *Cumhuriyet*, May 14, 1997. In August 1997, at a road checkpoint in Wan's Erdîş (Off. Erçis) district, heroin was also found in a civilian car driven by a sergeant who was on duty in Colemêrg province; see "Astsubayda 1.5 Trilyonluk Eroin [1.5 Trillion Worth of Heroin Found on a Sergeant]," *Milliyet*, August 20, 1997.

84. Güneş, *The Kurdish National Movement*.

85. In these on-field patrols and anti-smuggling ambushes, security forces often used their weapons to intercept the smugglers' convoys and consequently wound, maim, or kill smugglers. For a detailed analysis of these on-field ambushes, the killings committed by the security forces during these ambushes, and the criminal prosecutions of these killings, see Chapter 4.

86. In October 2007, the PKK guerrillas raided the Dağlıca Commando Battalion in Colemêrg's Gever district and killed twelve and abducted eight soldiers, and in October 2008, the guerrillas attacked Aktütün Gendarmerie Station in Colemêrg's Şemzînan district and killed fifteen soldiers. Media reports, which were often solicited commentaries from the retired military commanders who led the counterinsurgency war in the 1990s, underlined that the existing military stations, which were originally built in the 1950s and the 1960s, had aimed to prevent smuggling and intervene in ordinary crimes rather than facilitate counterinsurgency. For this reason, the criticisms argued, the stations were built on valley floors to monitor border passage to villages and thus became easy targets for the PKK forces. For examples of such criticisms, see Sarızeybek, "Aktütün"; Yayman, "Terörle Mücadelenin Zaafı Jandarma Karakolları"; Yayman, "Terörle Mücadelenin Yumuşak Karnı."

87. The Defense Ministry stated that by October 2013, twenty-one of the twenty-two planned stations and twenty-six of the thirty planned surveillance towers had been completed on the Turkish-Iranian border in Wan province. In the same period, the authorities completed only sixteen stations and four surveillance towers in other provinces across

the Turkish-Iranian and Turkish-Iraqi borders. These figures were provided as a response to a parliamentary inquiry submitted by pro-Kurdish BDP parliamentarian Nazmi Gür on October 7, 2013. For the response, see https://www2.tbmm.gov.tr/d24/7/7-25652c.pdf.

88. Using satellite images from February to May 2019, a report detected thirty-three checkpoints had a metal overhead (Kandelaki, "Roadblocks in Turkey's New Southeast Strategy").

89. "İnsansız Kontrol Noktasıyla Teröre Geçit Yok [No Passage to Terrorism with an Unmanned Checkpoint]," *Anadolu Ajansı*, November 25, 2016, https://www.aa.com.tr/tr/turkiye/insansiz-kontrol-noktasiyla-terore-gecit-yok/692885.

90. On December 28, 2021, the Bitlis Governorship announced that gendarmeries began using body cameras at the road checkpoints in Elcewaz (Off. Adilcevaz) district, which connected Wan province to the central Anatolian provinces, see http://www.bitlis.gov.tr/adilcevaz-cimenli-yol-kontrol-uygulamasinda-jandarma-ekipleri-aselsan-tarafindan-uretilen-akilli-yaka-kameralarini-kullanmaya-basladi.

91. For a detailed account of smugglers' journeys from Gever to Wan and of tactics to bypass road checkpoints, including the use of joker cars and back roads, see Özcan, "Yüksekova'da Sınır Deneyimleri."

92. There was a special market for vehicles that were strong enough to carry smuggled items on roads with tough conditions and also had low operating and maintenance costs. Some dealers traveled around the country, bought these kinds of vehicles in western Turkey, and sold them to smugglers. In fact, the smuggling economies created very dynamic markets for pack animals and vehicles typically used in smuggling campaigns. Another aspect of the use of particular vehicles was that they could be easily identified by the state security forces. There were several cases in which the gendarmeries or soldiers fired at these vehicles (e.g., an Isuzu NPR mini-truck or Ford Transit minivan) as they approached the road checkpoints.

93. For an analysis of Kurdish smugglers' targetability and the bribes that smugglers offered in exchange for safe passage, see Chapter 5.

94. For a detailed analysis of these corridors and their political and theoretical implications in the context of state sovereignty and extraction regimes, see Bozçalı, "Corridors of Countersovereignty."

95. For the case of the apprehended smuggler, see Chapter 5.

Chapter Two

1. The government authorities first referred to the talks with Öcalan under the name of "Resolution Process," but they later started calling it the "National Unity and Fraternity Project" (*Milli Birlik ve Kardeşlik Projesi*). The Kurdish public called the talks the "Peace Process."

2. For a timeline of the Resolution Process, see Aktan, "Çözüm Sürecinin Kronolojisi."

3. Cited in Küçük, "Terör Bitme Noktasına Geldi." Translation is mine.

4. *Adalet ve Kalkınma Partisi.*

5. Following the military coup of 1980, the military government and successive civilian government led by Turgut Özal introduced a series of harsh neoliberal economic restructuring reforms. During this era, financial liberalization was consolidated: citizens

were allowed to open foreign currency accounts; the inter-bank money market, as well as Istanbul Stock Exchange, was launched; and market-determined exchange rates were eventually constituted. During the 1990s, however, the Turkish economy suffered from constant recession and astronomical inflation and interest rates. Because of state corruption and the expenses of the counterinsurgency war, the increasing government debt and large-scale external and domestic borrowing led to recurring economic crises. One of the most devastating economic crises hit the Turkish economy in 1994. From January to April 1994, the Turkish lira devalued by more than 130 percent.

6. The authorities provided this estimation in their letter of intent that they submitted to the IMF on September 29, 1999. The letter is available at https://www.imf.org/external/np/loi/1999/092999.htm.

7. The crisis (on November 22, 2000) first began among private banks that had difficulty finding external borrowing; their inability to borrow put extra pressure on the foreign exchange reserves in the country. With the outbreak of a political disagreement and crisis between the Turkish prime minister and president (on February 19, 2001), the increased pressure on foreign exchange reserves evolved into the second wave of the crisis and brought a drastic devaluation of Turkish lira; see Uygur, "Krizden Krize Türkiye."

8. Abdullah Öcalan prepared six different legal defense texts from 1999 to 2010. In 1999, Öcalan submitted a legal defense against his prosecution at İmralı Island in which he received capital punishment, and his defense text was published as a separate book (Öcalan, *Kürt Sorununda Demokratik Çözüm Bildirgesi*). Öcalan also prepared a legal defense for a criminal case regarding the PKK's organization in Riha (Off. Urfa) province, and this text was also published (Öcalan, *Dicle-Fırat Havzasında Tarih*). Öcalan wrote another legal defense text to be submitted to the ECtHR in 2001 and published this defense in two volumes (Öcalan, *Sümer Rahip Devletinden*). Öcalan submitted a new legal defense text to an Athenian court in 2003 and wrote another legal defense text for the ECtHR's Grand Chamber in 2004. These legal defenses were also published as separate books (Öcalan, *Özgür İnsan Savunması*; Öcalan, *Bir Halkı Savunmak*). In 2009 and 2010, Öcalan also penned legal defense texts for another case at the ECtHR and published them in five volumes (*Demokratik Uygarlık Çözümü*).

9. For a detailed analysis of Öcalan's new politics and how it has transformed the PKK, see Jongerden and Akkaya, *PKK Üzerine Yazılar*.

10. Although the exact time and location of the secret talks were not known, these talks are believed to have taken place as early as 2006 in different locations, including Oslo, Norway, and Brussels, Belgium, and may have continued until 2011 (Kadıoğlu, "The Oslo Talks").

11. The other party that gained seats in the parliament was the secularist Republican People's Party (CHP, *Cumhuriyet Halk Partisi*).

12. The pro-Kurdish candidates bypassed the election threshold for the first time in the 2007 elections by running as independent candidates.

13. The Constitutional Court banned the *Refah* (Welfare) party in 1998 and its successor, the *Fazilet* (Virtue) party, in 2001. While the *Saadet* (Felicity) party was established to replace the *Fazilet* party, a group of former party members pursued a moderate political agenda and founded AKP.

14. Merging conservative politics with neoliberalism, the AKP conceived Islamic liberalism and presented it as a new model of Islamist politics and neoliberal economic development, especially in the aftermath of Arab revolts in the 2010s. For a critical analysis of this model, see Tuğal, *The Fall of the Turkish Model.*

15. For the AKP MP Halil Özyolcu's parliament speech on July 10, 2003, see 22. Dönem, 1. Yasama Yılı, 105. Birleşim, Cilt 2, *TBMM Tutanak Dergisi.*

Except for the smuggling of "astronomically valued items," the new law replaced prison sentences with heavy fines. To decrease the number of court cases and the workload of the legal system, the law also introduced a new system of pre-trial settlement: If defendants paid the minimum amount of the heavy fines for the alleged crime, the case would not be referred to the court and would be dropped. Although the previous law dictated that any vehicles and equipment involved in smuggling were to be impounded, the new law introduced restrictions on impoundment.

16. *Enerji Piyasası Düzenleme Kurumu.*

17. Prior to the introduction of the Oil Market Law (Law 5015), the oil sector had been mainly regulated through the Turkish Oil Law (Law 6326), which divided the oil sector into two sectors: the crude oil sector (production and transportation of crude oil) and the oil products sector (production, distribution, and consumption of oil products, such as gas, diesel fuel, and fuel oil). While crude oil continued to be governed through the Turkish Oil Law, the new Oil Market Law was designed to govern the market for refined oil.

The EPDK was initially established as the Electricity Market Regulatory Authority by Law 4628, which was legislated in February 2001; it was restructured as the Energy Market Regulatory Authority to regulate both national electricity and national natural gas markets by Law 4646, legislated in April 2001.

The law also introduced the national oil marker (*ulusal marker*) system, a new anti-smuggling measure. The distribution of oil marker to gas stations was launched in 2007. For a discussion of the oil marker system and its contestation by Kurdish oil smugglers and lawyers, see Chapter 3.

18. This anti-smuggling vigilance was exemplified by a parliamentary research commission that investigated oil smuggling in the country. After a three-month research period in which the commission members talked to various retired and employed state officers and representatives of the oil sector, the commission published a report on the scope of the contraband oil market in Turkey in March 2005 (The Grand National Assembly of Turkey, "Akaryakıt Kaçakçılığının Ekonomiye, İnsan ve Çevre Sağlığına").

19. The government even initially tried to authorize the army (i.e., ground forces) to investigate smuggling cases in addition to law enforcement agencies, namely the police, gendarmerie, coast guard, and customs officers. However, authorizing the army to conduct law enforcement contradicted the Criminal Procedural Law and compromised the constitutionality of the new law. For this reason, the idea was dropped during the legislative process. See 22. Dönem, 5. Yasama Yılı, 77. Birleşim, Cilt 150, *TBMM Tutanak Dergisi.*

20. The oil marker was a particular chemical composition that was required to be mixed into legal oil and could be detected in a laboratory test. Although the marker was first introduced in 2003 through the Oil Market Law (Law 5015), the actual implementation of

the national marker was launched in 2007. For how Kurdish oil traders and their lawyers contested the oil marker system, see Chapter 3.

21. The increased prison sentence for tobacco smuggling was introduced by an amending law (Law 6455), which was passed in March 2013; the increased sentence for oil smuggling was legislated in June 2014 by an amending law (Law 6545).

22. The criminal procedural law allowed courts to postpone prison sentences that were less than twenty-four months for a five-year probationary period. If the convict did not commit another crime during this period, the prison sentence was erased. Before the 2013 change, thus, it was possible for courts to reduce a two-year prison sentence for tobacco smuggling to fifteen months, given mitigating circumstances, and postpone prison sentences for the probationary period.

23. The neoliberal policies and market economy reforms often served to facilitate, rather than contradict or undermine, counterinsurgency schemes. Scholars have demonstrated that neoliberal logics, which range from managerial techniques to the use of private military forces or subcontractors, were integrated into regimes of counterinsurgency; see Khalili, "Counterterrorism and Counterinsurgency in the Neoliberal Age."

24. Erdinç, *Overdose Türkiye*.

25. As an example of criminalizing the PKK through drug trafficking, the Turkish police presented, during a meeting in Antalya, Turkey, in June 1994, a report that connected the PKK with heroin smuggling and distribution in Europe. See Şardan, "PKK Raporu Interpol'de."

26. For the resolution, see United Nations Security Council, *Resolution 1373*, September 28, 2001, https://www.unodc.org/pdf/crime/terrorism/res_1373_english.pdf.

27. In 1996, Alex P. Schmid presented an early formulation of these links as a security field to the UN Crime Prevention and Criminal Justice Branch; see Schmid, "Revisiting the Relationship between International Terrorism."

28. U.S. President George W. Bush designated the PKK as a "foreign drug trafficker" under the Foreign Narcotics Kingpin Designation Act (known as Kingpin Act), https:// georgewbush-whitehouse.archives.gov/news/releases/2008/05/20080530-5.html.

29. See note 18 above.

30. "PKK'ya Kaçakçılıktan 100 milyon Euro Gelir [100 Million Euros Income from Smuggling to PKK]," *Yeni Şafak*, August 23, 2013.

31. "Sigara Kaçakçılığı Terörle Bağlantılı [Cigarette Smuggling is Linked to Terrorism]," *Sabah*, October 27, 2011.

32. Strozier and Frank, *The PKK*.

33. "*Kandil'in 1 Numarası Açıkladı: 1 PKK'lının Maliyeti* [Kandil's Number One Announced: The Cost of A PKK Member]," *EnSonHaber*, December 20, 2011, https://www.ensonhaber.com/gundem/kandilin-1-numarasiacikladi-1-pkklinin -maliyeti-2011-12-20.

34. Çöggün, "Terörle Mücadelenin bir Parçası Olarak Kaçakçılıkla Mücadele," 42. Translation is mine.

35. The seven geographical regions were introduced in 1941 and served to discursively Turkify the national territory by eliminating the Ottoman provincial names with ethnic and religious references, such as Lazistan, Kurdistan, or Pontus (Jongerden, "Crafting

Space, Making People"). Eastern and Southeastern Anatolia covered most, albeit not all, of northern Kurdistan (Bakur).

36. The term "honor killing" refers to the killing of female kin by male family members under the accusations that the woman brought dishonor upon the family.

37. Koğacıoğlu, "Knowledge, Practice, and Political Community," 189.

38. State officials identified and co-expressed these proxy terms through derogatory expressions, such as savage/savagery, bigot/bigotry, or ignorant/ignorance (Yarkın, "Turkish Racism Against Kurds").

39. Koğacıoğlu, "Knowledge, Practice, and Political Community," 204.

40. Koğacıoğlu, "Knowledge, Practice, and Political Community."

41. Bayir, *Minorities and Nationalism in Turkish Law.*

42. Turkish courts sentenced Kurdish rights defenders for racist propaganda because they advocated the existence of the Kurdish language and culture (Bayir, *Minorities and Nationalism in Turkish Law*). Although those in Turkish nationalist circles have advocated for the racial superiority of Turks and for genocidal acts against non-Turks, no one from these circles has received a criminal sentence for racism. In 1944, a group of Turkish nationalists received a sentence for racism in a local criminal court, but this sentence was reversed by the Appeals Court and the defendants were acquitted in the retrial (Bayir, *Minorities and Nationalism in Turkish Law*).

43. Anthropologist Ayşe Parla (*Precarious Hope*) has suggested, in the context of immigration of Turks from Bulgaria to Turkey, translating *soy* and *soydaş* as "racial kin" rather than "ethnic kin" to emphasize how the term evokes racial connotations and racialized practices.

44. Under this neutrality-claiming yet racialized citizenship order, the Turkish law grants ethnically Turkish citizens and noncitizens legal privileges, such as the right to enter military schools (Yıldız, *Ne Mutlu Türküm Diyebilene*) or legally migrate to Turkey and acquire Turkish citizenship, in easier and faster ways than non-Turkish noncitizens can access these privileges (Bayir, *Minorities and Nationalism in Turkish Law*; Parla, *Precarious Hope*).

45. Although "Kurdish" and "Kurdistan" were erased, this erasure has become marked. Anthropologist Deniz Duruiz ("Erasure and Affect in Race-Making in Turkey") has called this marking "erasure of erasure" in reference to Jacques Derrida's (*Of Grammatology*) conceptualization of *sous rature*, or "under erasure" in Gayatri Chakravorty Spivak's translation. In explaining the term, Spivak states that it means "to write a word, cross it out, and then print both word and deletion. (Since the word is inaccurate, it is crossed out. Since it is necessary, it remains legible)" ("Translator's Preface," xiv). In this way, terms that are struck through acquire an absent presence in texts or discourses. They are erased but their erasure is also made visible or sensible. Duruiz's "erasure of erasure," in that sense, diverges from accounts that frame Turkish state discourses and related public discourses as oscillating between orders of recognition and denial. Sociologist Mesut Yeğen ("The Kurdish Issue in Turkey"), for example, addresses how Ottoman authorities and the Ankara government led by Mustafa Kemal promised recognition of Kurdish autonomy in the late 1910s and early 1920s and how the Republican authorities began strictly denying Kurdish rights and identity in the mid-1920s and continued to do

so until the 1990s. In this shift from recognition to denial, Yeğen notes that Kurdishness/ Kurdistan was erased; the Kurdish in the Kurdish question became crossed out, which is why he uses the term, "~~Kurdish~~ question." Yeğen thus articulates the crossed-out Kurdishness as a simple denial. In contrast, Koğacıoğlu's ("Knowledge, Practice, and Political Community") articulation of "nonrecognizing recognition" or Duruiz's "erasure of erasure" theorizes a specific mode of racialization that goes beyond simple denial or a strict binary of recognition and denial.

46. Çöğgün, "Terörle Mücadelenin bir Parçası Olarak Kaçakçılıkla Mücadele," 43–44. Translation is mine.

47. The association of Kurdish borderlands and Kurdish smugglers with terrorism further helped security officers frame their use of violence as acts of self-defense and legally justify the killings of unarmed Kurdish smugglers in courts; see Chapter 4.

48. High-security (F-type) prisons replaced wards (fifty-person capacity dormitories) with one- or three-person cells for those convicted of terrorism, organized crimes, and drug trafficking offenses. Prisoners resisted the F-type prisons with hunger strikes and death fasts (*ölüm orucu*) in 1996 and 2000; for a detailed analysis of the death fasts, see Bargu, *Starve and Immolate*.

49. For how carceral power and practices are central to colonialism, see Khalili, *Time in the Shadows*.

50. Meeker, *A Nation of Empire*.

51. Anthropologist Elif Babül (*Bureaucratic Intimacies*, 43) defines "the social imaginary as repertoires of meaning-making available in a given society" in reference to Cornelius Castoriadis (*The Imaginary Institution of Society*).

52. The judge and prosecutor candidates took classes in the Justice Academy in Ankara and completed a training program. After a failed coup in 2016, the Justice Academy was restructured in 2018, including the dismissal of Academy trainers and thousands other judges and prosecutors who the authorities alleged to be connected with the coup attempt.

53. Koğacıoğlu, "Conduct, Meaning and Inequality in an İstanbul Courthouse"; Babül, *Bureaucratic Intimacies*.

54. Comaroff and Comaroff, "Law and Disorder in the Postcolony."

55. A 1973 constitutional amendment first introduced the State Security Courts to the Turkish legal system, but the amendment was canceled by the Constitutional Court in 1976. The 1982 Constitution, which was prepared following the military coup of 1980, reintroduced these special courts.

56. The State Security Courts were also authorized to prosecute drug trafficking allegations.

57. While martial law was lifted in most of the provinces in the mid-1980s, emergency rule replaced it in most of the Kurdish provinces; see Chapter 1.

58. The KCK trials, for instance—the leading anti-Kurdish lawfare campaigns during my fieldwork—were conducted in these courts. For an analysis of KCK trials, see Hakyemez, *Lives and Times of Militancy*.

59. In court sessions, the court criers acted as default interpreters for citizens who could not speak Turkish. Yet, in the court cases in which Kurdish politicians, activists,

journalists, or even lawyers were put on trial, such as during the KCK trials, judges often did not allow court criers to translate for Kurdish-speaking defendants and denied the defendants' request to speak in Kurdish or to have an interpreter (Bayir, *Minorities and Nationalism in Turkish Law*). In these cases, the judges often denoted Kurdish language as an unknown or a foreign language in court records.

60. The indirect marking of Kurdishness and Kurdistan through the categories of terrorism and terrorist reflected "anti-Kurdish state racism," in which the Kurdish population and lands are identified with terrorism and thus rendered expendable (see Chapter 4 for a further discussion). I understand the anti-Kurdish state racism as a specific manifestation of the state authorities' racialization of Kurds without naming them under the undeclared colonial rule in Kurdistan.

61. Article 10 of the Turkish Constitution declared the principle of procedural equality before the law for citizens and noncitizens, and the higher courts, the Appeals Court and the Constitutional Court, closely enforced this procedural equality.

62. In examining the citizenship order in Brazil, for example, anthropologist James Holston has also shown how the formally inclusive Brazilian citizenship operated with an unequal and differentiated "substantive distribution of the rights, meanings, institutions, and practices that [formal citizenship] entails to those deemed citizens" (*Insurgent Citizenship*, 7).

63. My framing of the cunning of state law is inspired by anthropologist Elizabeth Povinelli's (*The Cunning of Recognition*) conceptualization of "the cunning of recognition," which builds on Hegel's idea of the "cunning of reason" in his *Lectures on the Philosophy of History*. Povinelli has conceptualized cunning of recognition to explain "how late liberal ideology works through the passions of recognition, tries to develop its worth without subjecting itself to the throes of contestation and opposition" (*The Cunning of Recognition*, 16). In smuggling court cases in Kurdistan, the Turkish law's cunning also deployed procedural equality to impose substantive inequality on its Kurdish citizens without deserting its claims for impartiality and citizenship order neutrality for ethnicity, religion, gender, and class. For a related conceptualization of "the cunning of judicial reform" and a discussion on how judicial reforms deployed discourses of access to justice to justify and expand the power of state law in India, see Baxi, "Access to Justice and Rule-of (Good) Law."

64. The anti-smuggling legislation provided only the minimum and maximum levels of penal and administrative fines and prison sentences, so judges assessed the specific cases and determined the proper fine, prison sentence, or postponement for each case.

65. The Turkish version is: "*Yörede sigara ve akaryakıt kaçakçılığının geçim kaynağı haline gelecek derecede yaygın oluşu da gözetilerek aynı zamanda cezanın caydırıcı ve önleyici etkisini sanık üzerinde göstermesi gerekliliği yanısıra adaletin gerçek anlamda ancak bu şekilde tecelli edeceği de düşünülerek.*"

66. See Law 5607, Article 5.

67. In 2020, the article on effective remorse in the anti-smuggling law was amended to allow defendants to show effective remorse by paying a fine during prosecution as well. Although the amendment resembled the judges' legal interpretation in Wan central courthouse, I do not know whether the judges' interpretation played a role in the change.

Chapter Three

1. The search for sufficient, certain, and convincing evidence in Turkish courts was based on the legal principle of *in dubio pro reo*: Defendants could not be convicted by the court if there was still doubt about their guilt. Although this principle is not expressed explicitly in Turkish Criminal Law, the Turkish Courts of Appeal has established and enforced it through its decisions. Article 38 of the 1982 Turkish Constitution, which says that "no one shall be considered guilty until proven guilty in a court of law," has also been cited as legal justification for *in dubio pro reo* and the search for sufficient, certain, and convincing evidence.

2. Nonguilty decisions must be understood as being different from both innocent and guilty decisions.

3. Both types of not-proven verdicts were issued under Article 223, Clause 2, Item e of the Turkish Criminal Procedure Law (No. 5271, CMK 223/2e). This article mandates an acquittal "if it has not been proven that the accused committed the charged crime (*yüklenen suçun sanık tarafından işlendiğinin sabit olmaması, hallerinde . . .*)." Although this provision directly applies to the first type of not-proven cases, courts often referenced it when issuing the second type of decisions (nonillegality decisions), noting that the crime could not be proven with sufficient evidence beyond a reasonable doubt.

4. My articulation of nonillegality differs from the concepts of "extralegal" (Lazarus-Black, *Legitimate Acts and Illegal Encounters*) and "not-yet-(il)legal" (Smart and Zerilli, "Extralegality"), which refer to practices or situations that are not (yet) addressed by or lie outside of the law or legal system. In the oil smuggling cases that I examine, however, the decisions of not-proven guilty and allegedly contraband oil's nonillegality emerged only after, and as a result of, the court process. To emphasize the constitutive role of the court process, I call these cases nonillegality decisions instead of extralegal or not-(yet)-illegal. For a discussion of the use of "extralegal" as being synonymous with "illegal," see Nordstorm, *Global Outlaws*; Smart and Zerilli, "Extralegality."

5. Despite the ubiquity of police surveillance in Wan city center, the police seldom conducted raids in crowded public places, such as Cumhuriyet Avenue and nearby areas that hosted many street vendors selling contraband in their stalls, during the day because such raids might trigger resistance from onlookers. For an example of this, see the failed attempt to detect a contraband cigarette seller, depicted at the beginning of Chapter 2. Police forces could not easily patrol every neighborhood either. Neighborhoods on the peripheries of the city center were particularly challenging for a single police car to enter and patrol. Forcibly displaced people built these neighborhoods and turned them into strongholds of the Kurdish Freedom Movement, particularly of the PKK. For this reason, law enforcement could enter these neighborhoods through the use of special forces units with armored vehicles.

6. For the smuggled cigarettes, fraudulent holograms might help circumvent road checkpoints or even court verdicts, although courts would eventually conduct authenticity inspections on the holograms. However, the smugglers viewed fraudulent holograms as an unnecessary burden that weakened key marketing advantages of cigarette smuggling: low investment costs and time efficiency. Unlike a campaign of smartphone smuggling (a smartphone cost a few hundred dollars), cigarette smuggling did not require large

capital investments because of the cigarettes' relatively low cost (a package cost less than one U.S. dollar). In contrast to oil products that mostly required a vehicle to carry them or a larger storage unit to sell them, lightweight cigarettes could easily be carried around and traded everywhere. The fraudulent holograms, however, would put additional financial cost on the smuggled cigarettes. It would also require additional time to repackage the cigarettes with the fraudulent holograms.

7. The high-degree criminal courts had a panel that was often composed of three judges. If the number of defendants was high, five or more judges might be involved. There was no jury system in the Turkish Criminal Law.

8. The provincial court commissions updated and published the list of authorized experts who would provide expert witness testimonies to the courts on an annual basis.

9. Torpey, *The Invention of the Passport*.

10. In the case of medical documentation practices in Mozambique, Ramah McKay ("Documentary Disorders") has shown how the use of multiple documents with multiple functions led to a documentary disharmony that opened up contending spaces of agency for patients, health workers, state authorities, and nongovernmental organizations.

11. For how migrants used authentic yet false documents to negotiate the legality of their stay in Italy, see Tuckett, *Rules, Paper, Status*.

12. Although judges and prosecutors considered the content inspection results reliable material evidence to finalize smuggling trials, they were aware that defendants could bribe court experts or lab workers to manipulate the results of the content inspections. In fact, I came across an oil smuggling case that predated the oil marker system in which a worker at a university laboratory in a different province was convicted for taking bribes and manipulating chemical test results.

13. İŞARETR is a made-up word that combines the Turkish word *işaret*, which means marker, with TR, the international country code (the ISO 3166 code) for Turkey.

14. *Türkiye Bilimsel ve Teknolojik Araştırma Kurumu.*

15. "Ulusal Markerin 1 Milyonuncu Litresi Teslim Edildi [1 Million Liter of National Marker Has Been Delivered]," *TÜBİTAK Bülten*, 2013, 136: 18–20.

16. Another inspection device, Marker K, was introduced for the oil distribution companies' storage facilities. Through these devices, the companies could test the level of the national marker and ensure that each cargo of legally processed oil products contained the national marker at the desired level. Additionally, the EPDK established an online data collection center, as a centralized surveillance system, to follow and inspect these companies' storage tanks.

17. Latour, *Pandora's Hope*, 23.

18. See the energy minister's written answer to a parliamentary question on the use of counterfeit national oil marker, Answer No. B. 15.0 SGB02-610, Dated May 27, 2008. The energy minister confirmed the studies on identifying the national marker with DNA codes but also mentioned, in his written answer to the parliamentary question, that it would require more research, development, and investment.

19. "Tanklarda Ulusal Marker, İsopiropil Alkol ve Akaryakıt Dışında Ürün Yok [There Are No Products in the Tanks Other than the National Marker, Isopropyl Alcohol, and

Fuel]," October 17, 2009, *Vatan* https://www.gazetevatan.com/ekonomi/tanklarda-ulusal
-marker-isopiropil-alkol-ve-akaryakit-disinda-urun-yok-265249.

20. Several news websites also published the expert witness report. I accessed the report
online on October 14, 2014, at http://www.habervaktim.com/foto-galeri/iste-sahteciligi-
ortaya-cikaran-belgeler-1777-p6.htm.

21. Examining the politics around oil economies, a number of studies also unpacked
the materiality of oil and showed how its material qualities, such as its transportability
through pipelines and oil tankers, created opportunities and predicaments for different actors, from oil-producing governments to oil workers (Mitchell, *Carbon Democracy*;
Barry, *Material Politics*) and corporations (Rogers, "The Materiality of the Corporation").
Drawing on these studies, I here show how the material content of oil itself became a field
of struggle in which state authorities, oil traders, and their lawyers tried to enforce or
undermine the borders of the national oil market. I unpack how the chemical uncertainty
and unpredictability of certain chemicals enabled specific technical, legal, and therefore political configurations and consequences; for a similar analysis, see Sawyer, "Crude
Contamination." Relatedly, I suggest oil chemistry as another site for "chemo-ethnography" and examining political, economic, and affective engagements with modern chemistry (Shapiro and Kirksey, "Chemo-Ethnography").

22. "EPDK'dan İşaretleme Duyurusu [An Announcement on the Marker by the
EPDK]," *Petrol Dünyası* Vol. 36, June 2007: 21–23.

23. Because the courts referred to the market quality inspections in oil smuggling
trials and some of these inspections included chemical tests that relied on probabilistic
estimates, the national oil market had been sealed by probabilistic borders before the
introduction of the oil marker and mobile inspection devices.

24. Salter, "Theory of the /," 736.

25. Because national territories and borders can also be imagined as three-dimensional
volumes, such framing can allow for dividing and bordering a volumetric territory ver-
tically rather than horizontally. For instance, at the Camp David negotiations in 2000,
U.S. President Clinton suggested a partition plan in which the basement and ground
floors of certain buildings in the Old City could be used by Palestinians and the upper
levels would be under Israeli jurisdiction; for a detailed analysis of the plan, see Weizman,
Hollow Land. My articulation of probabilistic border and border crossing as an incident
of degree or likelihood also differs from the volumetric framing of borders and territories,
as the latter tends to understand border crossings as definitive, either/or phenomena.

26. Michelle Murphy (*Sick Building Syndrome*) has made this argument in relation to
sick building syndrome, in referring to Ian Hacking's (*Historical Ontology*) conceptualization of historical ontology.

27. The Turkish Resettlement Law of 1934 exemplified such racial bordering by considering only people with Turkish race and descent as legitimate immigrants in Turkey;
in doing so, it created the Turkish race as a legal category (Yıldız, *Ne Mutlu Türküm
Diyebilene*; see also Parla, *Precarious Hope*). In the 1920s, U.S. borders were also politically
and legally reimagined through particular ethnic and racial terms in which Asian and
Mexican immigrants were deemed alien even when they attained U.S. citizenship (Ngai,
Impossible Subjects).

28. Sociologist Chris Rumford has conceptualized "borderwork" to denote the ways in which ordinary people, companies, and civil society organizations enforce physical borders or "seek to dismantle, shift, or construct [physical borders] anew" to emphasize the state borders' constant maintenance and the involvement of multiple actors in addition to governments in border enforcement ("Towards a Multiperspectival Study of Borders," 898). Although Rumford's framework considers the state as a bounded actor and presumes a strict boundary between state and society even though border enforcement crosscuts these boundaries (Rumford, "Introduction"; see also Rumford, "Towards a Multiperspectival Study of Borders"; Rumford, "Towards a Vernacularized Border Studies"), my conceptualization of borderwork departs from his analysis and instead attends to the work that the state-society boundary and the construction thereof do (see Mitchell, "The Limits of the State"). For an alternative articulation of "border work" that examines the making of state borders and territoriality as ongoing, multi-scalar, multi-actor, and contingent processes, see Reeves, *Border Work*.

29. Uncertainty does not necessarily undermine modern state governance, though. As the modern understanding of linear and ever-expanding time has replaced cyclical temporality, modern statecraft has come to claim its authority through governing future uncertainties (Koselleck, *Futures Past*). The emergence of modern statecraft became possible and unfolded with the development of modern probabilistic calculations as well as the creation and collection of statistical data, both in the metropoles and colonies (Cohn, *Colonialism and Its Forms of Knowledge*; Hacking, "How Should We Do the History of Statistics?"). Kurdish oil traders and their lawyers' technolegal tactics, however, show how these calculations and the management of uncertainty can also lead to unexpected forms of political and legal agency that counteract modern governance and state control.

30. While Max Weber (*Economy and Society*) has suggested that modern states claim a monopoly on the legitimate means of violence, John Torpey (*The Invention of the Passport*) has taken Weber's formulation to argue that modern states also monopolize the "legitimate means of movement" within and across borders.

31. Andersson, *Illegality, Inc.*; Guiraudon and Lahav, "A Reappraisal of the State Sovereignty Debate"; Menjívar, "Immigration Law Beyond Borders."

32. Local bordering practices may also include the creation of gated residential communities or identifying and branding some local cultural practices or products as *sui generis* (Rumford, "Introduction").

33. For rebel groups' or road bandits' control and capitalization of trade traffic in Africa and elsewhere, see Roitman, *Fiscal Disobedience*; Schouten, *Roadblock Politics*. For borderland communities' bordering practices in defiance of state borders, see Galemba, *Contraband Corridor*.

34. Janet Roitman calls this logic of exclusion and extraction "the epistemological foundations of state power and the exigencies of the exercise of state power" (*Fiscal Disobedience*, 198).

35. I occasionally encountered lawyers who were hesitant to share their casework with their colleagues, especially if it involved high-profile political trials such as the KCK trials, which prosecuted elected politicians from the pro-Kurdish party high-profile political cases. Because many lawyers used courtroom statements and performances in these

high-profile cases as a platform to build political credibility within the broader Kurdish movement, their reluctance to share their casework was often a reflection of the lawyers' competition for positions within the pro-Kurdish party or candidacy in parliamentary or municipal elections under the party lists.

36. For political trials and anti-Kurdish lawfare campaigns, see Chapter 2.

37. For a detailed analysis of Kurdish political defenses in the 1980s and onward, see Gündoğan, *Kawa Davası Savunması*; Hakyemez, *Lives and Times of Militancy*; Hakyemez, "Margins of the Archive."

38. Vergès, *Savunma Saldırıyor*; see also Hakyemez, "Margins of the Archive."

39. Hakyemez, "Margins of the Archive."

40. For published legal defense texts, see Öcalan, *Bir Halkı Savunmak*; Öcalan, *Demokratik Uygarlık Çözümü*; Öcalan, *Özgür İnsan Savunması*; Öcalan, *Dicle-Fırat Havzasında Tarih*; Öcalan, *Kürt Sorununda Demokratik Çözüm*; Öcalan, *Sümer Rahip Devletinden*.

Chapter Four

1. İHD was Turkey's leading human rights organization and was established by families of political prisoners in 1986 (Babül, *Bureaucratic Intimacies*). As İHD became a leading base for Kurdish human rights lawyers, these lawyers also became forerunners of the human rights movement in Turkey; see the Introduction for an overview.

2. See Chapter 2 for how the Turkish judiciary protected state authorities in Kurdistan.

3. As the Turkish security forces also targeted Kurdish smugglers from Iran, the families of Iranian citizen smugglers could also hire a Turkey-based Kurdish lawyer and pursue criminal prosecutions in Turkish courts against the raids by Turkish soldiers that resulted in death. Iranian border patrols also attacked both Turkish and Iranian citizen smugglers. While I encountered several cases in Turkish courts that Kurdish lawyers pursued on behalf of their clients based in Iran, I did not come across any case in which the families of Turkish citizen smugglers pursued any prosecution against Iranian forces.

4. The incident has been referred to as the 33 Bullet (33 *Kurşun*) incident, named after a poem by renowned poet Ahmed Arif that lamented the slain villagers, and as the Sefo River Massacre (*Qirkirinê Geleyê Sefo*). For a detailed account of the incident and an exploration of how it is remembered in the region, see Özgen, *Van-Özalp ve 33 Kurşun Olayı*.

5. Ulugana, *Ağrı Kürt Direnişi ve Zilan Katliamı*.

6. The governing AKP spokesperson, Hüseyin Çelik, who was originally from Wan, referred to the air bombardment as an "operation accident" the day after the massacre, see "Çelik: Bir Operasyon Kazası Vardır [Çelik: There Was an Operation Mistake]," *Milliyet*, December 29, 2011, https://www.milliyet.com.tr/siyaset/celik-bir-operasyon-kazasi -vardir-1482031.

In justifying the air bombardment decision, military officials asserted that it was difficult for aerial drones to differentiate smugglers from guerrillas, especially during the nighttime. Yet, these justifications were hardly compelling. The military commanders and soldiers stationed in the military post closest to Roboski were aware of the smuggling convoys and the specific border passages these convoys used. A quick exchange and confirmation with the military post could have prevented the attack. For a statement by the Turkish Chief of General Staff, see "Genelkurmay'dan Uludere Açıklaması [Chief of General Staff's Statement on Uludere Incident]," *Sabah*, December 29, 2011, https://web.archive.org/web/20160322050442/http:/www.sabah.com.tr/gundem/2011/12/29/genelkurmaydan-aciklama.

7. In the 2010 constitutional reforms, the Constitutional Court was authorized to accept and assess individual applications regarding accusations of state authorities violating individual rights and freedoms defined in the Turkish Constitution as well as the European Convention on Human Rights. The individual complaint mechanism, modeled on the ECtHR, was introduced as an effective domestic legal remedy that Turkish citizens must exhaust before applying to the European Court of Human Rights. To many of my interlocutors, the Constitutional Court's individual application (*bireysel başvuru*) mechanism was a new means to distract complainants and delay potential applications to the ECtHR, which was already worried about the volume of applications filed from Turkey.

8. In addition to Turkey's Kurdish borderlands, across the Iraqi-Iranian borderlands, Kurdish smugglers had also been systematically targeted and killed by Iranian security forces, and the Iranian authorities merely dismissed the majority of these killings without formally investigating and sanctioning them. For an analysis of these killings, see Soleimani and Mohammadpour, "Life and Labor on the Internal Colonial Edge."

9. The Wan MP, Nazmi Gür, who was also a member of the pro-Kurdish BDP, submitted the parliamentary question after I shared my initial research findings on the smuggler killings with him. For the response to the parliamentary question, see https://cdn.tbmm.gov.tr/KKBSPublicFile/D24/Y3/T7/WebOnergeMetni/e17bf25f-ad99-4eda-b87b-04bceocdfode.pdf.

10. I conducted these fact-finding visits on behalf of the working group of Van Bar Association's Human Rights Commission. For the visits, I compiled all the smuggler killings that local media and human rights organizations had reported. I cross-checked these reports with official statements and then visited border towns and villages to interview residents to confirm the reported incidents and record unreported ones. Based on these visits, I created a map of stings and killings and prepared a fact-finding report for the commission. For the map, see Bozçalı, "Proving Injustice."

11. See Chapter 2.

12. The Turkish military occasionally used mules to transport ammunition and food during counterinsurgency operations (Gürcan, "Ordunun 'Organik' Yük Taşıma Sistemi").

13. See Chapter 5.

14. In this way, I came across some incidents in which smuggler animals had saved the lives of their owners, their smuggler human partners. For an analysis of the animal-human collaborations in the smuggling economies in Kurdistan, see Bozçalı, "Partners in Crime."

15. The size of these plastic containers varied, from a 60- to 240-liter carrying capacity. Typically, a mule or a horse carried two to six *jelikan*, depending on their size. Although the origin of the term *jelikan* is not clear, it always made me think it as a version of English term "jerrycan" or "jerrican."

16. The agreement between the Republic of Turkey and the Iranian State on the Safety of the Border Zone as well as Resolution of the Disputes in the Border Zone (*Türkiye Cumhuriyeti ile İran Devleti Şahinşahisi arasında Hudud Mıntıkasının Emniyetine ve Mezkur Mıntıkada Çıkan Hadise ve İhtilafların Tesviyesine ait Mukavelename*) was signed on March 14, 1937.

17. For an analysis of state authorities' strategic practice of nonrecording in addition to recording, see Kalir and van Schendel, "Introduction."

18. Chatterjee, "The Impunity Effect," 125; see also Drexler, "History and Liability in Aceh, Indonesia."

19. Arguments invoking the landscape to justify state violence are not specific to the Kurdish borderlands. Scholars have shown how in the U.S.–Mexico borderlands state authorities have used the landscape as "a moral alibi" (Doty, "Bare Life," 600) to deny the role of border-enforcement policies that force people to undertake deadly border crossings. The state's violent bordering practices thus became "a killing machine that simultaneously uses and hides behind the viciousness of the Sonoran Desert" (De León, *The Land of Open Graves*, 3).

20. Weizman proposed this concept in his *Forensic Architecture* (20). The book is named after the research agency he established and directed at Goldsmiths, University of London. The agency utilized a range of techniques and bodies of expertise from multiple fields, including law, human rights, architecture, art, and journalism, to investigate various incidents of state and corporate violence from around the world. These incidents included mass killings, police violence, drone attacks, detention and torture, land grabs, enforced displacements, environmental contamination, toxicity, and forest fires. In fact, the Diyarbakır Bar Association commissioned the Forensic Architecture ("The Killing of Tahir Elçi") to conduct a comprehensive analysis of the 2015 murder of the Bar Association's president, Tahir Elçi.

21. If the offender—a state official, solider, or gendarmerie—shot at and killed a smuggler by following an unlawful order, the court would confirm the unlawfulness of the killing but maintain the impunity of the perpetrator. Although state officials were held criminally responsible for executing orders that involved a criminal act, such as an order to kill, according to the Turkish Criminal Procedural Law, they would not receive a punishment if the executed order was in violation of the law, such as an order to shoot when shooting was considered to be a nonproportional use of force. Rather than acquit the official, the court would decide that there was "no need for imposing conviction (*ceza verilmesine yer yoktur*)." While sanctioning the killings, these no-need-for-conviction decisions still confirmed the state authorities' misconduct (i.e., the unlawful order) and thus might substantiate the financial compensation claims of slain smugglers' families in civil courts. For an analysis of compensation claims for smuggler killings, see Bozçalı, "Money for Life."

22. For an articulation of how the proportionate use of violence leads to effective legalization of extensive violence and more violent law enforcement interventions, see Akarsu, "We're Tired of This Weber Guy!"

23. Stepputat, "Introduction," 4.

24. Can, "Human Rights, Humanitarianism, and State Violence"; Ferrándiz and Robben, *Necropolitics*; Rojas-Perez, *Mourning Remains*; Rosenblatt, *Digging for the Disappeared*; Wagner, "Identifying Srebrenica's Missing"; Sanford, *Buried Secrets*; Ferrándiz, "Exhuming the Defeated"; Schwartz-Marin and Cruz-Santiago, "Forensic Civism"; Cruz-Santiago, "Lists, Maps, and Bones."

25. Sekula, "Photography and the Limits of National Identity," 29.

26. Weizman, *Forensic Architecture*, 64. Because political violence is imposed in various forms, which can range from extrajudicial killings to environmental destruction and dispossession, counterforensics also involves a variety of investigative tactics for claiming rights, such as Palestinian surveyors' use of Ottoman land registrations to challenge the Israeli state's land grabs (Kohlbry, "Palestinian Counter-forensics").

27. My interlocutors' vernacular-counterforensic examination of the judicial impunity work also challenges understanding impunity as a lack of criminal prosecution given the legal immunity that authoritarian rulers and judicial inactivity self-impose (Sikkink, *The Justice Cascade*). As scholars have demonstrated, impunity can also be produced through legal investigations. Examining the prosecutions of anti-Muslim violence in India, for example, Moyukh Chatterjee ("The Impunity Effect"; *Composing Violence*) has shown that police reports were created in ways that revealed violence while leaving the perpetrators unidentified. Regarding torture claims in Turkey, Başak Can ("Human Rights, Humanitarianism, and State Violence") has illustrated that forensic and medical evidence can be used to deny, rather than reveal, state-committed violations, even though the documentation of such evidence can allow future technoscientific reinterpretations that contest the initial denial. My analysis of judicial impunity work and its counterforensic examination joins and expands these studies by showing not only how impunity is legally produced but also how rights advocates can develop (vernacular counterforensic) practices to expose and contest the legal authorities' impunity work.

28. While counterforensic practices in other contexts have often exposed state-committed violations retrospectively (Rubin, "Exhuming Dead Persons"), Kurdish complainants and their lawyers documented not only past state crimes but also the judiciary's violations, such as noncollecting specific pieces of evidence, in real-time, as they occured during the criminal investigations and prosecutions. This was made possible by their vernacular counterforensic work and sustained yet critical engagement with state forensics.

29. Sally Engle Merry's conceptualization of "vernacularization" (or "vernacularization of rights") is a multistage process in which activists "vernacularized" the global ideas and strategies by prioritizing and rearticulating those that speak to their local needs and that seem more compatible with local cultures (or ideologies) ("Transnational Human Rights and Local Activism"). Although the activists, in Merry's ("Transnational Human Rights and Local Activism") articulation, seem to view ideas and values as legitimate, my interlocutors questioned the political legitimacy of human rights legal practices and institutions, such as international courts or advocacy organizations, while engaging with them. This critical yet sustained engagement with international (and domestic) rights practices and institutions is the primary way my articulation of vernacular counterforensics differs from Merry's framing of vernacularization ("Transnational Human Rights and Local Activism").

30. Hansen, "Governance and State Mythologies," 240.

31. For a detailed analysis of this legal cunning, see Chapter 2.

32. For the conceptualization of state racism, see Foucault, *Society Must Be Defended*. I consider "anti-Kurdish state racism" to be a particular version of the "racialization without naming," a specific modality of racialization through which the Turkish state authorities racialized the Kurds and Kurdistan by using proxy terms and avoiding the terms "Kurd," "Kurdish," or "Kurdistan" under the undeclared colonial rule in Kurdistan. For a discussion of this modality of racialization, see Chapter 2. In the anti-Kurdish state racism, terrorism emerged as a main proxy term that denoted and thus racialized the Kurds and Kurdistan but particularly rendered them killable or destroyable.

33. Foucault, *Society Must Be Defended*, 241.

34. For an analysis of modern states' monopolization of prosecutorial roles and legitimate means of forensics as part of its biopolitical management of the living and dead, see Stepputat, "Introduction."

35. This trend has been amplified by the post-9/11 global "war on terror," which has led to the identification of certain bodies, profiles, and behaviors as being potentially linked to terrorism and to subjecting them to specialized legal regimes and state violence (Hussain, "Hyperlegality"; Eckert, *The Social Life of Anti-Terrorism Laws*; Mamdani, *Good Muslim, Bad Muslim*).

36. For the mobility across Kurdish highlands and how the PKK guerrillas temporarily yet consistently restricted the army's land forces' access to certain parts of the highlands, see Chapter 1. For the ways in which the PKK guerrillas opened free passage corridors to smugglers in the areas they controlled, see Bozçalı, "Corridors of Countersovereignty"

37. Greenberg, "Law, Politics, and Efficacy," 428.

38. Darıcı and Hakyemez, "Neither Civilian nor Combatant," 73.

39. Kelly, *This Side of Silence*, 149.

40. Kurban, *Limits of the Supranational Justice*.

41. A few days after the incident, on January 2, 2012, the vice prime minister, Bülent Arınç, declared that the smugglers were not killed intentionally, that any negligence behind the incident would be investigated, and that compensation would be paid to the families of the murdered smugglers; see "Özür Yok, Kasıt Yok, Tazminat Var [No Apology, No Intent, But There is Compensation]," *Bianet*, January 3, 2021, https://bianet.org/haber/ozur-yok-kasit-yok-tazminat-var-135180.

42. The initial criminal investigation began at the Diyarbakır prosecutor's office. In June 2013, after an eighteen-month investigation, the prosecutor claimed that the deaths were the result of negligence rather than deliberate intent, even though the prosecutor's office confirmed that the smugglers were discernible in the drone footage recorded hours before the attack; see "Prosecutor Confirms Villagers Could Be Discerned in UAV Footages," *Bianet News in English*, August 6, 2012, https://web.archive.org/web/20140107205439/http://www.bianet.org/english/human-rights/140149-prosecutor-confirms-villagers-could-be-discerned-in-uav-footages. Given the negligence and possibility of a mistake in executing the military order, the prosecutor decided on non-jurisdiction (*görevsizlik kararı*) and sent the case to the military prosecutor. Lawyers for the Roboski families objected to the non-jurisdiction decision by stressing that killing with

negligence was still a crime in the Turkish Criminal Law, not a military crime, so the deaths must not be investigated and prosecuted in the military courts; see "İHD: Roboskî katliamı insanlığa karşı işlenmiş bir suçtur, örtbas edilemez [İHD: The Roboskî Massacre is a crime against humanity, it cannot be covered up]," İnsan Hakları Derneği (İHD) Diyarbakır Şubesi, January 8, 2014, https://ihddiyarbakir.org/tr/post/14221/ihd-roboski -katliami-insanliga-karsi-islenmis.

43. *Encü ve diğerleri*. B. No: 2014/11864, 24/2/2016, Anayasa Mahkemesi (2016). https://kararlarbilgibankasi.anayasa.gov.tr/BB/2014/11864.

44. The Roboski families and human rights activists accused the Constitutional Court and ECtHR of producing and maintaining impunity for those involved in the Roboski massacre by using procedural mistakes as an excuse; see "Joint Statement on Roboski Massacre Decision of the ECHR," Diyarbakır Bar Association, Human Rights Association [İHD], Human Rights Foundation of Turkey [TİHV], Mülkiye Human Rights Center, May 24, 2018, https://ihd.org.tr/en/joint-statement-on-roboski-massacre -decision-of-the-echr/. Some also blamed the lawyer who submitted the medical report and the Şırnak Bar Association (Sak, "Roboski Katliamı'nın 10. yıl dönümü"). A human rights lawyer and scholar, Kerem Altiparmak ("Roboski and Procedural Rules"), who had joined the legal team preparing the families' application to the ECtHR, also argued that both the Constitutional Court and ECtHR, instead of the families or their lawyers, made separate procedural mistakes in reaching the inadmissibility decision.

Chapter Five

1. Kelly, "In a Treacherous State," 183.

2. Politicians and scholars have defined "deep state" in a variety of ways that range from the military and military tutelage to a crime organization that bridges crime syndicates, bureaucrats, and politicians (Gingeras, *Heroin, Organized Crime*; Sabuktay, "Tracing the Deep State"; Söyler, *The Turkish Deep State*).

3. Özar et al., *From Past to Present a Paramilitary Organization in Turkey*.

4. Smuggling or other illegal economies can be considered socially legitimate in specific contexts. For example, Rebecca Galemba ("Corn Is Food, Not Contraband"; *Contraband Corridor*) has shown how the smuggling of corn was justified in the Mexican-Guatemalan borderlands because corn was widely seen as a food item central to daily subsistence. Ieva Jusionyte ("On and Off the Record") has demonstrated that borderland communities across Argentina, Brazil, and Paraguay justified the smuggling of electronics by arguing that the Argentine state's taxes on those goods were excessive. While illegal activities can be viewed as legitimate for generating small amounts of wealth and thus reproducing (rather than disrupting) the existing socioeconomic hierarchies (Bocarejo, "Thinking with (Il)Legality"), the changing socioeconomic structures and emergence of new inequalities and injustices, such as a shift from planned economy to market economy, can also render socially unaccepted illegal economies, such as the cultivation of hashish, tolerable (Botoeva, "Multiple Narratives of Il/legality and Im/morality"). The ways of spending illegally obtained wealth might also have a role in its social justifications or dismissals. In contrast to extravagant expenditures, for example, investing such wealth into one's household or community may

also establish social legitimacy (De Boeck, "Domesticating Diamonds and Dollars"; Donovan, "Magendo").

5. For these trials, see Chapter 2.

6. The incident was also reported in the national newspapers; see "VIP Sevkiyat [The VIP Shipment]," *Yeni Şafak*, January 21, 2013, https://www.yenisafak.com/gundem/vip-sevkiyat-459774.

7. In analyzing the contested and uneven aspects of the sovereignty power in "sensitive spaces," such as borders or refugee camps, where different sovereignty-claiming forces overlapped and challenged each other, Elizabeth Cullen Dunn and Jason Cons have articulated the concept of aleatory sovereignty as "literally rule by chance, or the constant making and remaking of shifting landscapes of unpredictable power with which both the governed and the governing must contend" ("Aleatory Sovereignty," 102). In this formulation, "sovereignty . . . appears not just contingent (which implies that if only all the historically or contextually specific factors are known, the outcome can be explained) but aleatory and often inexplicable from the perspective of individual actors, who cannot know everything about how and why the other people in sensitive space act" ("Aleatory Sovereignty," 102).

8. In criminal prosecutions, the courts established a fixed payment for the lawyers involved in the case. The lawyers, especially senior, experienced lawyers, considered these court-imposed fees too low and often requested additional lawyering fees from their clients.

9. In June 2012, Kurdish guerrillas launched a military campaign to block the Turkish military's access to Şemzînan, a border district between Iraq and Iran that was connected to Turkey by two mountain passes. The guerrillas controlled one of these passes for several weeks, which resulted in most permanent checkpoints in Wan and Colemêrg provinces to be unattended or only partially functional during the daytime. See Chapter 1.

10. Dunn and Cons, "Aleatory Sovereignty."

11. I use the phrase "moral economy" to refer to a set of obligations and norms that stem from specific modalities of exchange and valorization embedded in economic activities (for a similar conceptualization, see Carrier, "Moral Economy"). For various ways in which the concept has been understood and used, see Götz, "Moral Economy."

12. See "Bitlis'te Korucunun Öldürülmesini PKK Üstlendi [PKK Claims Responsibility for the Killing of a Village Guard in Bitlis]," *Bianet*, October 28, 2014, https://bianet.org/bianet/insan-haklari/159493-bitlis-te-korucunun-oldurulmesini-pkk-ustlendi. The other village guard leader's body was found in September 2012. The PKK forces blamed that village guard for participating in the killing of the same women guerrilla unit in March 2012; see "YJA Star: Ali Yum tarafımızca cezalandırıldı [YJA Star: We punished Ali Yum]," *ANF News*, October 1, 2012, https://firatnews.com/guncel/yja-star-ali-yum-tarafymyzca-cezalandyryldy-8699.

13. For a definition of "moral contract" in the context of revolutionary and national liberation movements, see Wilson, *Sovereignty in Exile*.

14. Anthropologist Marlene Schäfers invokes the concept of the "moral bargain" in describing how Kurdish subjects "navigated within a space of hegemony that centrally determined how they were able to render their undertakings politically and morally

legitimate" instead of the concept of moral contract, since the latter framing tends to presume independent actors who engaged in a contract with the liberation movement ("Walking a Fine Line," 129).

15. Kapıköy was the only border passage located inside Wan province. In addition to the Kapıköy border passage, there were two other border passages between Turkey and Iran: the Gürbulak border passage, which was located in the Bazîd district of Agirî province and neighbored Wan to the north, and the Esendere border passage, which was located in the Gever district of Colemêrg province and neighbored Wan to the south.

16. The amending law (Law 6360) changed the metropolitan municipalities law (Law 5216) to reorganize the metropolitan municipality as a Province-wide administrative body, extend its authority at the expense of the appointed governor's authority, and add villages and other rural settlements to a single electoral district of the metropolitan municipality. The legislation upgraded Wan province, alongside twelve other provinces, to a Metropolitan Province (*Büyükşehir*).

17. The state security forces exhibited tortured bodies of the murdered militants as a performance of unleashed sovereign power from the 1990s onward. During the clashes between the PKK forces and youth militants, in two different incidents, one in Gimgim (Off. Varto) of Mûş province in August 2015 and the other in Şirnex city center in October 2015, the security forces exhibited the tortured lifeless bodies of murdered PKK militants.

18. In February 2017, three years after the elections, the central government appointed the district governor in lieu of the democratically elected mayor.

Conclusion

1. The HDP's electoral success had come at a heavy cost. During campaigns from April to June, ISIS (the Islamic State of Iraq and Syria), paramilitary groups (e.g., Kurdish Hizbullah), and state security forces targeted party rallies and members in more than a hundred attacks. In this period, five people were killed and hundreds more were wounded.

2. Until 2017, Turkey was governed through a parliamentarian system in which the president performs representative roles with some limited executive and overseeing powers and in which the prime minister and the Council of Ministers perform the main executive roles. The AKP founder and leader, Erdoğan, was elected as a non-executive president in August 2014, after having served as prime minister for eleven years. Because the presidency office was mainly representative and non-executive at the time, Erdoğan left his party after he was elected as the new president. Following the regime change that introduced the executive presidency, President Erdoğan joined the AKP and became its leader again in 2017.

3. During the Syrian civil war, Kurdish forces led by the PYD (Democratic Union Party, *Partiya Yekîtiya Demokratîk*), which the Turkish state viewed as a PKK branch and designated as a terrorist organization, created self-defense forces and declared three autonomous cantons, Afrin, Kobanê, and Jazeera, in western Kurdistan (Rojava) in 2014.

4. ISIS, which is also referred to as the Islamic State of Iraq and the Levant (ISIL) and the Islamic State (IS), is a transnational militant group that follows the Salafi jihadist

ideology. It originated from a jihadist insurgency that broke out in Baghdad in 2004, following the occupation of Iraq by the U.S.-led coalition. After breaking ties with the Sunni-Salafi militant organization Al-Qaeda in 2013, ISIS seized control of territories in northern Iraq and acquired U.S.-supplied military equipment from the Iraqi army. Using this sophisticated military equipment, ISIS expanded its control over eastern Syria amidst the ongoing war in Syria. The Kurdish PYD, along with its armed wings, the YPG (People's Defense Units, *Yekîneyên Parastina Gel*) and the YPJ (Women's Defense Units, *Yekîneyên Parastina Jin*), took the lead in resisting ISIS's expansion. With the help of airstrikes and military equipment that the U.S.-led international joint force air-dropped, the PYD-led coalition ended the siege of Kobanê in January 2015, after it had fiercely defended the city center against ISIS for months. The coalition also regained most of the territory that ISIS had previously controlled in North and East Syria. In October 2015, the PYD-led coalition was reorganized and became known as the Syria Democratic Forces. Subsequently, in September 2018, the Autonomous Administration of North and East Syria, which consists of self-governing sub-regions, was established.

5. Reflecting this sense of distrust, the Assembly framed the self-rule declaration as a civilian act of self-defense; they stated that they "do not reject the state" but "the state institutions lost their legitimacy in their eyes." See "Şırnak Halk Meclisi öz yönetim ilan etti [The Şırnak People's Assembly declared self-governance]," *T24*, August 11, 2015, https://t24.com.tr/haber/sirnak-halk-meclisi-demokratik-ozerklik-ilan-etti,305805.

6. These militias were organized under YDG-H (Patriotic Revolutionary Youth Movement, *Yurtsever Demokratik Gençlik Hareketi*).

7. The Office of the United Nations High Commissioner for Human Rights reported that at least 2,000 people were killed during the urban warfare, while the International Crisis Group estimated that over 3,300 people were killed between June 2015 and July 2016. See The Office of the United Nations High Commissioner for Human Rights, "Report on the human rights situation in South-East Turkey: July 215 to December 2016," *United Nations*, February 2017, https://www.ohchr.org/sites/default/files/Documents/Countries/TR/OHCHR_South-East_TurkeyReport_10March2017.pdf. For the Crisis Group's report see Crisis Group, "Türkiye's PKK Conflict: A Visual Explainer," March 15, 2023, https://www.crisisgroup.org/content/turkeys-pkk-conflict-visual-explainer. The International Crisis Group recorded that at least 6,561 people, armed and unarmed from all parties, were killed between July 2015 and March 2023.

8. With the support of the Turkish government and various politicians, Fethullah Gülen and his followers, beginning in the 1980s, created a network of schools, civil society organizations, and media outlets inside and outside of Turkey. While the Gülen movement has long been criticized for infiltrating the high state bureaucracy, particularly the police, judiciary, and military, and hiding their Gülenist affiliations, the AKP government cooperated with the movement to undermine secularist, Kemalist, and nationalist government workers during the 2000s and early 2010s. However, as the Gülen movement gained power, indirect disputes with the AKP government began. One of the first disputes emerged as early as 2008, when the AKP developed a new Kurdish policy and initiated peace talks with the PKK. Audio recordings of secret talks between PKK representatives and the Turkish intelligence agents that occurred in 2009 were leaked

in September 2011. Based on these recordings, a Gülenist prosecutor invited the head of Turkish intelligence to give his testimony; the prosecutor allegedly planned to arrest him in February 2012. In December 2014, the Gülenist prosecutors also launched corruption investigations against the AKP government that pressured the judiciary to remove these prosecutors from their posts.

9. "Van'da gözaltına alınan 6 hakim ve savcı tutuklandı [Six judges and prosecutors detained in Van were arrested]," *Memurlar.net*, July 27, 2016, https://www.memurlar.net/haber/599364/van-da-gozaltina-alinan-6-hakim-ve-savci-tutuklandi.html.

10. In February 2024, the Turkish justice minister reported that around four thousand prosecutors and judges were dismissed after July 2016; see "Adalet Bakanı Tunç: Mesleklerine geri dönen 387 isimle (hakim ve savcı) alakalı HSK olarak yeniden inceleme başlattık [Minister of Justice Tunç: We, as the HSK, have initiated a new investigation regarding the 387 individuals (judges and prosecutors) who have returned to their professions]," *Anadolu Ajansı*, February 17, 2024, https://www.aa.com.tr/tr/gundem/adalet-bakani-tunc-mesleklerine-geri-donen-387-isimle-hakim-ve-savci-alakali-hsk-olarak-yeniden-inceleme-baslattik/3140278. It was reported that, in May 2006, the total number of judges and prosecutors was 15,899; see Ünlü, "2016 yılı Mayıs ayına göre kamu personel sayıları."

11. According to the Turkish Ministry of Justice's 2024 Performance Program, the total number of judges and prosecutors was 23,797 as of November 2023; see Ministry of Justice, *Performans Programı: 2024.*

12. I observed these phases through my ethnography, which began during the escalated clashes between the Turkish military and the PKK in the summer of 2012 and witnessed the ceasefire and indirect peace talks. Although I left the field during these talks, which had already begun to stall by the end of the 2014 summer, I visited the region again in 2015 and remained in contact with several interlocutors during the period of urban warfare and resumed counterinsurgency in Kurdistan.

13. Scheppele, "Autocratic Legalism"; de Sa e Silva, "Good Bye, Liberal-Legal Democracy."

14. For an example of the analysis of "democratic backsliding" in Turkey, see Kirişçi and Sloat, "The Rise and Fall of Liberal Democracy in Turkey." Others have used similar expressions, such as "authoritarian drift" (Akyol, "Turkey's Authoritarian Drift") or "the drift toward competitive authoritarianism" (Özbudun, "Turkey's Judiciary and the Drift").

15. For a similar critique of liberal legalism in the Turkish context, see Gökarıksel and Türem, "The Banality of Exception?"

16. In authoritarian regimes, from Egypt to Russia and China, marginalized groups have used the state courts to challenge state-committed rights violations; see Moustafa, *The Struggle for Constitutional Power*; Stern, *Environmental Litigation in China.*

17. Goodale, *Reinventing Human Rights.*

18. For examples of such engagements, see Kirsch, "Juridification of Indigenous Politics"; Sapignoli, *Hunting Justice.* For the use of liberal law as long as it advances independently set and pursued political goals by Indigenous groups, see Speed, *Rights in Rebellion*; Hernández Castillo, *Multiple Injustices.*

19. Hale, "Using and Refusing the Law," 619.

20. Hale, "Using and Refusing the Law."

21. Hale, "Using and Refusing the Law," 620.

22. Mora, "(Dis)Placement of Anthropological Legal Activism."

23. Hale, "Using and Refusing the Law," 623.

24. For calls on domestic or international courts to try border enforcement agents for unlawful deportation or detention of migrants across Australian, U.S., and European borders, see Altholtz, "Elusive Justice"; Chetail, "Is There Any Blood on My Hands?"; Mann, "Border Violence as Crime." For the recent uptake of environmental or climate change litigations in domestic and international courts, see Peel and Osofky, "Climate Change Litigation"; Setzer and Vanhala, "Climate Change Litigation."

25. Anthropologist Justin Richland has suggested that "cooperation without submission (CWS)" (which was originally coined by Richland's mentor Emory Sekaquaptewa, a Hopi linguist, lawyer, and anthropologist) is a mode of interaction that Indigenous nations develop to recognize each nation's sovereignty, a mode based on the autonomy of each nation's "ways of valuing [or "norming"], knowing, and relating to the world" (*Cooperation without Submission*, 4). Richland has further argued that the Indigenous peoples deployed CWS in their interactions with the U.S. government agencies as a distinct discursive act to refuse U.S. sovereignty superiority and enact their own "juris-diction" and hence sovereignty (*Cooperation without Submission*, 4). For other works on Indigenous people's practices of refusal in the context of Turtle Island (North America), see Coulthard, *Red Skin, White Masks*; Simpson, *Mohawk Interruptus*.

26. Browne (*Dark Matters*) has conceptualized "dark sousveillance" by building upon Steve Mann's articulation of "Veillance Plane," in which an axis of surveillance and "anti-surveillance" is juxtaposed with an axis of sousveillance and anti-sousveillance" (see Mann et al., "Sousveillance").

27. For "militarized global apartheid," see Besteman, "Militarized Global Apartheid"; for data-driven capitalism, see Shoshana Zuboff's articulation of "the age of surveillance capitalism" (*The Age of Surveillance Capitalism*).

BIBLIOGRAPHY

Abraham, Itty, and Willem van Schendel. "Introduction." In *Illicit Flows and Criminal Things: States, Borders, and the Other Side of Globalization*, edited by Willem van Schendel and Itty Abraham. Indiana University Press, 2005.

Açıksöz, Salih Can. *Sacrificial Limbs: Masculinity, Disability, and Political Violence in Turkey*. University of California Press, 2019.

Agamben, Giorgio. *Homo Sacer: Sovereign Power and Bare Life*. Translated by Daniel Heller-Roazen. Stanford University Press, 1998.

Agamben, Giorgio. *State of Exception*. Translated by Kevin Attell. University of Chicago Press, 2005.

Akad, Lütfi Ömer, dir. *Hudutların Kanunu*. Dadaş Film, 1967.

Akarsu, Hayal. "'We're Tired of This Weber Guy!'—Force Experts, Police Reforms, and the Violence of Standardization." *American Anthropologist* 127, no. 1 (2025): 5–19. https://doi.org/10.1111/aman.28028.

Akçam, Taner. *A Shameful Act: The Armenian Genocide and the Question of Turkish Responsibility*. Metropolitan Books, 2006.

Aker, A. Tamer, Ayşe Betül Çelik, Dilek Kurban, Turgay Ünalan, and Hatice Deniz Yükseker. *Türkiye'de Ülke İçinde Yerinden Edilme Sorunu: Tespitler ve Çözüm Önerileri*. İstanbul: TESEV Yayınları, 2005.

Akkaya, Ahmet Hamdi. "The 'Palestinian Dream' in the Kurdish Context." *Kurdish Studies* 3, no. 1 (2015): 47–63. https://doi.org/10.33182/ks.v3i1.391.

Aktan, İrfan. "Çözüm Sürecinin Kronolojisi [Chronology of the Peace Process]." *Bianet*, November 11, 2014. https://bianet.org/haber/cozum-surecinin-kronolojisi-160243.

Akyol, Mustafa. "Turkey's Authoritarian Drift." *New York Times*, November 10, 2015.

Altholz, Roxanna. "Elusive Justice: Legal Redress for Killings by U.S. Border Agents." *Berkeley La Raza Law Journal* 27 (2017): 1–39.

Altiparmak, Kerem. "Roboski and Procedural Rules: How the Truth about a Massacre Was Buried in the Pages of History." *New Journal of European Criminal Law* 11, no. 4 (2020): 489–503. https://doi.org/10.1177/2032284420913950.

Altuğ, Seda. "The Turkish-Syrian Border and Politics of Difference in Turkey and Syria (1921–1939)." In *Syria: Borders, Boundaries, and the State*, edited by Matthieu Cimino. Springer International Publishing, 2020.

Anand, Nikhil. *Hydraulic City: Water and the Infrastructures of Citizenship in Mumbai.* Duke University Press, 2017.

Anders, Gerhard. "Testifying about 'Uncivilized Events': Problematic Representations of Africa in the Trial Against Charles Taylor." *Leiden Journal of International Law* 24, no. 4 (2011): 937–59.

Andersson, Ruben. *Illegality, Inc.: Clandestine Migration and the Business of Bordering Europe.* University of California Press, 2014.

Andreas, Peter. *Blue Helmets and Black Markets: The Business of Survival in the Siege of Sarajevo.* Cornell University Press, 2008.

Andreas, Peter. *Smuggler Nation: How Illicit Trade Made America.* Oxford University Press, 2014.

Aras, Ramazan. *The Wall: The Making and Unmaking of the Turkish-Syrian Border.* Palgrave Macmillan, 2020.

Aydın, Delal. "Mobilising the Kurds in Turkey: Newroz as a Myth." In *The Kurdish Question in Turkey*, edited by Cengiz Gunes and Welat Zeydanlioglu. Routledge, 2013. https://doi.org/10.4324/9780203796450-5.

Babül, Elif. *Bureaucratic Intimacies: Translating Human Rights in Turkey.* Stanford University Press, 2017.

Babül, Elif. "Radical Once More: The Contentious Politics of Human Rights in Turkey." *Social Anthropology* 28, no. 1 (2020): 50–65. https://doi.org/10.1111/1469-8676.12740.

Baksi, Mahmut. *Teyrê Baz, ya da, Hüseyin Baybaşin, bir Kürt İşadamı.* Peri Yayınları, 1999.

Bargu, Banu. *Starve and Immolate: The Politics of Human Weapons.* Columbia University Press, 2014.

Barry, Andrew. *Material Politics: Disputes Along the Pipeline.* Wiley-Blackwell, 2013.

Baxi, Pratiksha. "Access to Justice and Rule-of (Good) Law: The Cunning of Judicial Reform in India." *Indian Journal of Human Development* 2, no. 2 (2008): 279–302. https://doi.org/10.1177/0973703020080202.

Bayir, Derya. *Minorities and Nationalism in Turkish Law.* Routledge, 2016.

Benjamin, Walter. "Critique of Violence." Translated by Edmund Jephcott. In *Walter Benjamin: Selected Writings Volume 1, 1913–1926*, edited by Marcus Bullock and Michael W. Jennings. The Belknap Press of Harvard University Press, 1996.

Berger, Margaret A., and Lawrence M. Solan. "The Uneasy Relationship Between Science and Law: An Essay and Introduction." *Brooklyn Law Review* 73, no. 3 (2008): 847–55.

Beşe, Ertan. "Geçici Köy Korucuları." In *Almanak Türkiye 2005: Güvenlik Sektörü ve Demokratik Gözetim*, edited by Ümit Cizre. TESEV Yayınları, 2006.

Beşe, Ertan. "Özel Harekat." In *Almanak Türkiye 2005: Güvenlik Sektörü ve Demokratik Gözetim*, edited by Ümit Cizre. TESEV Yayınları, 2006.

Beşikçi, İsmail. *Devletler Arası Sömürge Kürdistan.* Yurt Kitap Yayın, 1990.

Beşikçi, İsmail. *Doğu Anadolu'nun Düzeni: Sosyo-ekonomik ve Etnik Temeller.* E. Yayınları, 1970.

Besteman, Catherine. "Militarized Global Apartheid." *Current Anthropology* 60, no. S19 (2019): S26–38. https://doi.org/10.1086/699280.

Bhabha, Homi. *The Location of Culture.* Routledge, 1994.

Billé, Franck, ed. *Voluminous States: Sovereignty, Materiality, and the Territorial Imagination.* Duke University Press, 2020.

Biner, Zerrin Özlem. "Documenting 'Truth' in the Margins of the Turkish State." In *Law against the State: Ethnographic Forays into Law's Transformations,* edited by Julia Eckert, Brian Donahoe, Christian Strümpell, and Zerrin Özlem Biner. Cambridge University Press, 2012.

Biner, Zerrin Özlem. *States of Dispossession: Violence and Precarious Coexistence in Southeast Turkey.* University of Pennsylvania Press, 2019.

Birdal, Murat. *The Political Economy of Ottoman Public Debt: Insolvency and European Financial Control in the Late Nineteenth Century.* Tauris Academic Studies, 2010.

Björkman, Lisa. *Pipe Politics, Contested Waters: Embedded Infrastructures of Millennial Mumbai.* Duke University Press, 2015.

Bocarejo, Diana. "Thinking with (Il)Legality: The Ethics of Living with Bonanzas." *Current Anthropology* 59, S18 (2018): S48–59. https://doi.org/10.1086/696160.

Bonilla, Yarimar. "Unsettling Sovereignty." *Cultural Anthropology* 32, no. 3 (2017): 330–39. https://doi.org/10.14506/ca32.3.02.

Botoeva, Gulzat. "Multiple Narratives of Il/legality and Im/morality: The Case of Small-Scale Hashish Harvesting in Kyrgyzstan." *Theoretical Criminology* 25, no. 2 (2021): 268–83. https://doi.org/10.1177/1362480619880344.

Bovenkerk, Frank, and Yücel Yesilgöz. *The Turkish Mafia: A History of the Heroin Godfathers.* Milo Books, 2007.

Bozarslan, Hamit. "Kurds and the Turkish State." In *The Cambridge History of Turkey,* Volume 4, edited by Reşat Kasaba, 333–56. Cambridge University Press, 2008.

Bozarslan, Hamit. *Network-Building, Ethnicity and Violence in Turkey.* Emirates Center for Strategic Studies and Research, 1999.

Bozçalı, Fırat. "Corridors of Countersovereignty: Insurgency, Smuggling, and Post-Nation-state Politics in Turkey's Kurdish Highlands." *Anthropological Theory* 24, no. 3 (2024): 325–43. https://doi.org/10.1177/14634996241232755.

Bozçalı, Fırat. "Money for Life: Border Killings, Compensation Claims and Life-Money Conversions in Turkey's Kurdish Borderlands." In *Turkey's Necropolitical Laboratory: Democracy, Violence and Resistance,* edited by Banu Bargu. Edinburgh University Press, 2019.

Bozçalı, Fırat. "Partners in Crime: Smuggling Economies (Kaçak/Qaçax) and Human-Animal Collaborations in Turkey's Kurdish Borderlands." *Journal of Cultural Economy* 17, no. 2 (2024): 249–63. https://doi.org/10.1080/17530350.2023.2189144.

Bozçalı, Fırat. "Proving Injustice: Smuggler Killings, Impunity Work, and Vernacular Counterforensics in Turkey's Kurdish Borderlands." *American Anthropologist* 126, no. 4 (2024): 567–80. https://doi.org/10.1111/aman.28015.

Browne, Simone. *Dark Matters: On the Surveillance of Blackness*. Duke University Press, 2015.

Bryant, Rebecca E. "Sovereignty." In *International Encyclopedia of Anthropology*. Wiley, 2018. https://doi.org/10.1002/9781118924396.wbiea1868.

Burns, Robert P. *A Theory of the Trial*. Princeton University Press, 1999. https://doi.org/10.1515/9781400823376.

Çalı, Başak. "Human Rights Organizations in Turkey." In *The Oxford Handbook of Turkish Politics*, edited by Güneş Murat Tezcür. Oxford University Press, 2020.

Campt, Tina Marie. "Black Visuality and the Practice of Refusal." *Women & Performance* 29, no. 1 (2019): 79–87. https://doi.org/10.1080/0740770X.2019.1573625.

Can, Başak. "Human Rights, Humanitarianism, and State Violence: Medical Documentation of Torture in Turkey." *Medical Anthropology Quarterly* 30, no. 3 (2016): 342–58. https://doi.org/10.1111/maq.12259.

Carrier, James G. "Moral Economy: What's in a Name." *Anthropological Theory* 18, no. 1 (2018): 18–35. https://doi.org/10.1177%2F1463499617735259.

Castoriadis, Cornelius. *The Imaginary Institution of Society*. Translated by Kathleen Blamey. Polity, 1987.

Çelik, Adnan. "Challenging State Borders: Smuggling as Kurdish Infra-Politics During 'The Years of Silence.'" In *Kurds in Turkey: Ethnographies of Heterogeneous Experiences*, edited by Lucie Drechselová and Adnan Çelik, 159–84. Lexington Books, 2020.

Cemal, Hasan. *Kürtler*. Doğan Kitap, 2003.

Chatterjee, Moyukh. *Composing Violence: The Limits of Exposure and the Making of Minorities*. Duke University Press, 2023.

Chatterjee, Moyukh. "The Impunity Effect: Majoritarian Rule, Everyday Legality, and State Formation in India." *American Ethnologist* 44, no. 1 (2017): 118–30. https://doi.org/10.1111/amet.12430.

Chatterjee, Partha. *The Politics of the Governed: Reflections on Popular Politics in Most of the World*. Columbia University Press, 2004.

Chetail, Vincent. "Is There Any Blood on My Hands? Deportation as a Crime of International Law." *Leiden Journal of International Law* 29, no. 3 (2016): 917–43. https://doi.org/10.1017/S0922156516000376.

Chua, Lynette J. "Collective Litigation and the Constitutional Challenges to Decriminalizing Homosexuality in Singapore." *Journal of Law and Society* 44, no. 3 (2017): 433–55. https://doi.org/10.1111/jols.12037.

Clarke, Kamari Maxine. "Affective Justice: The Racialized Imaginaries of International Justice." *PoLAR: Political and Legal Anthropology Review* 42, no. 2 (2019): 244–67. https://doi.org/10.1111/plar.12307.

Clarke, Kamari Maxine, and Sara Kendall. "'The Beauty Is That It Speaks for Itself': Geospatial Materials as Evidentiary Matters." *Law Text Culture* 23, no. 1 (2019): 91–118.

Çöğgün, Mustafa. "Terörle Mücadelenin bir Parçası Olarak Kaçakçılıkla Mücadele." *İdarecinin Sesi* (Ocak-Şubat 2013): 39–44.

Cohn, Bernard S. *Colonialism and Its Forms of Knowledge: The British in India.* Princeton University Press, 1996.

Comaroff, John L., and Jean Comaroff. "Law and Disorder in the Postcolony: An Introduction." In *Law and Disorder in the Postcolony,* edited by J. L. Comaroff and J. Comaroff. University of Chicago Press, 2006.

Coulthard, Glen Sean. *Red Skin, White Masks: Rejecting the Colonial Politics of Recognition.* University of Minnesota Press, 2014.

Cover, Robert M. "Violence and the Word." *The Yale Law Journal* 95, no. 8 (1986): 1601–29. https://doi.org/10.2307/796468.

Cruz-Santiago, Arely. "Lists, Maps, and Bones: The Untold Journeys of Citizen-Led Forensics in Mexico." *Victims & Offenders* 15, no. 3 (2020): 350–69. https://doi.org/10.1080/15564886.2020.1718046.

Dağlı, Faysal. *Birakujî: Kürtlerin İç Savaşı.* Belge Yayınları, 1994.

Darıcı, Haydar. "Negotiating Smuggling: Tribes, Debt, and the Informal Economy in Turkish Kurdistan." *Journal of Cultural Economy* 17, no. 2 (2024): 165–77. https://doi.org/10.1080/17530350.2023.2259412.

Darıcı, Haydar, and Serra Hakyemez. "Neither Civilian nor Combatant: Weaponised Spaces and Spatialised Bodies in Cizre." In *Turkey's Necropolitical Laboratory: Democracy, Violence and Resistance,* edited by Banu Bargu. Edinburgh University Press, 2019.

De Boeck, Filip. "Domesticating Diamonds and Dollars: Identity, Expenditure and Sharing in Southwestern Zaire (1984–1997)." *Development and Change* 29, no. 4 (1998): 777–810. https://doi.org/10.1111/1467-7660.00099.

De León, Jason. *The Land of Open Graves: Living and Dying on the Migrant Trail.* University of California Press, 2015.

Degani, Michael. *The City Electric: Infrastructure and Ingenuity in Postsocialist Tanzania.* Duke University Press, 2022.

Demirel, Çayan, and Ertugrul Mavioglu, dirs. *Bakur: Inside the PKK.* Surela Film, 2015.

Derince, Mehmet Şerif. "A Break or Continuity? Turkey's Politics of Kurdish Language in the New Millennium." *Dialectical Anthropology* 37, no. 1 (2013): 145–52. https://doi.org/10.1007/s10624-013-9303-4.

Deringil, Selim. *The Well-Protected Domains: Ideology and the Legitimation of Power in the Ottoman Empire, 1876–1909.* I. B. Tauris, 1998.

Derrida, Jacques. "Force of Law: The Mystical Foundation of Authority." In *Deconstruction and the Possibility of Justice,* edited by Drucilla Cornell, Michael Rosenfield, and David G. Carlson. Routledge, 1992.

Derrida, Jacques. *Of Grammatology.* Corrected edition. Translated by Gayatri Chakravorty Spivak. Johns Hopkins University Press, 1997.

de Sa e Silva, Fabio. "Good Bye, Liberal-Legal Democracy." *Law & Social Inquiry* 48, no. 1 (2023): 292–313. https://doi.org/10.1017/lsi.2022.106.

Doğan, Taylan. *Savaş Ekonomisi.* Avesta Yayınları, 1998.

Donovan, Kevin P. "Magendo: Arbitrage and Ambiguity on an East African Frontier." *Cultural Anthropology* 36 no. 1 (2021): 110–37. https://doi.org/10.14506/ca36.1.05.

Doty, Roxanne Lynn. "Bare Life: Border-Crossing Deaths and Spaces of Moral Alibi." *Environment and Planning D: Society and Space* 29, no. 4 (2011): 599–612. https://doi .org/10.1068/d3110.

Drexler, Elizabeth. "History and Liability in Aceh, Indonesia: Single Bad Guys and Convergent Narratives." *American Ethnologist* 33, no. 3 (2006): 313–26. https://doi.org/10 .1525/ae.2006.33.3.313.

Dunn, Elizabeth Cullen, and Jason Cons. "Aleatory Sovereignty and the Rule of Sensitive Spaces." *Antipode* 46, no. 1 (2014): 92–109. https://doi.org/10.1111/anti.12028.

Duruiz, Deniz. "Erasure and Affect in Race-Making in Turkey." *POMEPS Studies* 44 (2021): 135–142.

Duruiz, Deniz. "Tracing the Conceptual Genealogy of Kurdistan as International Colony." *Middle East Report* 295 (Summer 2020). https://merip.org/2020/08/tracing -the-conceptual-genealogy-of-kurdistan-as-international-colony/.

Düzel, Esin. "Fragile Goddesses: Moral Subjectivity and Militarized Agencies in Female Guerrilla Diaries and Memoirs." *International Feminist Journal of Politics* 20, no. 2 (2018): 137–52. https://doi.org/10.1080/14616742.2017.1419823.

Eckert, Julia M., ed. *The Social Life of Anti-Terrorism Laws: The War on Terror and the Classifications of the "Dangerous Other."* Verlag, 2008. https://doi.org/10.14361/ 9783839409640.

Elden, Stuart. "Secure the Volume: Vertical Geopolitics and the Depth of Power." *Political Geography* 34 (2013): 35–51. https://doi.org/10.1016/j.polgeo.2012.12.009.

Engle, Karen. "A Genealogy of the Criminal Turn in Human Rights." In *Anti-Impunity and the Human Rights Agenda*, edited by Karen Engle, Zinaida Miller, and D. M. Davis. Cambridge University Press, 2016.

Erdinç, F. Cengiz. *Overdose Türkiye: Türkiye'de Eroin Kaçakçılığı, Bağımlılığı ve Politikalar.* İletişim Yayınları, 2004.

Ertür, Başak. *Spectacles and Specters: A Performative Theory of Political Trials.* 1st ed. Fordham University Press, 2022.

Ferguson, James. *The Anti-Politics Machine: "Development" Depoliticization, and Bureaucratic Power in Lesotho.* Cambridge University Press, 1990.

Ferrándiz, Francisco. "Exhuming the Defeated: Civil War Mass Graves in 21st-Century Spain." *American Ethnologist* 40, no. 1 (2013): 38–54. https://doi.org/10.1111/amet .12004.

Ferrándiz, Francisco, and Antonious Robben, eds. *Necropolitics: Mass Graves and Exhumations in the Age of Human Rights.* University of Pennsylvania Press, 2017.

Forensic Architecture. "The Killing of Tahir Elçi." February 8, 2019. https://forensic-architecture.org/investigation/the-killing-of-tahir-elci.

Foucault, Michel. *"Society Must Be Defended": Lectures at the Collège de France, 1975–1976.* Translated by David Macey. Picador, 2003.

Gal, Susan. "Language and the 'Arts of Resistance.'" *Cultural Anthropology* 10, no. 3 (1995): 407–24. https://doi.org/10.1525/can.1995.10.3.02a00060.

Galemba, Rebecca B. *Contraband Corridor: Making a Living at the Mexico-Guatemala Border.* Stanford University Press, 2018.

Galemba, Rebecca B. "'Corn Is Food, Not Contraband': The Right to 'Free Trade' at the Mexico–Guatemala Border." *American Ethnologist* 39, no. 4 (2012): 716–34. https://doi.org/10.1111/j.1548-1425.2012.01391.x.

Gallien, Max, and Florian Weigand, eds. *The Routledge Handbook of Smuggling*. Taylor & Francis, 2022.

Garapon, Béatrice, and Adnan Çelik. "From Tribal Chiefs to Marxist Activists: Kurdistan from 1946 to 1975." In *The Cambridge History of the Kurds*, edited by Hamit Bozarslan, Veli Yadirgi, and Cengiz Gunes. Cambridge University Press, 2021.

Ghobadi, Bahman, dir. *A Time for Drunken Horses*. MK2 Productions, Farabi Cinema Foundation, Bahman Gobadi Films, and Ferdosi Multimedia, 2000.

Gingeras, Ryan. *Heroin, Organized Crime, and the Making of Modern Turkey*. Oxford University Press, 2014.

Gökarıksel, Saygun, and Z. Umut Türem. "The Banality of Exception? Law and Politics in 'Post-Coup' Turkey." *The South Atlantic Quarterly* 118, no. 1 (2019): 175–87. https://doi.org/10.1215/00382876-7281684.

Göksedef, Ece. "90'larda Öldürülen Kürt İş Adamları Kimler, Sonraki Süreçte Neler Yaşandı? [Who Were the Kurdish Businesspeople Killed in the 90s, and What Happened in the Aftermath?]" *BBC News Türkçe*, May 27, 2021. https://www.bbc.com/turkce/haberler-turkiye-57257229.

Göner, Özlem. "Rightful Recognition of Kurdistan as a Colony and De-Colonizing Knowledge Production." *The Commentaries* 3, no. 1 (2023): 165–96. https://doi.org/10.33182/tc.v3i1.3147.

Good, Anthony. "Cultural Evidence in Courts of Law." *Journal of the Royal Anthropological Institute* 14, no. S1 (2008): S47–60. https://doi.org/10.1111/j.1467-9655.2008.00492.x.

Goodale, Mark. *Reinventing Human Rights*. Stanford University Press, 2022.

Gordillo, Gastón. "Hostile Terrain: On the Spatial and Affective Conditions for Revolution." *Territory, Politics, Governance* (2023): 1–16. https://doi.org/10.1080/21622671.2023.2172450.

Gordillo, Gastón. "Terrain as Insurgent Weapon: An Affective Geometry of Warfare in the Mountains of Afghanistan." *Political Geography* 64 (2018): 53–62. https://doi.org/10.1016/j.polgeo.2018.03.001.

Gören, Şerif, dir. *Katırcılar*. Uzman Filmcilik, 1987.

Götz, Norbert. "'Moral Economy': Its Conceptual History and Analytical Prospects." *Journal of Global Ethics* 11, no. 2 (2015): 147–62. https://doi.org/10.1080/17449626.2015.1054556.

Green, Linda. *Fear as a Way of Life: Mayan Widows in Rural Guatemala*. Columbia University Press, 1999.

Greenberg, Jessica. "Counterpedagogy, Sovereignty, and Migration at the European Court of Human Rights." *Law & Social Inquiry* 46, no. 2 (2021): 518–39. https://doi.org/10.1017/lsi.2020.40.

Greenberg, Jessica. "Law, Politics, and Efficacy at the European Court of Human Rights." *American Ethnologist* 47, no. 4 (2020): 417–31. https://doi.org/10.1111/amet.12971.

Gross-Wyrtzen, Leslie, and Alex A. Moulton. "Toward 'Fugitivity as Method': An Introduction to the Special Issue." *ACME an International E-Journal for Critical Geographies* 22, no. 5 (2023): 1258–72. https://doi.org/10.7202/1107308ar.

Guiraudon, Virgine, and Gallya Lahav. "A Reappraisal of the State Sovereignty Debate: The Case of Migration Control." *Comparative Political Studies* 33, no. 2 (2000): 163–95. https://doi.org/10.1177/0010414000033002001.

Gündoğan, Cemil. *Kawa Davası Savunması ve Kürtlerde Siyasi Savunma Geleneği*. Vate Yayınevi, 2007.

Güneş, Cengiz. *The Kurdish National Movement in Turkey: From Protest to Resistance*. Routledge, 2012.

Gunter, Michael M. "A de Facto Kurdish State in Northern Iraq." *Third World Quarterly* 14, no. 2 (1993): 295–319. https://doi.org/10.1080/01436599308420326.

Gupta, Akhil. "An Anthropology of Electricity from the Global South." *Cultural Anthropology* 30, no. 4 (2015): 555–68. https://doi.org/10.14506/ca30.4.04.

Gürcan, Metin. "Ordunun 'organik' Yük Taşıma Sistemi: Katırlar." *Al-Monitor*, January 27, 2016. https://www.al-monitor.com/tr/contents/articles/originals/2016/01/turkey-army-recruits-mules-for-transportations.html.

Gusterson, Hugh. "Drone Warfare in Waziristan and the New Military Humanism." *Current Anthropology* 60, S19 (2019): S77–86. https://doi.org/10.1086/701022.

Guyer, Jane I. *Marginal Gains: Monetary Transactions in Atlantic Africa*. University of Chicago Press, 2004.

Hacking, Ian. "How Should We Do the History of Statistics?" In *The Foucault Effect: Studies in Governmentality: With Two Lectures by and an Interview with Michel Foucault*, edited by Graham Burchell, Colin Gordon, and Peter Miller, 181–96. University of Chicago Press, 1991.

Hacking, Ian. *Historical Ontology*. Harvard University Press, 2002.

Hakyemez, Serra. "Lives and Times of Militancy: Terrorism Trials, State Violence and Kurdish Political Prisoners in Post-1980 Turkey." PhD diss., Johns Hopkins University, 2016.

Hakyemez, Serra. "Margins of the Archive: Torture, Heroism, and the Ordinary in Prison No. 5, Turkey." *Anthropological Quarterly* 90, no. 1 (2017): 107–38. https://doi.org/10.1353/anq.2017.0004.

Hale, Charles R. "Activist Research v. Cultural Critique: Indigenous Land Rights and the Contradictions of Politically Engaged Anthropology." *Cultural Anthropology* 21, no. 1 (2006): 96–12.

Hale, Charles R. "Using and Refusing the Law: Indigenous Struggles and Legal Strategies after Neoliberal Multiculturalism." *American Anthropologist* 122, no. 3 (2020): 618–31. https://doi.org/10.1111/aman.13416.

Handler, Joel F. *Lawyers and the Pursuit of Legal Rights*. Academic Press, 1978.

Hansen, Thomas Blom. "Governance and State Mythologies in Mumbai." In *States of Imagination: Ethnographic Explorations of the Postcolonial State*, edited by Thom Blom Hansen and Finn Stepputat. Duke University Press, 2001.

Hansen, Thomas Blom. "Performers of Sovereignty: On the Privatization of Security in Urban South Africa." *Critique of Anthropology* 26, no. 3 (2006): 279–95. https://doi.org/10.1177/0308275X06066583.

Hansen, Thomas Blom, and Finn Stepputat. "Sovereignty Revisited." *Annual Review of Anthropology* 35, no. 1 (2006): 295–315.

Harney, Stefano, and Fred Moten. *The Undercommons: Fugitive Planning & Black Study.* Wivenhoe: Minor Compositions, 2013.

Hecht, Gabrielle. *The Radiance of France: Nuclear Power and National Identity after World War II.* The MIT Press, 1998.

Hernández Castillo, Rosalva Aída. *Multiple Injustices: Indigenous Women, Law, and Political Struggle in Latin America.* University of Arizona Press, 2016.

Heyman, Josiah, ed. *States and Illegal Practices.* Berg Publishers, 1999.

Holston, James. *Insurgent Citizenship: Disjunctions of Democracy and Modernity in Brazil.* Princeton University Press, 2008.

Hovannisian, Richard G, ed. *Armenian Van/Vaspurakan.* Mazda Publishers, 2000.

Hussain, Nasser. "Hyperlegality." *New Criminal Law Review* 10, no. 4 (2007): 514–31. https://doi.org/10.1525/nclr.2007.10.4.514.

Işık, Ayhan. *Turkish Paramilitarism in Northern Kurdistan: State Violence in the 1990s.* Edinburgh University Press, 2024. https://doi.org/10.1515/9781399506007.

Jasanoff, Sheila. *Science at the Bar: Law, Science, and Technology in America.* Harvard University Press, 1995.

Jones, Andrew. "It's Not [Just] Cricket: The Art and Politics of the Popular – Cultural Imperialism, 'Sly Civility' & Postcolonial Incorporation." *Coolabah* 10, no. 10 (2013): 118–31. https://doi.org/10.1344/co201310118-131.

Jongerden, Joost. "Colonialism, Self-determination and Independence: The New PKK Paradigm." *The Peace in Kurdistan Campaign* 3 (May 2021). https://www.peaceinkurdistancampaign.com/pdf-colonialism-self-determination-and-independence-the-new-pkk-paradigm-by-dr-joost-jongerden/.

Jongerden, Joost. "Crafting Space, Making People: The Spatial Design of Nation in Modern Turkey." *European Journal of Turkish Studies: Social Sciences on Contemporary Turkey* 10 (2009). https://journals.openedition.org/ejts/4014.

Jongerden, Joost. *The Settlement Issue in Turkey and the Kurds: An Analysis of Spatial Policies, Modernity and War.* Brill Academic Publishers, 2007.

Jongerden, Joost, and Ahmet Hamdi Akkaya. *PKK Üzerine Yazılar.* Vate Yayınevi, 2012.

Jongerden, Joost, and Zeynep Gambetti, eds. *The Kurdish Issue in Turkey: A Spatial Perspective.* Routledge, 2015.

Jusionyte, Ieva. "On and Off the Record: The Production of Legitimacy in an Argentine Border Town." *PoLAR: Political and Legal Anthropology Review* 36, no. 2 (2013): 231–48. https://doi.org/10.1111/plar.12024.

Kadıoğlu, İ. Aytaç. "The Oslo Talks: Revealing the Turkish Government's Secret Negotiations with the PKK." *Studies in Conflict and Terrorism* 42, no. 10 (2019): 915–33. https://doi.org/10.3316/agispt.20190808015262.

Kalir, Barak, and Willem van Schendel. "Introduction: Nonrecording States between Legibility and Looking Away." *Focaal* 77 (2017): 1–7. https://doi.org/10.3167/fcl.2017 .770101.

Kandelaki, Nino. "Roadblocks in Turkey's New Southeast Strategy: An Analysis." *Bellingcat*, 2019. https://www.bellingcat.com/news/mena/2019/07/03/roadblocks-in-turkeys-new-southeast-strategy-an-analysis/.

Karayılan, Murat. *Bir Savaşın Anatomisi: Kürdistan'da Askeri Çizgi*. Aram Yayıncılık, 2014.

Kelley, Robin D. G. "Black Study, Black Struggle." *Ufahamu* 40, no. 2 (2018): 153–68. https://doi.org/10.5070/F7402040947.

Kelly, Tobias. "In a Treacherous State: The Fear of Collaboration Among West Bank Palestinians." In *Traitors: Suspicion, Intimacy and the Ethics of State-Building*, edited by Sharika Thiranagama and Tobias Kelly. University of Pennsylvania Press, 2010.

Kelly, Tobias. *This Side of Silence: Human Rights, Torture, and the Recognition of Cruelty*. University of Pennsylvania Press. 2012.

Kelsall, Tim. *Culture under Cross-examination: International Justice and the Special Court for Sierra Leone*. Cambridge University Press, 2009.

Kesselring, Rita. *Bodies of Truth: Law, Memory, and Emancipation in Post-Apartheid South Africa*. Stanford University Press, 2017.

Khalili, Laleh. "Counterterrorism and Counterinsurgency in the Neoliberal Age." In *The Oxford Handbook of Contemporary Middle-Eastern and North African History*, edited by Amal N. Ghazal and Jens Hanssen. Oxford University Press, 2015. https://doi.org/ 10.1093/oxfordhb/9780199672530.001.0001.

Khalili, Laleh. *Time in the Shadows: Confinement in Counterinsurgencies*. Stanford University Press, 2012.

Kirişçi, Kemal, and Amanda Sloat. "The Rise and Fall of Liberal Democracy in Turkey: Implications for the West." *Brookings Institute*, 2019. https://www.brookings .edu/research/the-rise-and-fall-of-liberal-democracy-in-turkey-implications-for-the -west/.

Kirsch, Stuart. "Juridification of Indigenous Politics." In *Law Against the State: Ethnographic Forays into Law's Transformations*, edited by Julia Eckert, Brian Donahoe, Christian Strümpell, and Zerrin Özlem Biner. Cambridge University Press, 2012.

Klein, Janet. *The Margins of Empire: Kurdish Militias in the Ottoman Tribal Zone*. Stanford University Press, 2011.

Koğacıoğlu, Dicle. "Conduct, Meaning and Inequality in an İstanbul Courthouse." *New Perspectives on Turkey* 39 (2008): 97–127. https://doi.org/10.1017/S0896634600005082.

Koğacıoğlu, Dicle. "Knowledge, Practice, and Political Community: The Making of 'Custom' In Turkey." *Differences: A Journal of Feminist Cultural* 22, no. 1 (2011): 172– 228. https://doi.org/10.1215/10407391-1218283.

Kohlbry, Paul. "Palestinian Counter-forensics and the Cruel Paradox of Property." *American Ethnologist* 49, no. 3 (2022): 374–86. https://doi.org/10.1111/amet.13084.

Koselleck, Reinhart. *Futures Past: On the Semantics of Historical Time*. Translated by Keith Tribe. Columbia University Press, 2004.

Kruse, Corinna. *The Social Life of Forensic Evidence*. University of California Press, 2015.

Küçük, Mustafa. "Terör Bitme Noktasına Geldi [Terror has Come to End]." *Hürriyet*. April 25, 2013. https://www.hurriyet.com.tr/gundem/teror-bitme-noktasina-geldi-23129012.

Kühn, Thomas. "An Imperial Borderland as Colony: Knowledge Production and the Elaboration of Difference in Ottoman Yemen, 1872–1914." *MIT Electronic Journal of Middle Eastern Studies* 3 (Spring 2003): 5–17.

Kurban, Dilek. *Limits of the Supranational Justice: The European Court of Human Rights and Turkey's Kurdish Conflict*. Cambridge University Press, 2020.

Kurt, Mehmet. *Kurdish Hizbullah in Turkey: Islamism, Violence and the State*. London: Pluto Press, 2017.

Kurt, Mehmet. "'My Muslim Kurdish Brother': Colonial Rule and Islamist Governmentality in the Kurdish Region of Turkey." *Journal of Balkan and Near Eastern Studies* 21, no. 3 (2019): 350–65. https://doi.org/10.1080/19448953.2018.1497757.

Kurt, Mashuq, and Nilay Özok-Gündoğan. "The Decolonial Turn in Kurdish Studies: An Introduction." *The South Atlantic Quarterly* 123, no. 4 (2024): 655–64. https://doi.org/10.1215/00382876-11381065.

Latour, Bruno. *Pandora's Hope: Essays on the Reality of Science Studies*. Harvard University Press, 1999.

Latour, Bruno. *The Making of Law: An Ethnography of the Conseil d'Etat*. Translated by Marina Brilman and Alain Pottage. Cambridge: Polity, 2010.

Lazarus-Black, Mindie. *Legitimate Acts and Illegal Encounters: Law and Society in Antigua and Barbuda*. Smithsonian Institution Press, 1994.

Lazarus-Black, Mindie. "The Rites of Domination: Practice, Process, and Structure in Lower Courts." *American Ethnologist* 24, no. 3 (1997): 628–51. https://doi.org/10.1525/ae.1997.24.3.628.

Leachman, Gwendolyn M. "From Protest to Perry: How Litigation Shaped the LGBT Movement's Agenda." *UC Davis Law Review* 47 (2014): 1667–751.

Lefebvre, Henri. *Rhythmanalysis: Space, Time and Everyday Life*. Continuum, 2004.

Le Ray, Marie. "Experiencing Justice and Imagining State: Engaging the Law to Challenge the Rule of Exception in Tunceli." *European Journal of Turkish Studies: Social Sciences on Contemporary Turkey* 10 (2009). https://journals.openedition.org/ejts/4249.

Li, Tania. *The Will to Improve: Governmentality, Development, and the Practice of Politics*. Duke University Press, 2007.

Lloyd, David. "From the Critique of Violence to the Critique of Rights." *Critical Times* 3, no. 1 (2020): 109–30. https://doi.org/10.1215/26410478-8189873.

Lutz, Ellen L., and Kathryn Sikkink. "International Human Rights Law and Practice in Latin America." *International Organization* 54, no. 3 (2000): 633–59. https://doi.org/10.1162/002081800551235.

Lynch, Michael, and Simon Cole. "Science and Technology Studies on Trial: Dilemmas of Expertise." *Social Studies of Science* 35, no. 2 (2005): 269–311. https://doi.org/10.1177/0306312705048715.

Mamdani, Mahmood. "Amnesty or Impunity? A Preliminary Critique of the Report of the Truth and Reconciliation Commission of South Africa (TRC)." *Diacritics* 32, no. 3/4 (2002): 33–59. https://doi.org/10.1353/dia.2005.0005.

Mamdani, Mahmood. *Good Muslim, Bad Muslim: America, the Cold War, and the Roots of Terror.* Pantheon Books, 2004.

Mann, Itamar. "Border Violence as Crime." *University of Pennsylvania Journal of International Law* 42, no. 3 (2021): 675–736.

Mann, Steve, Jason Nolan, and Barry Wellman. "Sousveillance: Inventing and Using Wearable Computing Devices for Data Collection in Surveillance Environments." *Surveillance & Society* 1, no. 3 (2003): 331–55. https://doi.org/10.24908/ss.v1i3.3344.

Mannov, Adrienne. "Maritime Piracy and the Ambiguous Art of Existential Arbitrage." *Current Anthropology* 64, no. 2 (2023): 147–71. https://doi.org/10.1086/724981.

Marcus, Aliza. *Blood and Belief: The PKK and the Kurdish Fight for Independence.* New York University Press, 2007.

McCann, Michael W. *Rights at Work: Pay Equity Reform and the Politics of Legal Mobilization.* University of Chicago Press, 1994.

McGranahan, Carole. "Refusal as Political Practice: Citizenship, Sovereignty, and Tibetan Refugee Status." *American Ethnologist* 45, no. 3 (2018): 367–79. https://doi.org/10.1111/amet.12671.

McGranahan, Carole. "Theorizing Refusal: An Introduction." *Cultural Anthropology* 31, no. 3 (2016): 319–25. https://doi.org/10.14506/ca31.3.01.

McKay, Ramah. "Documentary Disorders: Managing Medical Multiplicity in Maputo, Mozambique." *American Ethnologist* 39, no. 3 (2012): 545–61. https://doi.org/10.1111/j.1548-1425.2012.01380.x.

McMurray, David A. *In and out of Morocco: Smuggling and Migration in a Frontier Boomtown.* University of Minnesota Press, 2001.

Meeker, Michael E. *A Nation of Empire: The Ottoman Legacy of Turkish Modernity.* University of California Press, 2002.

Menjívar, Cecilia. "Immigration Law Beyond Borders: Externalizing and Internalizing Border Controls in an Era of Securitization." *Annual Review of Law and Social Science* 10 (2014): 353–69. https://doi.org/10.1146/annurev-lawsocsci-110413-030842.

Merry, Sally Engle. "Transnational Human Rights and Local Activism: Mapping the Middle." *American Anthropologist* 108, no. 1 (2006): 38–51. https://doi.org/10.1525/aa.2006.108.1.38.

Mitchell, Timothy. *Carbon Democracy: Political Power in the Age of Oil.* Verso, 2011.

Mitchell, Timothy. *Rule of Experts: Egypt, Techno-Politics, Modernity.* University of California Press, 2002.

Mitchell, Timothy. "The Limits of the State: Beyond Statist Approaches and Their Critics." *American Political Science Review* 85, no. 1 (1991): 77–96. https://doi.org/10.2307/1962879.

Miyazaki, Hirokazu. *Arbitraging Japan: Dreams of Capitalism at the End of Finance.* University of California Press, 2013.

Mora, Mariana. "(Dis)Placement of Anthropological Legal Activism, Racial Justice and the Ejido Tila, Mexico." *American Anthropologist* 122, no. 3 (2020): 606–17. https://doi.org/10.1111/aman.13426.

Moustafa, Tamir. *The Struggle for Constitutional Power: Law, Politics, and Economic Development in Egypt.* Cambridge University Press, 2007.

Murphy, Michelle. *Sick Building Syndrome and the Problem of Uncertainty: Environmental Politics, Technoscience, and Women Workers.* Duke University Press, 2006.

Mutlu, Servet. "The Economic Cost of Civil Conflict in Turkey." *Middle Eastern Studies* 47, no. 1 (2011): 63–80. https://doi.org/10.1080/00263200903378675.

Narrain, Arvind, and Arun K. Thiruvengadam. "Social Justice Lawyering and the Meaning of Indian Constitutionalism: A Case Study of the Alternative Law Forum, Bangalore." *Wisconsin International Law Journal* 31 (2013): 525–65.

Ngai, Mae M. *Impossible Subjects: Illegal Aliens and the Making of Modern America.* Princeton University Press, 2004.

Nordstrom, Carolyn. *Global Outlaws: Crime, Money, and Power in the Contemporary World.* University of California Press, 2007.

O'Connor, Francis. *Understanding Insurgency: Popular Support for the PKK in Turkey.* Cambridge University Press, 2021.

Öcalan, Abdullah. *Bir Halkı Savunmak.* İstanbul: Çetin Yayınları, 2004.

Öcalan, Abdullah. *Demokratik Uygarlık Çözümü.* 5 vols. İstanbul: Amara Basım, 2015.

Öcalan, Abdullah. *Dicle-Fırat Havzasında Tarih, Kutsallık ve Lanetin Simgesi, Urfa.* Weşanên Serxwebûn, 2001.

Öcalan, Abdullah. *Kürt Sorununda Demokratik Çözüm Bildirgesi.* İstanbul: Mem Yayınları, 1999.

Öcalan, Abdullah. *Özgür İnsan Savunması.* İstanbul: Çetin Yayınları, 2003.

Öcalan, Abdullah. *Sümer Rahip Devletinden Halk Cumhuriyetine Doğru.* 2 vols. İstanbul: Mem Yayınları, 2001.

Oğuz, Zeynep. "Cavernous Politics: Geopower, Territory, and the Kurdish Question in Turkey." *Political Geography* 85 (2021): 102331. https://doi.org/10.1016/j.polgeo.2020.102331.

Olson, Robert W. *The Emergence of Kurdish Nationalism and the Sheikh Said Rebellion, 1880–1925.* University of Texas Press, 1989.

Ong, Aihwa. *Neoliberalism as Exception: Mutations in Citizenship and Sovereignty.* Duke University Press, 2006.

Ong, Andrew. *Stalemate: Autonomy and Insurgency on the China-Myanmar Border.* Cornell University Press, 2023.

Otero-Bahamon, Silvia, Simón Uribe, and Isabel Peñaranda-Currie. "Seeing Like a Guerrilla: The Logic of Infrastructure in the Building of Insurgent Orders." *Geoforum* 133 (2022): 198–207. https://doi.org/10.1016/j.geoforum.2021.10.009.

Özar, Şemsa, Nesrin Uçarlar, and Osman Aytar. *From Past to Present a Paramilitary Organization in Turkey: Village Guard System.* Translated by Sedef Çakmak. İstanbul: DİSA Yayınları, 2013.

Özbudun, Ergun. "Turkey's Judiciary and the Drift Toward Competitive Authoritarianism." *The International Spectator* 50, no. 2 (2015): 42–55. https://doi.org/10.1080/03932729.2015.1020651.

Özcan, Ömer. "Curfew 'Until Further Notice': Waiting and Spatialisation of Sovereignty in a Kurdish Bordertown in Turkey." *Social Anthropology* 29, no. 3 (2021): 816–30. https://doi.org/10.1111/1469-8676.13082.

Özcan, Ömer. "Yüksekova'da Sınır Deneyimleri: Bir 'Sınır Kaçakçılığı' Hikayesi ve Barış Süreci." *Toplum ve Bilim* 131 (2014): 162–85.

Özgen, Neşe. *Van-Özalp ve 33 Kurşun Olayı: Toplumsal Hafızanın Hatırlama ve Unutma Biçimleri*. İstanbul: TÜSTAV Yayınları, 2002.

Özgen, Neşe. "Sınırın İktisadi Antropolojisi; Suriye ve Irak Sınırlarında İki Kasaba." In *Gelenekten Geleceğe Antropoloji*, edited by Belkis Kümbetoğlu and Hande Birkalan Gedik. Istanbul: Epsilon Yayınları, 2005.

Öztan, Ramazan Hakkı. "The Great Depression and the Making of Turkish-Syrian Border, 1921–1939." *International Journal of Middle East Studies* 52, no. 2 (2020): 311–26. https://doi.org/10.1017/S0020743820000021.

Parla, Ayşe. *Precarious Hope: Migration and the Limits of Belonging in Turkey*. Stanford University Press, 2019.

Peel, Jacqueline, and Hari M. Osofsky. "Climate Change Litigation." *Annual Review of Law and Social Science* 16, no. 1 (2020): 21–38. https://doi.org/10.1146/annurev-lawsocsci-022420-122936.

Peterson, Kristin. *Speculative Markets: Drug Circuits and Derivative Life in Nigeria*. Duke University Press, 2014.

Povinelli, Elizabeth A. *The Cunning of Recognition: Indigenous Alterities and the Making of Australian Multiculturalism*. Duke University Press, 2002.

Prasse-Freeman, Elliott. "Resistance/Refusal: Politics of Manoeuvre under Diffuse Regimes of Governmentality." *Anthropological Theory* 22, no. 1 (2022): 102–27. https://doi.org/10.1177/1463499620940218.

Prasse-Freeman, Elliott. *Rights Refused: Grassroots Activism and State Violence in Myanmar*. Stanford University Press, 2023.

Quijano, Aníbal. "Coloniality and Modernity/Rationality." *Cultural Studies* 21, no. 2–3 (2007): 168–78. https://doi.org/10.1080/09502380601164353.

Reeves, Madeleine. *Border Work: Spatial Lives of the State in Rural Central Asia*. Cornell University Press, 2014.

Richland, Justin B. *Cooperation without Submission: Indigenous Jurisdictions in Native Nation-US Engagements*. University of Chicago Press, 2022. https://doi.org/10.7208/chicago/9780226608624.

Rogers, Douglas. "The Materiality of the Corporation: Oil, Gas, and Corporate Social Technologies in the Remaking of a Russian Region." *American Ethnologist* 39, no. 2 (2012): 284–96. https://doi.org/10.1111/j.1548-1425.2012.01364.x.

Roitman, Janet. *Fiscal Disobedience: An Anthropology of Economic Regulation in Central Africa*. Princeton University Press, 2005.

Rojas-Perez, Isaias. *Mourning Remains: State Atrocity, Exhumations, and Governing the Disappeared in Peru's Postwar Andes*. Stanford University Press, 2017.

Rosenblatt, Adam. *Digging for the Disappeared: Forensic Science after Atrocity*. Stanford University Press, 2015.

Rubin, Jonah S. "Exhuming Dead Persons: Forensic Science and the Making of Post-fascist Publics in Spain." *Cultural Anthropology* 35, no. 3 (2020): 345–73. https://doi.org/10.14506/ca35.3.01.

Rudi, Axel. "The PKK's Newroz: Death and Moving Towards Freedom for Kurdistan." *Zanj* 2, no. 1 (2018): 92–114. https://doi.org/10.13169/zanjglobsoutstud.2.1.0092.

Rumford, Chris. "Introduction: Citizens and Borderwork in Europe." *Space and Polity* 12, no. 1 (2008): 1–12. https://doi.org/10.1080/13562570801969333.

Rumford, Chris. "Towards a Multiperspectival Study of Borders." *Geopolitics* 17, no. 4 (2012): 887–902. https://doi.org/10.1080/14650045.2012.660584.

Rumford, Chris. "Towards a Vernacularized Border Studies: The Case of Citizen Borderwork." *Journal of Borderlands Studies* 28, no. 2 (2013): 169–80. https://doi.org/10.1080 /08865655.2013.854653.

Sabuktay, Ayşegül. "Tracing the Deep State." *Perspectives* 1, no. 1 (2012): 4–7.

Sak, Ferdî. "Roboski Katliamı'nın 10. yıl dönümü: Hukuki süreçte ihmal kimin? [The 10th Anniversary of the Roboski Massacre: Who Is Responsible for Negligence in the Legal Process?]." *Rûdaw*, December 12, 2021. https://www.rudaw.net/turkish/ kurdistan/281220211.

Salih, Mohammed A. "Internal Cultural Imperialism: The Case of the Kurds in Turkey." *The International Communication Gazette* 83, no. 8 (2021): 733–52. https://doi.org/10 .1177/1748048520928666.

Salter, Mark B. "Theory of the /: The Suture and Critical Border Studies." *Geopolitics* 17, no. 4 (2012): 734–55. https://doi.org/10.1080/14650045.2012.660580.

Sanford, Victoria. *Buried Secrets: Truth and Human Rights in Guatemala*. Palgrave Macmillan, 2003.

Sapignoli, Maria. *Hunting Justice: Displacement, Law, and Activism in the Kalahari*. Cambridge University Press, 2018.

Şardan, Tolga. "PKK Raporu Interpol'de [The PKK Report Has Been Submitted to the Interpol]." *Milliyet*, June 7, 1994.

Sarızeybek, Erdal. "Aktütün: Kimsesiz, Garip ve Yapayalnız bir Karakol [Aktütün: A Helpless, Isolated, and Completely Alone Outpost]." Interview by Alper Uruş and Hale Gönültaş. *Vatan*, October 5, 2008. https://www.gazetevatan.com/gundem/ aktutun-kimsesiz-garip-ve-yapayalniz-bir-karakol-201961.

Sawyer, Suzana. "Crude Contamination: Law, Science, and Indeterminacy in Ecuador and Beyond." In *Subterranean Estates: Life Worlds of Oil and Gas*, edited by Hannah Appel, Arthur Mason, and Michael Watts. Cornell University Press, 2015.

Schäfers, Marlene. *Voices That Matter: Kurdish Women at the Limits of Representation in Contemporary Turkey*. University of Chicago Press, 2023.

Schäfers, Marlene. "Walking a Fine Line: Loyalty, Betrayal, and the Moral and Gendered Bargains of Resistance." *Comparative Studies of South Asia, Africa, and the Middle East* 40, no. 1 (2020): 119–32. https://doi.org/10.1215/1089201X-8186126.

Scheingold, Stuart A. *The Politics of Rights: Lawyers, Public Policy, and Political Change*. Yale University Press, 1974.

Scheppele, Kim Lane. "Autocratic Legalism." *The University of Chicago Law Review* 85, no. 2 (2018): 545–84.

Schmid, Alex P. "Revisiting the Relationship between International Terrorism and Transnational Organised Crime 22 Years Later." The Hague: International Centre for Counter-Terrorism, 2018. https://www.icct.nl/publication/revisiting-relationship-between-international-terrorism-and-transnational-organised.

Schmitt, Carl. *Political Theology: Four Chapters on the Concept of Sovereignty.* Translated by George Schwab. University of Chicago Press, 2005.

Schnitzler, Antina von. "Citizenship Prepaid: Water, Calculability, and Techno-Politics in South Africa." *Journal of Southern African Studies* 34, no. 4 (2008): 899–917. https://doi.org/10.1080/03057070802456821.

Schnitzler, Antina von. *Democracy's Infrastructure: Techno-politics and Protest after Apartheid.* Princeton University Press, 2016.

Schouten, Peer. *Roadblock Politics: The Origins of Violence in Central Africa.* Cambridge University Press, 2022.

Schuster, Caroline E. "Gender and Smuggling." In *The Routledge Handbook of Smuggling,* edited by Max Gallien and Florian Weigand. Taylor & Francis, 2022.

Schwartz-Marin, Ernesto, and Arely Cruz-Santiago. "Forensic Civism: Articulating Science, DNA and Kinship in Contemporary Mexico and Colombia." *Human Remains and Violence: An Interdisciplinary Journal* 2, no. 1 (2016): 58–74. https://doi.org/10.7227/HRV.2.1.5.

Scott, James C. *Domination and the Arts of Resistance: Hidden Transcripts.* Yale University Press, 1990.

Scott, James C. *Weapons of the Weak: Everyday Forms of Peasant Resistance.* Yale University Press, 1985.

Sekula, Allan. "Photography and the Limits of National Identity." *Grey Room* 55 (2014): 28–33. https://doi.org/10.1162/GREY_a_00143.

Şenoğuz, H. Pınar. "Ahlaki Ekonominin Sınırları: Kilis'in Kayıtdışı Ekonomisi ve Yeni Zenginleri." *Toplum ve Bilim* 131 (2014): 105–35.

Setzer, Joana, and Lisa C. Vanhala. "Climate Change Litigation: A Review of Research on Courts and Litigants in Climate Governance." *Wiley Interdisciplinary Reviews: Climate Change* 10, no. 3 (2019): e580. https://doi.org/10.1002/wcc.580.

Shange, Savannah. "Black Girl Ordinary: Flesh, Carcerality, and the Refusal of Ethnography." *Transforming Anthropology* 27, no. 1 (2019): 3–21. https://doi.org/10.1111/traa.12143.

Shapiro, Nicholas, and Eben Kirksey. "Chemo-Ethnography: An Introduction." *Cultural Anthropology* 32, no. 4 (2017): 481–93. https://doi.org/10.14506/ca32.4.01.

Sikkink, Kathryn. *The Justice Cascade: How Human Rights Prosecutions Are Changing World Politics.* 1st ed. W. W. Norton & Co., 2011.

Simpson, Audra. "The Ruse of Consent and the Anatomy of 'Refusal': Cases from Indigenous North America and Australia." *Postcolonial Studies* 20, no. 1 (2017): 18–33. https://doi.org/10.1080/13688790.2017.1334283.

Simpson, Audra. *Mohawk Interruptus: Political Life Across the Borders of Settler States.* Duke University Press, 2014.

Smart, Alan, and Filippo M. Zerilli. "Extralegality." In *A Companion to Urban Anthropology,* edited by Donald M. Nonini. Wiley-Blackwell Publishing, 2014.

Sojoyner, Damien M. "Another Life Is Possible: Black Fugitivity and Enclosed Places." *Cultural Anthropology* 32, no. 4 (2017): 514–36. https://doi.org/10.14506/ca32.4.04.

Soleimani, Kamal, and Ahmad Mohammadpour. "Life and Labor on the Internal Colonial Edge: Political Economy of Kolberi in Rojhelat." *The British Journal of Sociology* 71, no. 4 (2020): 741–60. https://doi.org/10.1111/1468-4446.12745.

Söyler, Mehtap. *The Turkish Deep State: State Consolidation, Civil-Military Relations and Democracy*. Abingdon, Oxon: Routledge, 2015.

Speed, Shannon. *Rights in Rebellion: Indigenous Struggle and Human Rights in Chiapas*. Stanford University Press, 2008.

Spivak, Gayatri Chakravorty. "Translator's Preface." In *Of Grammatology* by Jacques Derrida. Corrected ed. Johns Hopkins University Press, 1997.

Stepputat, Finn. "Introduction." In *Governing the Dead: Sovereignty and the Politics of Dead Bodies*, edited by Finn Stepputat. Manchester University Press, 2014.

Stern, Rachel E. *Environmental Litigation in China: A Study in Political Ambivalence*. Cambridge University Press, 2013.

Strozier, Charles, and James Frank. *The PKK: Financial Sources, Social and Political Dimensions*. AV Akademikerverlag GmbH & Company KG, 2011.

Sundberg, Juanita. "Diabolic *Caminos* in the Desert and Cat Fights on the Río: A Posthumanist Political Ecology of Boundary Enforcement in the United States–Mexico Borderlands." *Annals of the Association of American Geographers* 101, no. 2 (2011): 318–36. https://doi.org/10.1080/00045608.2010.538323.

The Grand National Assembly of Turkey [Türkiye Büyük Millet Meclisi]. "Akaryakıt Kaçakçılığının Ekonomiye, İnsan ve Çevre Sağlığına Verdiği Zararın Araştırılarak Alınması Gereken Tedbirlerin Belirlenmesi Amacıyla Kurulan Meclis Araştırması Komisyonu Raporu [Parliamentary Research Commission Established to Investigate the Damage Caused by Oil Smuggling to the Economy, Human Health, and Environmental Health, and to Determine the Necessary Measures to be Taken]." Report No. 10/238, March 2005. https://www5.tbmm.gov.tr/sirasayi/donem22/yil01/ss978m.htm#_Toc108326421.

Torpey, John. *The Invention of the Passport: Surveillance, Citizenship and the State*. Cambridge University Press, 2000.

Tuckett, Anna. *Rules, Paper, Status: Migrants and Precarious Bureaucracy in Contemporary Italy*. Stanford University Press, 2018.

Tuğal, Cihan. *The Fall of the Turkish Model: How the Arab Uprisings Brought Down Islamic Liberalism*. Verso, 2016.

Turkish Ministry of Justice [T. C. Adalet Bakanlığı]. *Performans Programı: 2024*. September 11, 2023. https://sgb.adalet.gov.tr/Resimler/SayfaDokuman/19012024101409 Adalet%20Bakanl%C4%B1%C4%9F%C4%B1%202024%20Y%C4%B1l%C4%B1%20 Performans%20Program%C4%B1.pdf.

Ulugana, Sedat. *Ağrı Kürt Direnişi ve Zilan Katliamı: 1926–1931*. Peri Yayınları, 2010.

Üngör, Uğur Ümit. *Paramilitarism: Mass Violence in the Shadow of the State*. Oxford University Press, 2020.

Ünlü, Ahmet. "2016 yılı Mayıs ayına göre kamu personel sayıları [The total number of public officers as of May 2016]." *Yeni Şafak*, May 15, 2016. https://www.yenisafak.com/yazarlar/ahmet-unlu/2016-yili-mayis-ayina-gore-kamu-personel-sayilari-2029063.

Ünlü, Barış. "The Kurdish Struggle and the Crisis of the Turkishness Contract." *Philosophy & Social Criticism* 42, no. 4–5 (2016): 397–405. https://doi.org/10.1177/0191453715625715.

Ustundag, Nazan. "Kaçak as a Mode of Feeling and Being: Sovereignty, Fantasy, and the Undercommons." *Journal of Cultural Economy* 17, no. 2 (2024): 154–64. https://doi.org/10.1080/17530350.2022.2159493.

Uygur, Ercan. "Krizden Krize Türkiye: 2000 Kasım ve 2001 Şubat Krizleri." *Türkiye Ekonomi Kurumu*, 2001. http://www.tek.org.tr/dosyalar/KRIZ-2000-20013.pdf.

Vali, Abbas. *Kurds and the State in Iran: The Making of Kurdish Identity.* I. B. Tauris, 2011.

van Bruinessen, Martin. *Agha, Sheikh, and State: On the Social and Political Organization of Kurdistan.* Utrecht University Press, 1978.

van Bruinessen, Martin. "The Kurds Between Iran and Iraq." *Middle East Report* 141 (July/August 1986). https://merip.org/1986/07/the-kurds-between-iran-and-iraq/.

Vergés, Jacques. *Savunma Saldırıyor [De la stratégie judiciaire].* Translated by Vivet Kanetti. Metis Yayınları, 1988.

Vogt, Wendy A. *Lives in Transit: Violence and Intimacy on the Migrant Journey.* University of California Press, 2018.

Wagner, Sarah. "Identifying Srebrenica's Missing: The 'Shaky Balance' of Universalism and Particularism." In *Transitional Justice: Global Mechanisms and Local Realities after Genocide and Mass Violence*, edited by Alexander Laban Hinton. Rutgers University Press, 2011.

Watts, Nicole. "Institutionalizing Virtual Kurdistan West: Transnational Networks and Ethnic Contention in International Affairs." In *Boundaries and Belonging: States and Societies in the Struggle to Shape Identities and Local Practices*, edited by Joel S. Migdal. Cambridge University Press, 2004.

Weber, Max. *Economy and Society: An Outline of Interpretive Sociology.* University of California Press, 1978.

Weiss, Erica. "Refusal as Act, Refusal as Abstention." *Cultural Anthropology* 31, no. 3 (2016): 351–58. https://doi.org/10.14506/ca31.3.05.

Weizman, Eyal. *Forensic Architecture: Violence at the Threshold of Detectability.* Zone Books, 2017.

Weizman, Eyal. *Hollow Land: Israel's Architecture of Occupation.* Verso, 2007.

Westrheim, Kariane. "Taking to the Streets: Kurdish Collective Action in Turkey." In *The Kurdish Question in Turkey*, edited by Cengiz Gunes and Welat Zeydanlioglu. Routledge, 2014.

White, Benjamin Thomas. *The Emergence of Minorities in the Middle East: The Politics of Community in French Mandate Syria.* Edinburgh University Press, 2011.

White, Thomas. "Sparks from the Friction of Terrain: Transport Animals, Borderlands, and the Territorial Imagination in China." *Environment and Planning D: Society & Space* 41, no. 3 (2023): 433–50. https://doi.org/10.1177/02637758231184881.

Whitman, James Q. *The Origins of Reasonable Doubt: Theological Roots of the Criminal Trial.* Yale University Press, 2008.

Wilson, Alice. *Sovereignty in Exile: A Saharan Liberation Movement Governs.* University of Pennsylvania Press, 2016.

Wilson, Richard Ashby. "Expert Evidence on Trial: Social Researchers in the International Criminal Courtroom." *American Ethnologist* 43, no. 4 (2016): 730–44. https://doi.org/10.1111/amet.12387.

Wright, Sarah. "When Dialogue Means Refusal." *Dialogues in Human Geography* 8, no. 2 (2018): 128–32. https://doi.org/10.1177/2043820618780570.

Yadirgi, Veli. *The Political Economy of the Kurds of Turkey: From the Ottoman Empire to the Turkish Republic.* Cambridge University Press, 2017.

Yalçın, Soner. *Behçet Cantürk'ün Anıları.* Doğan Kitap, 2003.

Yalçın, Soner. *Binbaşı Ersever'in İtirafları.* Beyoğlu, Kaynak Yayınları, 1994.

Yarkın, Gülistan. "İnkâr Edilen Hakikat Sömürge Kuzey Kürdistan." *Kürd Araştırmaları* 1 (Güz 2019). https://www.kurdarastirmalari.com/yazi-detay-nk-r-edilen-hakikat-s-m-rge-kuzey-k-rdistan-26.

Yarkın, Güllistan. "Turkish Racism Against Kurds: Colonial Violence, Racist Slurs and Mob Attacks." *The Commentaries* 2, no. 1 (2022): 77–90. https://doi.org/10.33182/tc.v2i1.2218.

Yayman, Hüseyin. "Terörle Mücadelenin Yumuşak Karnı . . . [Achilles Heel of Counterterrorism]." *Hürriyet*, August 6, 2012. http://www.hurriyet.com.tr/terorle-mucadelenin-yumusak-karni-21157249.

Yayman, Hüseyin. "Terörle Mücadelenin Zaafı Jandarma Karakolları [Gendarmerie Stations: Soft Spot of Counterterrorism]." Interview by Murat Aksoy. *Yeni Şafak*, May 9, 2010. https://www.yenisafak.com/roportaj/terorle-mucadelenin-zaafi-jandarma-karakollari-256487.

Yeğen, Mesut. "The Kurdish Issue in Turkey: Denial to Recognition." In *Nationalisms and Politics in Turkey: Political Islam, Kemalism, and the Kurdish Issue*, edited by Marlies Casier and Joost Jongerden. Routledge, 2011.

Yıldız, Ahmet. *Ne Mutlu Türküm Diyebilene: Türk Ulusal Kimliğinin Etno-Seküler Sınırları (1919–1938).* İstanbul: İletişim Yayınları, 2001.

Yöndem, Bülent, and Mustafa Bakacak. "Bu Terör Bitmez [The Terror Will Not End]." *Milliyet*, November 5, 1993.

Yonucu, Deniz. *Police, Provocation, Politics: Counterinsurgency in Istanbul.* Cornell University Press, 2022. https://doi.org/10.1515/9781501762178.

Yonucu, Deniz. "The Absent Present Law: An Ethnographic Study of Legal Violence in Turkey." *Social & Legal Studies* 27, no. 6 (2018): 716–33. https://doi.org/10.1177/0964663917738044.

Yurdakul, Doğan. *Abi: Kabadayılar, Mafya ve Derin Devlet.* Kırmızı Kedi Yayınevi, 2012.

Zeydanlıoğlu, Welat. "Turkey's Kurdish Language Policy." *International Journal of the Sociology of Language* 2012, no. 217 (2012): 99–125. https://doi.org/10.1515/ijsl-2012-0051.

Zuboff, Shoshana. *The Age of Surveillance Capitalism: The Fight for a Human Future at the New Frontier of Power.* PublicAffairs, 2019.

INDEX

The authorized representative in the EU for product safety and compliance is:
Mare Nostrum Group
B.V Doelen 72
4831 GR Breda
The Netherlands

www.ingramcontent.com/pod-product-compliance
Lightning Source LLC
Chambersburg PA
CBHW030353270326
41926CB00009B/1092